For [illegible]
Mi

1

Xmas 2009

D0992882

My father taught at St Paul's School, London, gave talks for the BBC, and also taught in the USA. In 1993, at a party, I met one of his former pupils. He told me that John Usborne was one of his most inspiring teachers. 'You must write about him' he said. I set about collecting the reminiscences of other Old Paulines, thinking that I would make an anthology of my father's writing along with his pupils' stories about him. This memoir evolved, slowly and sometimes painfully, as I uncovered aspects of my father's life that I had not known about, or had not understood as a child growing up.

Like every human being, John Usborne had flaws, but he was also blessed with a gift for teaching and with irrepressible and dogged enthusiasm for what caught his interest and imagination. Somehow his love of language, his desire to impart knowledge, his delight in nature and the countryside always managed to come bubbling through despite the underlying domestic difficulties and the never-ending struggle to pay the bills. The testimony of those Old Paulines who remember him and his teaching methods, and the way he obviously won the hearts of his American students in the short time he was with them, complete a story of an unusual and unconventional man.

Other titles published

Portrait of Islington
1981, 1989

Portrait of Hampstead
1984

Portrait of Hampstead
1986

Published by
Damien Tunnacliffe

John Usborne,
schoolmaster

Published in Great Britain in 1999

by

Ann Usborne
118b Highbury Hill
London N5 1AT

Text Drawings by Ann Usborne

Designed by Oliver Hickey

ISBN 0 9537429 0 3

Printed in Great Britain by
Antony Rowe Limited
Bumper's Farm, Chippenham, Wiltshire SN14 6LH.

Contents

Acknowledgements

I am most grateful, first of all, to my family, especially my uncles Henry and Dick, my aunts Gerda, Margaret and Pam.

I am happy to say that I would not have started this book without the memories of my father's former pupils, too many to name here. His St Paul's colleagues John Allport, Robert Bennett, Guy Burn, Ted Gawne, Paul Longland, Philip McGuinness, Tony Retallack, Erik Sthyr and Richenda Stubbs gave me much of their time.

A special thanks to my father's friends Francis Barnes, Michael Barton, Richard Briscoe, Philip Brownrigg, Mary Clifford-Wolff, Ralph and Irene Gabriel, Kay Gimpel, Richard Hutchins, Robin Jacques, Dick Keen, John Leahy, Alex McCurdy, Jean and James MacGibbon, Vera McNair, John Padel, Mark Patterson, Robert Perceval, Helen Simpson, Milena Thomas and Lawrence Waddy.

Others whose help was invaluable were Norman Badderly, Nicolas Blackett, Barry Brooke, Carey Dickson, Jill Drew, Sally Greenhill, Sue Hunt, Basil Johnson, Maurice Keen, Charles Kimber, Richard MacKenzie, Simon May, Ann Monsarrat, Ian Robinson, Paul Stobart, Alan Tadiello, Neil Somerville at the BBC Written Archives Centre, Robert Sopwith, Vivian Spong and Pam Wilson.

Finally, one of the best things in my life has been the help and encouragement of my editor, Jill Sutcliffe.

Introduction

As a small child I was intrigued by my father's six-finger typing, on a funny old high typewriter, black with gold lettering on it. He learnt to do it the hard way, as a sub-editor in journalism. He was a teacher, but that was done out of my sight. He collected material like a jackdaw. Magazines and books were flagged and in neat piles. His three activities, teaching, writing and broadcasting cross-fertilised each other.

I never thought much about his teaching, whether he was as good or as bad as my own teachers. I wish now that I had been able to watch him teach. Certainly I would have understood him better if I had. It would have helped me to have seen him holding the attention of his pupils; to have been aware of his love of the spoken word and his sense of the power it could exert. It was a surprise to me to learn, in my research for this book, that he considered his first experiences of acting at school to have been some of the most seminal of his early life.

He used to say he became bored if he was required to write more than 2000 words on any subject. If he had lived, I doubt he would have produced a good memoir in his old age. ('It was right that John died,' said his brother Dick.) His trail of comments on walking, watching birds, talking to people on his travels, teaching, favourite literature, were best listened to crisp and fresh. Writing poetry for him was a sensual game to play, a puzzle to crack, a jolly - and sentimental - way to celebrate anything he chose to celebrate. Occasions would be drawn out of the air. My sister and I are lucky to have birthday poems for our first three years. My mother had superb wedding anniversary verses and Valentines. He wrote prayers for our village Sunday School during the war, cricket poems, political doggerel, doggerel for his pupils at St Paul's, doggerel written in competition with his siblings. He loved writing love poems; he was an incurable romantic, a lover, and he loved love.

I'm sure I disappointed him. From the age of ten, I was a problem child. Talents I showed up to that age fizzled out soon afterwards, never to return. I became a dreamer, losing some of my concentration. The enthusiasm that was my father's most appealing trait stopped engaging me. I remember well the time that I began to lose interest in the things that absorbed him. I was an avid reader, but not of poetry; I wanted to write but I became lazy; my piano lessons didn't fire me. Not a flicker of excitement did I show in politics. My father began to embarrass, even to irritate me. He appeared to me a bit odd, beaky, scruffily dressed. Why was he bald? Why wasn't he normal like my friends' fathers, who wore suits, had jobs in offices, and earned enough money? His friends and pupils - and even my friends - found him fun. Why didn't I? The reason, of course, was that my mother was off him at the time, and her feelings had filtered through to me.

He confided to friends that we were estranged. Poor man, I bore him an old grudge - that for me being at home wasn't fun - and he had to accept it. I was cruel, taking sides with my mother so completely, but I knew that I loved him, and I hope he knew it. Through all our separations I was carrying in me a flickering coal of knowledge that some day when he was old and sitting still, I would come home to talk to him, be grateful to him, and hear what he had to say to me, his first child.

For me, embarking on this book has been a journey of discovery: it was a revelation to have heard his pupils' memories of him, and to have read his writing. I have come to understand his difficulties, his side of the family argument, and the interests that kept him going. I hope I have brought him back to life for those who knew him.

Chapter One

An early memory of mine - and it's probably a common one - is of being read a bedtime story by my father. It was a winter evening late in 1947, when I was seven and my sister six. Our father, recently returned from the United States, had brought home with him a Knopf edition, bound in brown leatherette with gold tooling, of *Irish Folktales*. I remember, physically, lying tense in my bed under the window, listening. Julie, in hers, was on the warm side of the room, next to the hot water pipes. Daddy sat on a low stool, lankily, his eyes glinting. He was completely transported; it was a banshee he was reading about, and I asked him whether she could be flying outside our bedroom window...

As a fourteen-year-old my father had been too young to join his three elder brothers on a shooting holiday in Ireland, but he heard their talk about it afterwards. This must have sparked his interest, for he was to become bewitched by soft Irish voices and the distinctive literature and folklore of Ireland, even though there was no Irish blood in his family.

They originated, in fact, in Scandinavia. The surname, Usborne, comes from the Norse for 'Sacred Bear'. Asbjorn was a pre-Christian deity in Northern Europe. The Viking invasion of Northern France brought Asbjorns to Normandy, and eight of them are recorded as having crossed the Channel with William the Conqueror.

We know from parish records that Usbornes lived on the same site in Kent from the fourteenth century until the nineteenth. Thomas Usborne built Loddenden, a beautiful half-timbered manor house in Goudhurst in 1560. (Today it no longer belongs to our family but it is still a private house.) The family adopted a coat of arms with the motto 'Pax in Bello' (Peace in War) but in 1809, John Usborne, corn merchant of Broad Street in the City of London, was granted a new, rather pompous motto 'Virtus vincit Invidiam' (Virtue conquers Envy), with a crest of a stag on a green mound resting under a larch tree. During the Napoleonic Wars, my uncle Tommy surmised, he probably found 'Pax in Bello' distastefully pacifist.

The subject of this memoir, also John Usborne, was, unlike some of his ancestors, a determined pacifist. He was the fourth son of Charles Frederick Usborne of the Indian Civil Service, a shy, scholarly man, small and fine-boned. John's mother, Janet, was of Huguenot descent on her father's side and good Scottish on her mother's. Her parents lived comfortably, near Leamington, and did a good deal of shooting and fishing, some drinking, and were always said by the Usborne side to be totally unintellectual. Further back, however, they had a better record. Janet's great-great-grandfather, a sober country parson, was a fellow of All Souls (albeit as Founder's Kin); his wife was Jane Austen's close friend; his son married Jane's niece; and his nephew was Tom Lefroy, Jane's one-time swain, who eventually became Lord Chief Justice of Ireland, and on whom Mr Darcy is said to be based. Janet met Charles Usborne in Lahore, the capital of the Punjab. A cousin of her father, Bishop Lefroy, was there and needed a housekeeper. So, in her late twenties and still single, Janet was dispatched in what became known as the 'fishing fleet', to find a husband among the British expatriates. She was a large, statuesque woman, six feet three inches tall, dark, blue-eyed, with a wide mouth and a slightly hooked nose. John, of all her sons inherited both her looks and height. He was proud of his Huguenot blood, and it amused him sometimes to use as a pseudonym her maiden name, Lefroy.

Charles (known as Charlie), John's father, did not want to follow his father as a broker on the Baltic Exchange. Friends, colleagues, nieces remembered his charm, his wicked sense of humour, his rebellious streak - but he was reclusive by nature. Kipling's stories of the British in India were the favourite popular reading when he was a boy at Charterhouse, and these set him dreaming of a life as a soldier.

His schooling, exclusive and Classics-orientated, was preparing him for his career. At Balliol College, Oxford in the 1890s Charlie was a victim of the influence of the legendary Master, Benjamin Jowett, who thought that the knowledge his undergraduates were acquiring was the ideal intellectual equipment for rulers in India. Charlie - and many others in his generation - resented Jowett's aging propaganda (he was 76 when he died in Charlie's second year) and his cultivation of the sons of the rich. But Charlie didn't stand a chance of doing what he wanted. At Woolwich he had two tries to earn an Army commission; when he learnt, after months of training, that his height, five feet seven inches, was against him, he dutifully did his year's probation for the Indian Civil Service, and passed. As he only got a third-class degree and 'the Heaven-born', as ICS officers were known, generally required a first, this was something of an achievement.

In 1898, aged 24, Charlie Usborne arrived in the great wheat-growing province of the Punjab. In Lahore he had lessons in Punjabi for a month before he started work - as Assistant Commissioner, 3rd Grade. As a young bachelor, on his solitary evenings in camp after inspecting his districts, Charlie sat at his teapoy and wrote comic verses for English-speaking children. Some of these were published in *The Times of India* under the pseudonym 'Multani' - Multan, a notoriously hot, inhospitable place being his second station. Later, when his wife and children were back in England, reading and writing poetry were his greatest consolation.

John was born on 15 September 1914, in the Indian hill station of Dalhousie. He was a big baby of 10 lbs, with a mole in front of his left ear. His mother and the three older boys, with eight or nine servants, were by this time in a house rented for the hot weather. A month later they all returned to the Punjabi plains, to join Charlie, who was Deputy Commissioner in the town of Hissar.

As John was to say 37 years later in a talk for the BBC's Home Service: 'I've travelled a little in several countries. In India I spent two years within reach of Mount Everest and its Abominable Snowman, of Kashmir with its long valley plastered with rhododendrons and azaleas. But I cared for none of these things. For I travelled mainly by perambulator and my stomach was my only waking concern.' He would have loved to have had his own memories of India, but he was taken away from it in infancy, never to return. Nevertheless his visions of the beautiful landscapes of the Himalayan foothills with their warmth and intense colours were to stay in the recesses of his mind all his life - to echo in the discovery of his own paradises. Each of these would seem to him more beautiful than the last: starting at the age of twenty-three with the Sabine Hills in spring, he would add the Allegheny foothills when he was thirty-three, rural Virginia when he was thirty-six, the mountains of Herzegovina when he was forty, and British Columbia when he was forty-four. Hot sunshine on his back as he walked alone along a country road looking at a new landscape and listening to its birdlife was his idea of bliss from his young adulthood to his death.

In April 1916 the whole family sailed for home from Karachi. They were accompanied by Nurse Clifford and Hugh Whistler, a bachelor friend on leave from the Indian Police. Hugh carried on board 'Our Owl', a fledgling owl in a wooden box. They all enjoyed, according to Janet, 'a quiet voyage, no enemy submarines seen'. The family has a photograph, taken on deck by Hugh, of the boys. John, with a head of wispy curls, is wearing an oversized knitted coat, obviously a hand-me-down. The older three, in shoulder-buttoned navy sweaters and long shorts, have been told to see that he didn't go over the side; Dick is laughing, with an arm clamped round his smallest brother's neck, wrenching his head round to face the camera.

Charlie was to have a well-earned long leave - he had been involved in putting down the Ghadr Conspiracy, a potentially dangerous German-Sikh plot to subvert British rule. Tommy, the eldest son, now aged eight, was to start at Summer Fields School, Oxford, in September. Hugh Whistler's parents lived in Battle, Sussex, and they eased the way for Charlie and Janet to buy a rambling Georgian house there: 2, Upper Lake, Senlac Hill.

Janet was happy to be back in England. She was a practical, determined woman and had never liked being an idle memsahib. Margaret, the last child, her longed-for girl, was born in October 1917, a month after her father returned to India.

On clear days, like distant thunder, the faint rumble of the guns in France could be heard in Battle. During the first three years of their life there, without their father, Tommy, Henry and Dick, one after the other, went off to Summer Fields, their father's prep school, leaving the two youngest children at home with their mother. Janet taught both John and Margaret to read and write.

Janet was intelligent, though not academically trained. Her parents had regarded the appropriate accomplishments for a daughter to be singing, playing the piano and speaking French. She was ill at ease with intellectuals, and quite likely suspicious of them. She was probably disappointed that her husband was a radical and an agnostic, with advanced views about India being governed by Indians, but she never admitted this to her children. She was evidently proud that he was a scholar, a poet and a linguist; it was inconceivable to her that her children should grow up without their own pride in their father's learning and principles. From her Scottish Calvinist mother Janet had inherited her belief in the orderliness imposed on a household by religion. For John and Margaret the parish church played an important part in their early childhood. A family friend remembers Janet proudly leading her children to the family pew on Sundays, with John bringing up the rear.

During the last two years of the First World War the atmosphere in the north of India was tense and dangerous, with frequent bloody riots as the Muslims and Sikhs became stronger and fought for their rights against the Hindus. From the entire sub-continent, more than half of the Indian soldiers recruited for the war came from the Punjab. (Had he been an officer of the Indian Army, Charlie, a good Hindustani-speaker, would have gone to Mesopotamia with his mule and camel-drivers.) While the province simmered, he was a tireless commissioner, one of a handful of Englishmen working non-stop through the debilitating heat of that summer of 1918 in the Plains. Many ICS men collapsed from overwork coupled with ill health. Charlie had a physical and mental breakdown in December 1918.'

In 1919, at the end of April, still suffering deep depression and weakened by virulent Asian flu, he went home on sick leave. The Amritsar Massacre, happening three weeks before his departure, further compounded his misery. What future was there for him in India?

Charlie arrived, and soon decided that the household was being run competently without him. His unhappiness clouded the air; nothing could be done to please him. Tommy disliked his father's old-fashioned methods when he coached him in Latin, and he was disappointed that the bandages on his father's head were not covering war wounds but boils.

Familiar with her husband's tendency to depression, Janet urged him to see one of the first psychiatrists working in London. My three uncles remembered the September evening of the day their father went up for his appointment. Their mother, adored by them all, was reading to them from Kipling's *Jungle Books* in the drawing room. The front door slammed; he was back. Janet had a look of horror on her face, having guessed rightly that Charlie had refused to see the doctor. He was beyond the ability to help himself. On 6 November, during a weekend of grouse-shooting in the Yorkshire Dales – the last stop on a tour with Janet of her relatives, planned for him as a change of scene – he shot himself in the church-yard of the village of Wensley.

To Janet it was a great sadness, but a relief; long before his death Charlie had had suicide in mind. To his youngest sister Dorothy, his confidante, he had, over the years, often threatened it – and out of sorrow and despair, she had not tried very hard to discourage him. He had realized that the conditions in India might drive him to it. Probably he had realized also that his marriage (he married Janet, I was told, because he wanted tall sons) was a mismatch.

That their father had died in this manner was not known by any of the children at the time. Tommy and Henry were told by the headmaster at Summer Fields merely that he had died. Their mother assumed that they had been told it was suicide. Revering his father's memory, and afraid to upset his mother, Tommy did not broach the subject of his death to her until ten years later. He was astonished to hear the truth.

John was exposed to poetry from the age of two, hearing his mother reading to his brothers. They grew up knowing that their father wrote his verses and translated Punjabi stories mostly during the lonely times in his life in India. He was a romantic man in the memory of his children, and all their lives they were proud of his skill.

Janet's gentle influence on her smallest son was developed while he was out of the range of his brothers' teasing, during their term-time. She encouraged his interest in music; she had a good contralto voice herself, and loved singing hymns in church. As a small boy John sang hymns with gusto, often out of tune. The pomp – even of an Anglican Sunday service – appealed to him: as a six-year-old he wrote little 30-word sermons, and would continue to write them until he was eight. He made good progress with piano lessons. The chance to play the organ of the girls' school in Battle Abbey was offered to him; his solitary walks to the Abbey along the Ghost Walk at the age of seven had a lasting effect. Battle and its ghosts fed his imagination and gave him his vivid sense of history. He was never to feel lonely walking on his own.

The 31 chap 1st verse to psalms of Davie

text In they O Lord, do I put my trust
Subject: Do you no wy we must put our
trust in God.
Well think what he has done
for us. He helps us to fight satin
with all our might and strength
and won the great Battle of
the Lords.
And so you must put all your
faith and trust in him.

Sermon by John, aged eight.

John had his first real lessons at home, with a governess, Miss Mabel Coles. His classical syllabus for the ensuing sixteen years was given its foundation not only from hearing his brothers conjugating their Latin verbs - but with the help of one of the series called the *Piers Plowman Histories*, Junior Book Two. From this book he learnt about Romulus and Remus, Leonidas the Spartan, Phaedippides the Runner, and The Childhood of Horatius. Moreover, he lived within an arrow's flight of the site of the Norman Conquest - a good start for a boy with a fertile imagination.

Tommy, Henry and Dick were all about a year apart in age, but there were almost four years between Dick and John, due to the short life of another brother, David, during that time. Good-natured teasing was directed at John and Margaret by their three brothers. Margaret, being the only girl, had her mother's skirts to hide in, but John retaliated by making them laugh. He learnt early not to mind being laughed at, and was a natural comedian. Being younger, he was obviously much smaller than the other three, but in his teens he overtook them all in height very rapidly, to earn the nickname Tiny.

The British government provided well for the officers of its Indian Civil Service. Charlie had invested his pension for the children's education, worrying that it was not sufficient for the schools he wanted for them without the benefit of scholarships. Janet had no money of her own. After Charlie's death she kept an exact account of every penny she spent. She used to warn the family that they 'would be in the workhouse' if they were extravagant; they did in fact have very little left after enjoying the most expensive educations. She was determined that this should come first of all priorities. Mercifully they were admitted to Summer Fields at reduced fees, and three of them got scholarships to their public schools.

At the age of twelve Henry learnt from *The Big Book for Boys* how to develop and print photographs. His brothers also learnt, at a bench Henry rigged up in his bedroom. John's first photographs, taken at the age of ten with his new VPK (Vest Pocket Kodak), were comic - of birds' nests, a blurred spaniel on the lawn, distant bandeau-ed women in a Hastings tennis tournament - but they give us a good idea of the contentment of his early childhood and the fun he had with his brothers. His sense of composition was never very good, but he was always keen to record the family's activities. The hobby helped to develop his other interests. Though their careers were to be very different, he and Henry had a special bond. Henry, the family do-it-yourselfer, can be thanked for making John's range of interests so wide. John tried everything if he had half a chance.

Hugh Whistler and his widowed mother were good neighbours to the Usbornes. Hugh's father had been in the Indian Army and the family had befriended Charlie in the lonely years before he married. Hugh, a few years younger than Charlie, was a well-known ornithologist by the time he retired from the Imperial Indian Police. His superiors in India had never discouraged his passion for birds because the search for them took him to out-of-the-way places which none of his colleagues wanted to inspect. His book *A Popular Handbook of Indian Birds* is masterly, a classic of its kind; there are small stuffed birds donated by him on display in the Natural History Museum.

Home in Battle for good in 1926, and now married, Hugh was editing his mass of bird-notes, working hard towards publishing his book. He called on the Usbornes often. He was a dapper, trim man with a moustache - but he was shy. The children were very fond of him. He helped Henry to make a birdbox to attract nuthatches to the garden. He taught Dick to draw birds. In the winter he took the boys on expeditions to see curlews and grey wagtails at Cox's Mill; and he introduced them to the thrill of watching the migrants arriving on Romney Marsh in the early spring. John was always very keen. For this interest, as for ancient history, he was in an ideal environment. Warblers were always a special love of his: whitethroats and willow warblers are names I remember him mentioning constantly during my own childhood.

There was a tennis-court behind the Usbornes' house, and Janet - all the while knitting socks and pullovers for the boys - would often watch the children play. As they grew up, a tennis four within the family had its advantages - and what glamour for the local girls! The boys followed the tournaments in 'Stings' - as they called Hastings - where the female players were watched as avidly as the male ones. At the age of fifteen John played in a tennis tournament himself, at Fleet, Hampshire. (He met another 15-year-old there, Michael Barton; they were to become the greatest of friends. Michael remembers that they both wore white trousers and trilbies to play.)

Shooting, like cricket, was in the blood. Tommy, Henry and Dick had been taught by their father to use his Two-two rifle in India. Dick remembered that when he was just six, they all went out shooting, Tommy entrusted with the gun. Their father would give each boy six 'dust-shots' (the smallest size shot, the type which Hugh Whistler kept handy in his pocket for bringing down small birds) and one proper bullet. If one of them shot a peacock or a monkey, apart from the statutory small birds, he was expected to show it to him. The gun was used frequently at Battle. Jack Stow, an ICS child the same age as Dick, who, with his sister Cynthia was a paying guest of Janet's, remembered: 'John was good at most games - cricket, tennis, and a deadly shot with an airgun. I think he was persuaded not to shoot robins.' Janet was brought up used to seeing animals killed - she had been taught how to kill rabbits. She was quoted in the Battle newsletter as saying - after the local hunt had driven a fox into her cellar and the hounds had pulled it to pieces there - 'I don't mind what happened to my flowering rose tree; all I wished was that my family had been at home to join in the fun.' An attitude that nowadays would not be thought politically correct, but at the time showed a sporting spirit.

John was merely keeping up with his brothers. For a boy an interest in birds in those days implied birds-nesting and shooting as well as watching. He knew that birds migrating north to Britain would be habitually shot by ornithologists - for examination - as they arrived over the south coast.

A few days before his eighth birthday John started at Summer Fields. Henry and Dick were still there, aged twelve and eleven, to keep an eye on him. John had been well schooled in Summer Fields' customs by his brothers so was braced for the fierce barks of the headmaster 'Bear' Alington, and his Black Book for misdemeanours on Sundays.

Summer Fields was founded in 1864 by Gertrude Maclaren, a 29-year-old wife and mother. She was a remarkable figure for her time. Her husband had founded the Oxford University Gymnasium. Her knowledge of the Classics and her determination were astonishing. The school was to aim high, preparing boys for entrance to the top public schools; her husband would be responsible for keeping them fit.

The Maclaren family lived on the outskirts of Oxford, in Summertown. Their house - close to the river Cherwell, surrounded by fields - was one of the older ones in the village, low, painted white, with a rose-covered verandah and a beautiful garden. One wall of this house is still the core of the main complex of the school.

Mrs Maclaren's first two pupils joined the lessons she gave her two small daughters. Her great triumph, in 1868, after six years of her own steady teaching, was to win her first Eton scholarship for the son of Alexander Macmillan, the founder of the publishing firm. Macmillan's enthusiasm for Mrs Maclaren's teaching was such that he gave the school the publicity it needed. Its tradition has always been to give its pupils a thorough grounding in the Classics; five years of intense work that can get an intelligent boy into Eton, preferably as a scholar with reduced fees.

The Reverend Hugh Alington, John's headmaster, acquired his nickname 'Bear' because he behaved like one: he was huge, he wore a black gown, he growled, grunted and roared. He had flowing white hair, white whiskers, a red face and round, protruberant eyes. He smoked revolting pipes, and smelt of Old Shag tobacco. He had been brought up, the youngest of ten brothers, in a remote Lincolnshire rectory, to believe in an Old Testament God and the Ten Commandments. Like most inhibited people, he was very emotional. His temper was terrifying, but he was in turn terrified by emotion displayed by others. Poor Bear, he had been taught through fear, so he believed he should teach that way himself. It was simple: the Classics were very hard, therefore the Classics were the best preparation for life. All Summer Fields masters at that time were eccentric; highly individual, old-fashioned, remote - but not cruel.

Bear has gone down in history as an arch-eccentric headmaster. He is lovable to read about now, a colourful character. All boys learnt how to keep out of his way, but in class he talked to them as men of the world, and illuminated his subject in a way that is still remembered. Each boy, to earn his approval, had to make good progress towards getting his scholarship, and to be a keen sportsman (Bear coached cricket and football apart from his teaching). Woe betide you if you made a howler in your Latin Unseen or funked a tackle on the football pitch! A mixture of English and Greek invective would be let fly, or at mildest, a long-drawn sniff. But his puritanical upbringing, his simplicity, meant he was honest, sincere and altruistic. He hummed hymns. There was a sense of humour there, simple and unsophisticated, usually on the theme of little boys and their comic remarks. It pleased him, as he walked past a boy, to give him his one-finger salute, a signal that he was soon to award him his cricket or football colours.

The most charismatic figure at Summer Fields for John was the Irishman Leonard Strong. 'He was a ray of sunshine!' said Dick. (For a one-year spell only, John's last, the 23-year-old Cecil Day-Lewis teaching Latin was no less inspiring.) When Leonard gave up teaching in 1930 he was already an established writer and poet - better known as L.A.G.Strong - and he went on to publish verse, novels, short stories, textbooks and to become a director of the publishing house Methuen.

Leonard had been an undergraduate at Wadham College, Oxford, when he first started teaching at Summer Fields. He was twenty-six when John arrived as a pupil, and had already shown the old diehards that there was no harm in being a friend to the boys. He took each one seriously, treating him as an adult, never talking down to him. He knew that they all needed light relief from the crushing pressure on them. What better than to play them songs from his collection of records of the D'Oyly Carte Company? (Leonard had been on the stage himself a few times, in the Dublin music-halls.) He played John McCormack's songs too - and sang himself, and performed little sketches, and generally enjoyed himself making the boys laugh. This was his entertainment for them out of hours; but his lessons were just as entertaining: he read W.B.Yeats, James Joyce, Oscar Wilde, and his own Oxford contemporaries, Aldous Huxley, T.S.Eliot, A.E.Coppard; he read Wilde's *The Importance of Being Earnest,* taking all the parts himself ('it was a tour de force,' said Dick). Bear put his head round the door one day during one of the readings, and later accused Leonard of being degenerate - he was doing all the work, the boys were 'too comfortable'.

Just after the First World War, the staff at Summer Fields was made up of mostly old men, and each taught a bit of everything, including sports coaching, having eased himself into his own 'menu'. The Eton authorities decreed suddenly that the English paper would count radically in the placing of scholarship candidates. Leonard, who had managed to mix English with Classics for his degree, was asked by the headmaster to take Scholarship English; and he did this until he left the school. The ground was hard for him at first, because in the study of the Classics the mechanical technique was considered the only method of learning which worked; but over the years he had great success in encouraging the boys to develop their own ideas, not to be too reverent, to draw their own conclusions from their set books, to think for themselves. They must do this, he believed, if they were to write essays.

John loved sport, an important component of the syllabus – a thing that Plato had insisted on for completing the man. Soccer was Bear's Football (he was respected for being an Oxford soccer blue), but he had sanctioned the beginning of rugger under another young master, John Evans, in 1920. There was Boxing. There was Fives. With big brothers John's competitive spirit developed at an early age. In his first photograph album, on the adjoining page to a photo of himself as one of Sergeant Morley's gym group, is one cut out of a national newspaper showing the winners of the 1927 Test Match; it includes the great Sussex bowler Maurice Tate, his boyhood hero. (John and his brothers regularly watched the Hastings Week matches in June. All four played the game with great delight, having good practice in the back garden at home). At Summer Fields you played with obtaining your colours in mind. John won his cricket colours in his third and fourth years and his football ones in his third.

Several years later, for Old Boys' Day in July 1959, he was highly amused to have the opportunity to write an article teasing Summer Fields for an extraordinary turnout of distinguished alumni, gathered together on a beautiful summer day to play cricket. The opposing teams were captained by the Right Reverend Robert Mortimer, Bishop of Exeter, and the Right Honourable Harold Macmillan, Prime Minister. (Henry Usborne captained the Prime Minister's team in his absence.)

'In the field the Prime Minister's team were right on their toes from the bell. The Admiral was castled for a blob in the first over. The Lord-in-Waiting, unable to castle another governor of the school in the first four balls of his over, appealed to the umpire: 'Umpire, surely it's over. You're not going to let me have another ball, are you?' 'I dare say', said an umpire aged 12 to a 45-year-old bowler who has not given up cricket and doesn't intend to for 30 years, 'this is the first time you've played cricket for a long time, isn't it, sir?' Runs, runs, runs. The Member for Argyll swung his arm vigorously in the outfield and was put on to bowl. A ball trickled off a bat in the direction of The Regular Cricketer in the gully... three wickets fell in quick succession and the tallywag said only 35. The Deputy Captain [Henry] murmured to his youngest brother [John], 'Do we want to win or shall I put Julian Amery on to bowl?'...'The eldest Usborne [Tommy], playing for the Governors, after getting a few boundaries, was finally caught by the youngest Usborne to the third Usborne's [Dick] bowling and the great delight of the second Usborne, who had fixed a trap.'

He couldn't help it; the network of contacts started at Summer Fields. In John's second year Ben Nicolson, the elder of Harold Nicolson and Vita Sackville-West's sons became a friend. His best friend, Ken Trevaskis, a tubby little boy, later became Governor of Aden. There was Derek Rawnsley, the grandson of the founder of the National Trust, who became an entrepreneur, and gave John his first job... Summer Fields kept tabs on them all, and later, with great charm, John would use these contacts for all they were worth.

The Matron, Miss Peirce, was fierce, but a great personality. She gave her doses with relish - one memoir describes her standing outside the dining-room to pop quinine pills into the boys' mouths as they emerged. A statutory order of hers was the boys' morning visit to the Vinery Rush, the school latrine, an open sewer with compartments built over it. One morning, Usborne or Trevaskis set light to a bundle of Bronco and, 'mindful of Cadiz', launched it on the stream, to scorch a few behinds as it floated by.

The boys wore short trousers until they were a certain height, and sweaters and 'little coats' (jackets). They always wore their caps out of doors in the winter. (I have a photograph taken by John of Moorhouse and Trevaskis in winter, sitting on a log near the Atco mower, swotting, in greatcoats and caps). On Sundays, for the service in the parish church, they wore blue suits, shirts with stiff Eton collars and white ties. Afternoons at the weekends were spent playing games; and in the summer swimming in the river, bug-hunting, and tending to the little allotments which two boys would share. There were no natural history lessons at all.

John did enjoy the Classics. In the fifth form he was taught them superbly for his scholarship by Geoffrey Bolton. (At that stage exams called 'Sham Schols' were laid on for top boys.)

'The right time to begin with the dry grammar and syntax,' John remembered, writing for *School and College* in 1958, 'was between 8 and 11, when the little mind is at its gayest and most absorptive and most competitive.

'There was a game we played in the dormitories when we were well under 11. After lights-out the boy whose turn it happened to be would test the others in Latin grammar and some Greek. Any boy who answered all the questions was automatically given the Top Winchester Schol: the next best got the Top Eton Schol, and so on to the bottom, who was always given as a consolation prize the Top Schol at Giggleswick, a school which in our arrogance and ignorance none of us believed really existed outside the music halls.'

John's father had known about Bradfield College, the Berkshire public school, as a small boy, for he was brought up in a large house a mile or so away. In India he had noticed that Henry, his second son, was not showing promise in the

Classics, but had a strong practical bent. He and his wife had discussed this; Charlie was interested in good teaching and, for his time, had an unusually creative approach to the education of his four sons. Because Bradfield was gaining a reputation for its science department, he decided to break the pattern; it seemed sensible to alternate the four boys between Charterhouse and Bradfield.

Although John, for a while, wanted to go to Eton with his friends Ben Nicolson and Ken Trevaskis, he was easily weaned from that idea by Henry's enthusiastic descriptions.

On a day in the Easter vac of 1928, during his first year at Cambridge, Henry – on his mother's instructions – drove John, aged $13\frac{1}{2}$, in the family's new Austin Seven from Summer Fields to Bradfield College, to sit the scholarship exam. John was noisy and very frisky on that drive, Henry remembered. He was already passionate about birds and knew that he would be encouraged to focus that interest at Bradfield. The nightjar in the copper beech tree opposite Army House, the freedom Henry had had to explore the fields and woods, the brilliant soccer coach John Moulsdale, the prospect of a new headmaster – made the school sound fun after the intense cramming of the last few months at Summer Fields.

John won First Scholarship in the summer, and was Bradfield's first scholar from Summer Fields. He won it easily; it wasn't a great feather in Summer Fields' cap, but Bradfield was pleased to have a boy so well trained in the Classics.

'A funny old gentleman who tied a school up with a church,' said Benjamin Jowett in the 1880s, of Thomas Stevens, the founder of Bradfield College. Stevens founded Bradfield as a choir school. Ironically, it was only at the end of the last century, when it opened its Modern Side, that it was put on the academic map. (Nowadays Bradfield is not known as an academic school.) Its setting – a lush, secluded stretch of the valley of the River Pang in Berkshire – remains as beautiful as when Stevens knew it as a boy in the early nineteenth century.

Among the new boys arriving in September 1928 at Army House with John were John Leahy, Alec McCurdy, Andrew Wardrop, John Gaye, George Govan and Edward Thompson. Andrew Wardrop, a classicist like John, and later a sinologist, was to be a lifelong friend; John Gaye was a sportsman and a keen naturalist; beyond their studies he and John enjoyed exploring the environs together, punting, climbing the local weir, birds-nesting and photographing. Another good friend made, Morrice James, was from another house. He was a brilliant classicist, and would become a distinguished diplomat and statesman.

'It's pretty bum here,' John wrote home to his mother. Even to a resilient boy, Bradfield was a rough place for the first year. Fagging was no less harsh than it had been in Henry's day. John was obliged to wear a gown and mortarboard on Sundays. The food was basic. And an absence of motherly women added to the austere atmosphere. Though as a school Bradfield was no longer isolated since the arrival of the motor-car, to John it must have seemed cut off from civilisation. He was on his best behaviour: Desmond Wilton, junior by a year to John, remembered him as 'a fairly quiet, introspective person'; Leslie Farmiloe, who, like John, was in Army House, remembered him as 'tall, good-looking, personable and well-mannered'.

The Officer Training Corps was an important element in the syllabus of public schools in the 1920s. Bradfield was paid a commission by the Government for recruiting boys into the Army. The weekly drill was tedious; 'Ronnie' Wathen, who had been a territorial major in wartime, should not by rights have worn his uniform, but it made him feel important...'Wake up, you boiled owl!' Lyonulph Tollemache, an aristocratic Wykehamist, better known as 'Tolly', commanded the parades in his loud, booming voice. Field Days, held each term at a different site, were looked forward to by the boys. A sergeant major came in from outside to mastermind them. A comic, blurred photograph of one of these occasions gives a good impression: one can imagine the asides from the boys as they were marched off, with the band playing - (John played the drum) eyes right at the war memorial in the quad on their way out to the road. The sergeant major's echoing commands could be heard by older boys in their classrooms as the cadets marched up Buscot Hill. *The Bradfield Chronicle*, the school magazine, reports the events of John's first Field Day, cold and windy, on 6 November 1928, thus: '...the question rises to the lips of any who possesses an enquiring mind - 'What does all this mean...?' Furthermore, if the day is then well spent those in power may decide the battle lost, won or drawn, and give orders for the fall in for the return march. The Army spirit is once again restored by the collection of blanks, the joys of the 'pull-through' and the rapture of the homeward march under the stars, to find that the same efficient hand that catered for the army at midday on the battle-field, is now again ready to distribute an excellent dish of 'sausage and mash'.'

John went on the OTC summer camps three times, to Tidworth, to Salisbury Plain, and as a corporal, to Tweseldown in 1932. He enjoyed being photographed in the Lines, wearing his fatigue trousers, singlet and peaked cap, standing lankily outside Tent Number Ten. (As I pored over the old photos, I saw that with the comedian, he had the actor in him, rather grave: he liked to be photographed in costume, so I discovered that at 16 he was aware of his good looks. I never noticed that trait in him at all - to me almost always he looked a bit of a scarecrow, the harassed schoolmaster - but all his family and friends remember his clothes and his little affectations regarding them. At Bradfield, Alec McCurdy remembered a good-naturedly rebellious touch: John liked to wear his shirt collar open, over the lapels of his coat.)

In fact John was taking an interest in his appearance, and in girls, four years before this, as an anecdote of his brother Dick's shows. Their Lefroy grandfather had bought a brewery for his only son Hugh, a bit of a wastrel. Drink had got the better of Hugh and he had retired to Bideford on the north coast of Devon with his rich wife Helen and their daughter Mary, who was a year older than Tommy. Several times Aunt Helen had invited the Usborne children to stay during the summer holidays. The house was a pretty Regency villa with white shutters. Tennis parties were arranged, and picnics on the beach. Some subtle matchmaking was going on! There are several photographs - a bevy of nubile girls in Jantzen bathing suits, bronzed, perched on the rocks; the few boys amongst them have towels modestly draped round the bottom halves of their suits. There was another Mary, aged 13 like John, the most beautiful girl; she was lusted after by Tommy, 20, Henry, 19, and Dick, 17, and they had all, Dick said, made advances to her. He told the story: on a warm evening in August 1927, they were all finishing a sumptuous picnic supper on the sand at Westward Ho! The sun was gilding everything with long rays. The sea at low tide looked inviting, but the party felt languid. Suddenly John jumped up and suggested to Mary that they have a last swim. All eyes were fastened on the couple - looking like young people from another world

- as they walked, chatting, towards the water's edge. Dick remembers that they were just perceptible, wading out, close to each other. John's arms started flailing about. What was his strange technique? Later, when his brothers asked him about it, he told them: 'I was showing her my latest bowling action.' He was getting his own back. Tiny was growing up.

Dick Usborne in 1993

The Usborne children knew for some time that their mother was ailing. But she kept from them the fact that she had breast cancer, and that she faced death at the age of 50. The boys were away at school and university; only Margaret, aged 10, was still at home with her in Battle. During her last months, unable to sleep in her bed, Janet organised her life round her reclining chair at the bedroom window. (Now in her '80s, Margaret still finds herself looking up at that window when she visits Battle.)

On 19 April 1929, in the Easter holidays, knowing that she had only days left, Janet packed two small suitcases for John and Margaret. She planned that, with their cocker spaniel Gerry and their cat Jummy, they should be away staying with their Watson cousins in Surrey when she died. Her 22-year-old niece Mary Lefroy had come from her parents' home in Bideford to help her run the household, and her uncle Pat Smythe, Provost of St Ninian's in Perth, had come down from Scotland to comfort her and give her spiritual consolation. Tommy was away, staying with a university friend; John was away too, staying with his friend Ben Nicolson; Dick was pottering at home. Henry, driving his mother's Morris Cowley, took Uncle Pat and Margaret to Rye for tea with friends, the Burra family (their daughter Anne was his current girlfriend). Mary telephoned Henry there

21

to tell him that their mother had died. Her last words, to Uncle Pat, were 'Something wonderful is happening to me.' Her religion and her pride in her family had given her her courage. It was astonishing to her children that she had kept the truth from them. Tommy and Henry went to the family doctor a few days later to have her illness explained.

Years earlier, when he and Janet had started their family in India, Charlie had made his youngest sister, Dorothy, the unofficial guardian of his children. Although Dorothy had a way of making her feel inferior, Janet had accepted this pact and came to be grateful that she and her husband would legally adopt her children in the event of her death.

The Usborne children were unbelievably fortunate. Uncle Hubert, as he was called by that generation of Usbornes, and later by his great-nephews and -nieces, was a heaven-sent guardian. He was four years older than their father; he had been brought up and educated at Harrow School, where his father had been a house-master. His mother was a member of the Digby family. Money had come from silk, and later, carpet manufacture, in Kidderminster; and when Hubert was a boy, a friend of his father's (a mysterious man - none of Hubert's children was allowed to know his name) had left a large amount of money to the family to be divided between him, his brother and four sisters. Hubert's own achievements were notable, but for the times, and for his circumstances, predictable: head boy at Harrow, First in Greats and a cricket blue at Balliol, a career in the ICS with his last few years as Deputy Commissioner of the Punjab. Both he and his brother-in-law were, as a result of their classical education, accomplished versifiers - and also lovers of cricket. The differences: he was cushioned financially, his parents were still alive and able to give him moral support, he was of tougher stuff physically and mentally, and he was content in his marriage. He felt that ahead of him, when he returned from India, life was offering him exciting opportunities. He had known Charlie and his brother and three sisters as a young man in England. Dorothy, 17 years younger than he, had accepted his proposal of marriage after he had been rejected by her older sister, Helen.

Hubert Watson, Dorothy, and their children Ursula, 6, Jennifer, 4, Pamela, 2, and Michael, 6 months, returned to England early in 1919. Hubert was aware of his good fortune in having been safe in India, spared the horror and danger of the First World War in Europe. He was looking for some voluntary work which, he said, 'should be of human service'. On 19 May, stirred by a 42-year-old spinster's appeal at the Albert Hall for support of her newly-founded 'Save the Children Fund', he promptly donated a substantial sum. He loved children and he was moved by the plight of the millions of them all over Europe, orphaned, helpless and starving in the aftermath of the war. In October of that year he was appointed honorary trea-surer of the Fund. Eglantyne Jebb, the Fund's founder and driving force, was to call him 'its linchpin'. The two of them were close associates; both were practical humanitarians, both enthusiastic writers of verse. In 1924 he was active in persuad-ing the League of Nations to adopt her brainchild, the Declaration of Children's Rights. He became the Fund's Chairman in 1930, and retired fifteen years later. There had been talk of a knighthood - which he would have accepted 'For the good of the cause' - but Aunt Dorothy persuaded him to refuse it.

A few months after Janet's death in 1929, Uncle Hubert bought a larger house

to accommodate his family and its addition of five more boisterous young people. Called 'Windrush', it was a handsome 10-bedroom Queen Anne mansion in
the village of Inkpen, close to the South Berkshire Downs. It came with 15 acres
of land, including a small paddock, a large rambling garden, stables, and married
quarters for a groom. Wiry little Aunt Dorothy, aged 43, her faithful 'Nurse' (the
children's nanny), and the Harris family - all servants - made the move from
Surrey together. The pets came too: the ponies Dodger and Nigger (who didn't
get up on Sundays because he knew he wouldn't be be needed to draw the trap):
Jane the donkey, the cats Bumble and Jummy and the dogs Juggins, Tim and Buzz.
At the start of the Depression, Uncle Hubert and the Save the Children Fund
were suffering hard times. Nevertheless he and Aunt Dorothy immediately made
of Windrush a wonderful home for all nine children.

Since acquaintance had been made soon after the Watsons' and Usbornes'
arrival in Inkpen, John was intrigued by some neighbours, the Padels, a musical
family with four children. They had their own string quartet. John's cousin
Michael, being a musical boy, soon got to know them and spent happy times playing their piano - but John, for fear of teasing by his three hearty brothers, stayed
away. The second of the three Padel boys, another John, remembered John
Usborne being the friendliest of his family; he never knew, until I told him in
1996, that he had wanted to join in their music-making. John Padel's pacifist
father was brought up in York, the son of a Moravian refugee. Though he and his
wife spent a great deal of their time running a kindergarten and doing good
works, because of his eccentric clothes he was considered in conservative Inkpen
very bohemian and - especially in the political climate of the time - rather suspect. 'He wore sandals!' exclaimed Dick when I asked him about Mr Padel.
Windrush had a field behind it and one day Dick was out there with Buzzy looking for partridges: he aimed his gun at a bird above Mr Padel while he was hoeing
in his raspberry patch across the road (Dick liked to remember that he actually shot
through Mr Padel's sunhat). The shot was brought round to the front door of
Windrush with a demand for an apology.

Music was one of the best things about Bradfield. John's voice broke early. He
sang in the chapel choir and the 'Glee Club', and he was on the Music
Committee in his last year. As one of the chorus in the Messiah in March 1930,
he sang 'Worthy is the Lamb' and 'Amen' with the combined choirs of Reading
University and Wellington College.

This performance was the result of some ambitious and dynamic teaching by
Douglas Fox, a man who is now a legend; a man whose courage in accepting an
appalling handicap endeared him to everybody. In 1918, at the age of 25, he was
asked to be Director of Music at Bradfield. He had been a brilliant organ scholar at
Oxford, and his progress had been watched with excitement by the music
establishment. In Normandy in 1917 he was badly wounded in the right arm, and
it had to be amputated. His determination to return immediately to his life as a
musician precluded learning how to use an artificial arm. He quickly learnt to be
self-reliant with one hand; in his organ and piano-playing he adapted, improvised,
and re-interpreted the music to suit his disability. The boys were amused by him
(John, in his middle age, mimicked him as he had learnt to do as a schoolboy);
Alec McCurdy and John Leahy remember his skill at the piano while teaching

the choir; and in taking the top off a boiled egg. Many described his hair-raising driving along the local lanes in his open two-seater Morris Cowley - changing gear at high speed, his elbow on the wheel while lighting his pipe. He invited to the school soloists of note, such as Leon Goossens and Myra Hess. From the day he arrived he started to build a reputation for Bradfield as a musical school.

'I rather tremble for John's half-term report,' Janet had written to Dick in February 1929, a few weeks before she died. She had heard that he was threatened with the loss of his scholarship after the first year. This event is a shady period in John's life. (He and his siblings never knew the outcome.) Dick's theory was that if the scholarship was withdrawn, the general lapse in John's Classics was to blame - a reaction after the intense Summer Fields cramming - and that he played too much cricket. Another possibility was that the financial stringency of the time was making the school look for ways to save money.

Norman Saunders was John's form master, a strict disciplinarian but a man who won his respect. He was 28 when John arrived, and was to watch him develop very closely during the five years he was his pupil, culminating in the last one in his own Classical Sixth Form. A classicist with the mind of a first-class scholar, Saunders found time for all the creative arts; he was musical, and painting fascinated him, particularly that of the the the Renaissance. He enthused to his pupils - and most definitely awakened John's sensibilities to visual art. There was no art teaching at Bradfield until 1936. I'm thankful for Saunders' enthusiasm: as John's daughter, I can sense the influence this man's purist tastes had on him at that impressionable age. For me, the big Phaidon linen-bound monographs on Botticelli and Manet, with their chalky sepia photogravure plates, bought at Blackwells while my father was at Oxford, were part of the furniture at home. Jane Austen's writing was a keen interest of Saunders, and John may have boasted about his connection to her through his mother.

'I spent five years as a boy at a very good public school, but I'm not at all sure that my few months' rehearsing and acting a tiny part in Sophocles' inspiring play, the *Antigone*, in Greek, wasn't worth all the other years put together.' These were John's words in 'Putting It Across', a talk he gave on the BBC in May 1954. (In 1890, after a visit to Epidauros, Hubert Branston Gray, a classicist who became headmaster after the founder's departure, built Bradfield's Greek Theatre in a disused chalk pit in the grounds. It is still the school's principal claim to fame.) Alec McCurdy, who sold programmes at the four performances of the *Antigone* in June 1931, remembered John clearly: as the Herald he stood on the road at the top of the steps down to the Greek Theatre, tooting into a four-foot long trumpet and chanting the standard greeting in Greek to the arriving guests. Barefoot, his legs painted brown, and thonged, and wearing a short white tunic piped with satin ribbon, he introduced the play with the words 'Euphemeite O Politi!' ('Silence please, Citizens!').

Often for the reason that Oxford and its specialists were nearby, lectures at Bradfield were original and lively: in March 1930 Dr Habberton Lulham talked to the boys on 'Rustic Life and Humour' with reference to Sussex gypsies and the lurcher curs they kept for catching rabbits. John Leahy remembered this prompting John to give some vulgar, and also - being a modest boy - he thought, disgusting imitations of the vernacular of some Inkpen locals. (All his life, my father loved talking to country people and listening to their speech. He may have been patronising at first, but if it started as a game – perhaps to entertain his brothers – it soon became a consuming interest. His father, from whom he inherited his love of language and zany sense of humour, had enjoyed talking to the Punjabi peasants in India. I remember well my father's sport of manoeuvring and tweaking his conversations with all sorts of people, strangers and friends, to produce the phrases he wanted to hear; words too: at the end of his life, he told me, laughing, how difficult it had been in Virginia, having once heard a woman talking of a 'spurnge' (sponge), to guide her to repeat the word. Journalism, with the latitude it allowed anyone who could express himself with ease (he later wrote some verse and short verses in the school magazine), began to intrigue him early. In October 1929 a journalist from *The Times*, P.L. Wetherby, came to speak about his paper, its offices and its foreign correspondents, showing slides 'excellently thrown on the screen by the new College lantern'.

Ornithologists from an Oxford society gave talks on particular birds and advice on how best to study and photograph them. A.P. Gardiner, alias 'Sniffers', the chemistry and biology teacher, took the boys on wonderful field trips: plovers, grasshopper-warblers, snipe, redshank were all to be seen on the marshes on the far side of the Pang; a nightjar was still nesting in the copper-beech tree opposite Army House. As a small boy, Hugh Whistler's descriptions of birds were part of John's ornithological education. No doubt using as reference the beautiful watercolour plate from a bird manual bought by his mother for his fourteenth birthday, John and Alec McCurdy saw their first Lesser Redpoll together. Later in life, John noted down sightings of this bird in his beloved Peterson/Mountfort/Hollom *Field Guide to the Birds of Britain and Europe*.

John was a 'cheese' (a Bradfield term for a hard-working or over-enthusiastic person), but he couldn't resist the sports opportunities. Cricket flourished and John was in the First Eleven in his last year. His brother Dick said he had a 'wristy' approach. 'I never connected him with large scores, but clearly he could have got them,' he told me. 'Why didn't he get them?' I asked. 'He was too good-looking.' he answered, meaning that he loved to strike attitudes, 'as we all did'. The four brothers were all Classicists by training and heredity, and – with their robust health – sportsmen too. Tommy – like his father – became a good rackets player. They were all good cricketers and tennis-players (John was in the Bradfield First Six) and all but Henry, keen soccer-players. Dick earned a squash-rackets blue at Balliol. John, with the leanest frame, was the most athletic.

Bradfield is a soccer school. In its early days it had its own version of the game. John Moulsdale was his soccer coach (John got into the Second XI in his last year), and History and English teacher. History had been his subject at Cambridge – and he had won a Soccer blue; he had been a Welsh International player. For this reason he was popular with the boys and something of a celebrity in Bradfield village. In the middle school he was John's history teacher. In 1928 he was given the assignment of starting the English Department for the school. Moulsdale was enthusiastic and his excitement in his own prodigious reading infected the boys. (So John came in on the earliest English teaching of public schools.) He had a fertile imagination and the power to articulate, and he understood the boys' minds well. John Moulsdale's enjoyment of his subject contributed, as had Leonard Strong's, to John's decision, although he may not have recognised it at the time, to read English at Oxford.

Cyril Bailey, the Classics don at Balliol College, came from Oxford to preach to the boys in 1931, on a Sunday in June. There is no concrete evidence now to show that John became religious at about this time, and that for the first year at Oxford he thought seriously of joining the Church. We know that he did. Cyril Bailey, who was religious himself, was without doubt an influence on him.

Eighteen-year-old John, a school-leaver, enjoyed his summer. His caption to a photograph 'Chaps at the Aldershot Tattoo', shows his schoolfriends grinning in the sunshine in their best Oxford bags and trilbies, under a hoarding advertising 'Guinness for Strength'. There were punting picnics at Pangbourne. John had taken part in three weeks of expert coaching in tennis, on the new school courts, by the revered Major Moss (who had been lent by Charterhouse - where he coached regularly - to promote tennis in schools for the Lawn Tennis Association.) As an Old Bradfieldian cricketer he played for the 'Stragglers of Asia' against the Bradfield Waifs for two days in August.

At Windrush that summer of 1933, John and his younger cousin Michael, already one of Harrow's best cricket players at fourteen, were the only boys at home with the four girls: Tommy was away learning German, staying with a family in the Harz Mountains; Henry was working for Viyella in Nottingham; Dick had landed in Advertising - the agency Pritchard Wood and Partners - having been turned down for jobs in the Far East and the Police. Margaret, now aged fifteen, was at Cheltenham Ladies College.

Chapter Two

As John prepared to go up to Balliol, a political cloud was creeping over the horizon. Hitler had become Chancellor of Germany in January, and it was dawning on Europe that there was insanity in his greed for power. There seemed no way out of his tightening grip except through another war. John would be profoundly affected, but for the moment he was single-mindedly looking forward to life as an undergraduate.

His mother, uncle, aunt and elder brothers had made him feel he had a rightful place at Balliol since he was first aware of its existence; it was now his turn to get down to work. His rooms, for his first two years at the college, were on the first floor, Staircase 4, overlooking Broad Street, in Alfred Waterhouse's Brackenbury Building. He was excited, naturally: he took a snap of the view from one of his windows. The higgledy-piggledy eighteenth century roofscape above the little shops opposite is still easily recognisable, almost exactly as it was that day, Sunday 8 October, 1933.

The college has always had a reputation for being the most radical of the university - but also the most liberal; its thinking has been, since its founding, original, even during two centuries of near-obscurity after the Reformation. Balliol, then, was seen as a hotbed of Papists; at least two Balliol men were hanged and martyred for their 'seditious' beliefs. Benjamin Jowett, who was Master from 1870 until 1893, made the college a more secular place than it had ever been; he brought in Science, English, History and other new degree subjects. While encouraging originality and academic brilliance, he placed great emphasis on leadership and duty. (The East India Company, from 1806, had run its own school, Haileybury in Hertfordshire, to train boys for its Civil Service. After the Indian Mutiny of 1857 - which put an end to the despotic East India Company - the control of British India passed to the Crown. Jowett, then a Classics tutor at Balliol, was an adviser to the Government commission which planned the training for Queen Victoria's new Indian Civil Servants).

The Master of Balliol during John's time was A.D.Lindsay, the second of two successive Masters who were supporters of adult education for working-class men. He abhorred the idle rich. The votes of the youngest, most radical Fellows probably swung his election in 1924. He was a Scottish Calvinist by faith, and he wrote on Classical ethics.

'Balliol is a broad-minded college,' John's brother Dick told me. 'Chapel on Sundays was not obligatory. Tutorials, two a week, were in the mornings; meals were in Hall. Pubs were out of bounds. You could never be out after midnight without permission (but the scouts usually turned a blind eye). In the afternoon you were your own boss. Lectures permitting, you could play your chosen sport on the Master's Field, ten minutes' away. Back to the Junior Common Room for tea and crumpets (cucumber sandwiches in summer); or, as a treat, you could order a Devon Tea, with a Palm Court Orchestra playing, at the Cadena Café in 'the Corn' (Cornmarket Street, Oxford's old shopping street).

'Your scout – there was one for the undergraduates living on each staircase – looked after your comforts. For most of us, he was the first person in our lives to treat us as adults. He laid your fire and kept it going. He brought you hot water in the morning. He made your bed and tidied your rooms. He sent your sheets and dirty clothes out to the laundry and checked them back in. He sold you secondhand a teapot and a gown, and he would find you a bicycle to rent. If you'd been sick after drinking too much and he had cleared up, you gave him, as a tip, a chit for four pints at the Buttery. If your chamber pot was full in the night you had to go out in all weathers to Lady Periam's, the latrines in the quad (so called because the original site had been lodgings donated by a distinguished Elizabethan lady). When you wanted a bath you walked to the far end of the college, to the lower reaches of Staircase 21, where one-armed Cornell, in clouds of steam, found you a recently vacated bath-room, and chanted his cheerful hexameter: "Hurry up, gentlemen, please. We have lots of gentlemen waiting."'

Cyril Bailey had known that he would be John's tutor on his coming up to Balliol since he had seen him performing in the *Antigone* at Bradfield. Before John's first tutorial he had asked him to read Virgil for his Latin and Homer for his Greek. He set for translation some passages of Henry David Thoreau's *Walden* into Greek. Cyril – whose special studies were Lucretius, Epicurus and the religion of the Romans – was a 'phenomenal name inside the college' for his greatness as a teacher of Latin and Greek Composition. His professional commitments were many: he was elected Public Orator (the University's speechmaker, an office dating from the sixteenth century) in 1932; he sang with the Oxford Bach Choir; he played cricket, he loved mountaineering and cycling; he produced plays for the Oxford University Dramatic Society, and often took part in them. He had been tutor to both Tommy and Dick during their years at Balliol in the late 1920s.

Cyril was then in his sixties – six years away from retirement. Like John's father, he had been an undergraduate at Balliol under Benjamin Jowett. He was convivial and humorous – even in ceremonial Latin. All three Balliol brothers loved him; later each one had in his house the portrait etching of him by Andrew Freeth, and they all continued to meet him at Balliol dinners until his death in 1957.

Starting in 1933 with John was Richard Briscoe. He wrote: 'The College at that time was more varied in its undergraduates than many of the others. There were a good many from abroad, especially America, also a number from grammar schools as well as the traditional intake from Public Schools. Those from Public Schools tended to collect together socially, partly because one's background and origin were more influential than they are now, but also because of financial reasons. The grouping which included John and me were men with reasonably generous allowances, who could afford comfort and enjoyment, but not on any extravagant scale.

'Balliol was recognized as a college where you took your work seriously but not to the exclusion of other interests. Sport was not considered by us as of great importance. We did not contemplate taking up rowing. John did play in college football (soccer) and cricket teams, but it was not a matter of consuming interest. Our social life was very much centred on the college; and while we belonged to some university societies, I do not think John was much committed to them. The theatres (especially the Playhouse) and cinemas were cheap and we went regularly, but talking was what we liked to do, the beer in college was cheap and you did not have to worry if you drank too much, as you could manage, however late, to get back to your own bed. We did drink wine occasionally, but not, as I recall, spirits. Drugs were not thought about and anyway were not available.'

For Christmas after his first Michaelmas term John met his cousins Jenny and Pam, aged 19 and 17, at Château d'Oex, near Gstaad. The two youngest Watson sisters had spent three months 'learning French' with a family in Grenoble. This was John's first experience of skiing; he loved it so much that he contrived to be in the Alps every winter vacation while he was at Oxford. He usually assembled a group, and through the Wayfarers Travel Bureau had his own holiday free. He needed the exercise: beer being cheap at Balliol, he was becoming beefy.

By the New Year of 1934, the girls had gone home and John had joined a group of friends who had no Balliol connections, only one of whom I know about. Nicholas Monsarrat had stayed at Windrush, invited by Henry. They became friends in Nottingham, where they had been living in the same boarding-house. (At that time Monsarrat was about to leave his job as an articled clerk with his uncle's firm of solicitors, to write full-time; he would be publishing his first novel that year, *Think Of Tomorrow*.) A snapshot shows Nick and John skiing together on Kummi Ridge 'approaching lunch'; another shows Nick sprawling in the sunshine on the hotel balcony. (He dressed with panache, Dick remembered. 'He knew how to wear a thin scarf as a tie.') In his sixties, Nicholas Monsarrat wrote in his autobiography that since his schooldays 'indolence had never palled'. I remember my father saying to me when I was quite small that Nick was a lounge lizard and that he had pleaded an ankle injury so that he could stay behind with the girls.

John made many good friends at Balliol; the snaps show the chaps lined up on their skis at Adelboden; attending to a broken-down car on their way to a Balliol Players performance; standing among rocks on Snowdon on one of Cyril Bailey's reading parties; in ridiculous skaters' attitudes on a frozen pond. Ben Nicolson, Rawle Knox and Ralph Merton had popped up again, last seen at Summer Fields; Garrod Treverton, Richard Briscoe, Colum Gore-Booth, John McNair; Andrew Wardrop and Morrice James, who had been at Bradfield with him; Bill Davies, John Bailey, Cyril's son; Stuart Abbott, Oliver Bell, Marcus Goodall and Lawrence Waddy.

From California, where he now lives, Lawrence wrote to me: 'At Balliol, John was really a joy to be with. It is hard to pinpoint the memories, but I can still see every expression on his very expressive face: one of the best smiles in the world, a gentle humorous voice, backed by the twinkle in his eyes. He really loved life, so it was fun to be with him at breakfast in College or on the Master's Field, going to films, or just talking and talking. There can be few things which he and I did not discuss.'

There were girlfriends too, but for the moment, only in the vacations. An actress named Margery, a flaxen blonde with a look of Jean Harlow, was John's regular girlfriend for most of his second year. At Easter she posed in front of his Austin Seven, wearing a fur-trimmed black coat, with a clutch-bag and a rakish pill-box hat. The two of them became engaged in the summer. With Buzzy the dog beside her, Margery posed on the lawn at Windrush in a revealing striped playsuit. 'Ugh!' said my sister Julie, aged about twelve, looking at the photo, 'to think I could've come out of her!' Another girlfriend was Virgy Case, an American, met on the ski-slopes. (Pam still mimics her American pronunciation of her nickname, remembering, perhaps, her own teenage embarrassment about the fuss John made of her.) At that time – in his forties John was to tell the poet George Macbeth that it was a freudian lapse – any American girl with the name Virginia would have drawn him to her instantly.

What had cast this American spell on John? His American colleagues at Balliol? His brother Henry's talk after his trip to Illinois in 1932? Jeanette MacDonald singing 'Beyond the Blue Horizon'? Reading the first stories of Robert Benchley, James Thurber and Dorothy Parker in the *New Yorker?* (In the late 1920s at Balliol, Tommy and Dick used to pick that magazine out – apart from the *Daily Worker* and an English magazine called *Bally Hoo* – from the untidy pile on the table in the Junior Common Room.) All four brothers loved the American humorists, and gave to each other, and their sister Margaret, anthologies as birth-day presents.

At Bradfield John Moulsdale had taught John American history enthusiastically and positively, enjoying breaking through the old post-First World War preconception that the U.S. government was rough and insensitive, bleeding Europe dry with its demands for reparations. It was romantic to read about British families risking their lives and fortunes in the seventeenth century to settle in an uncharted country where they believed they would have civil and religious freedom. With the coming of the Talkies in 1930 – there were then very few English films – everything American, to the young, had 'glamor'. For young people the culture was irresistible. Permission to enjoy cynicism was given them by the jokes of Jewish comedians, told stridently in the colourful speech born out of a cosmopolitan melting-pot. Yet the space over there was limitless! America seemed to offer something for everyone. It was intoxicating for an eighteen-year-old at school in England during the austere early 1930s to hear of Roosevelt's plans for his New Deal.

Discovering that the youngest Usborne was as enthusiastic as his brothers about America and its culture, Cyril Bailey was not surprised that he was keen to join the Balliol Players. The amateur theatrical troupe was started in 1923 by two brothers, Godfrey and Robert Turton. Richard Briscoe recalled: 'At the end of the summer term the Players would make a two-week tour of western and southern England performing – usually in the open air – a Greek play in English translated by Professor Gilbert Murray. It was a strenuous business. The scenery – usually a temple façade – was transported in an ancient hired lorry and had to be erected for each performance. There were often crises! I remember once after an exhausting day and evening giving a performance at Battle Abbey, we struggled into our sleeping bags only to find in the morning that we were in full view of the girls' dormitories of the school.'

John took part in the tour of July 1934, for which the troupe had chosen to perform the *Ajax* by Sophocles, a tragedy. The main objective for them all, setting out, was to have a whale of a time (and they did; Lawrence Waddy remembers John as 'a quintessential Balliol Player'). They performed at the public schools Blundells, Sherborne, Whitgift and Lancing; and the Bishop's Palace at Wells and under the battlements of Corfe Castle. The team spirit was strong and the weather was good; publicans along the route knew them well.

However self-indulgent were John's first efforts at teaching, his acting experiences at Bradfield and Balliol made him project himself well. Walter Oakeshott, to be his headmaster at St Paul's at the start of his teaching career, had himself been at Balliol and had acted with the Players. About his role as Orestes in the *Oresteia* in 1924, performed for an audience of 700 against a vast starry sky at Corfe Castle, Oakeshott wrote 'the experience entered more deeply into one's being than any other aesthetic experience'.

John sat his Mods exam in 1935, and got a 3rd Class (as he would for his degree in 1937) - not good. But this was by now almost a family pattern. Dick, who reckoned he had worked harder than all his contemporaries for both his Mods and Greats, and also got thirds, felt strongly that there should have been some instruction on how to take the examinations. The examiners should have been Balliol dons, he thought, not dons from other colleges.

It was not considered advisable to change subjects after Mods, and the dons usually made it difficult. Perhaps in this case Cyril Bailey said, 'I don't think John Usborne will flourish at Greats...' giving John a chance to agree and to switch to English, on the whole seen as a soft option.

Roy Ridley was Balliol's first Fellow in English; he was elected in 1920. He was 45 when John became his pupil, and had been the college Chaplain for four years. As a brilliant Classics undergraduate of Balliol, he was unusual in his scholarship in subjects beyond the Classics. In 1913, when she was twenty, Dorothy Sayers watched him reading a poem on Oxford, and winning for it the Newdigate Prize for Poetry. 'Boyish, with fine sculptural bone-structure, a Roman nose, large grey eyes, sleek blond hair, thin lips' was her description of him. Though she had seen him only at a distance, she fell in love with him; she had been so intent on her search for a model for her hero that she was bound to fall on finding him. Three years later she published her book *Whose Body?* in which Lord Peter Wimsey made his first appearance.

Ridley was seen as a young don who, by the breadth of his tastes, was able to shake the literary prejudices out of his pupils. He is remembered for the emphasis he gave to the writing of clear and forceful essays. Here was a young tutor, vain and touchy certainly, but with an infectious fire in his teaching.

Some time during the Trinity term of 1936, probably at the 'Commem' Ball in June, John met a diminutive, vivacious Australian girl of nineteen. She had at least two suitors from Balliol, one of whom was John's friend Garrod Treverton. Garrod introduced them to each other. John - after his summer affair the year before with Margery - was more susceptible than all the other chaps to girls who practised being glamorous. Paula Halloran had never known austerity. Australian girls were very exotic at Oxford - they were usually free of parents, and they had travelled. They didn't have to be brainy (apart from one brainy one, Marghanita Laski, John never mentioned female undergraduates at Oxford) but they were healthy and tanned and sleek. I hope she stood up to him as he teased her about her Irish origins and her ignorance of cricket. He was very smitten. She was taken to Windrush to be shown off, as all girlfriends were. Pam remembers that she was beautifully dressed; and that when she was being offered a second helping of a rather substantial pudding, John answered for her: 'Paula's watching her figure.' None of the girls, heretofore, had met anybody who took her shape so seriously: but for the boys it was obviously an attraction.

Paula Halloran had been brought up in New South Wales, her parents moving house often. However, they lived mainly in Double Bay, Sydney. (An ancestor, Laurence Halloran, from County Sligo, had been Nelson's chaplain at the Battle of Trafalgar. Six years later, in 1811, he was transported for forging a tenpenny frank; he went on to found Sydney's first grammar school.) Ted, Paula's father, was from a racing family, and worked with his brother Jack as a stock and station agent in an office on O'Connell Street, Sydney. In 1910, on his horse Scopas, he won the Bong Bong Cup, run annually at the prestigious Bong Bong Picnic Races near Bowral, south west of Sydney. He fought with the Australian Cavalry at Gallipoli. He cut a dash with the ladies, not marrying until his late thirties. His heart was strained after the war, and when Paula was seven he died, of a burst aortic aneurysm. She had adored him, being his only child. To her he embodied Irishness. His shortcomings were part of his appeal; she was always proud of his horsemanship and his gambling.

Paula's mother, named Florence but nicknamed 'Haysie', or 'Hay' (her family name) was of Scottish stock, and married late for the time. She was thirty-five when Paula was born in Woollahra, Sydney. Hay was already successful at buying and selling property in the smartest residential areas of Sydney; after Ted's death she became quite a merry widow, and not having time for her child in the school holidays, she often sent her away to stay with Ted's glamorous aunt Allie Macphillamy, a noted hostess. Allie's husband ran 'Warroo', a sheep station near Forbes, 150 miles west of Sydney, and Paula loved its beautiful homestead and famous garden. There she was made a fuss of by her big boy-cousins, and rode the pony that was kept especially for her. At the age of fifteen she wanted to study Art, but her mother – being a social climber – had other ideas. Hay's own childhood had been spent in Sussex; several trips back to England had strengthened her resolve that Paula should be married well, and not to an Australian. So she was taken out of school a year early, and sent off, on her own, to a finishing school in Switzerland.

A spinster aunt living in the village of Long Crendon, near Chinnor, Oxfordshire, was to provide Paula with a base for her holidays during the year she spent at Le Grand Verger, in Lausanne. She was a very pretty girl, with a Celtic look about her – petite with short dark hair and hazel eyes – and she was a good tennis-player; it wasn't long – having been detailed by Paula's mother, her aunt was arranging meetings with young people locally and generally matchmaking – before she began to meet Oxford undergraduates. When she arrived she was sunny, excited, and completely unaffected by any post-Depression strictures or news of Hitler's sinister moves.

The first man to fall for Paula – during her first summer in England, when she was just seventeen – was Vivian Spong, a young subaltern in the Royal Tank Corps. Paula and her mother, on a short visit to see how Paula was faring, were staying in a guest house in Cowes in the Isle of Wight. Vivian and a cousin of Paula's, Bunny Crowle, also a subaltern, were both recovering from hayfever at Osborne House – at the time an Army officers' convalescent home. She spent

Christmas with Vivian's family. Within a year she had acquired a fiancé, a young man called Peter Watt, a Balliol undergraduate. (After her death I found a thick pile of his letters, tied up with white ribbon.) Her engagement was a whirl - Brands Hatch and the races and all the right things. Why that relationship ended she could not remember: 'I suppose I met Daddy!' Like the other girls at Le Grand Verger, she worked at acquiring the skills that would make her highly marriageable, and eventually - if she pulled it off - a grand lady. (She had little knowledge of cooking when she married; the skills were of the social kind, and included employing servants and household management. My socialist father used to make digs about that place.) Switzerland was a safe haven for the daughters of Jewish industrialists. Were those girls aware, at the end of 1934, of the gathering clouds? Did they hear of the 12,000 Russians who were exiled to Siberia by Stalin as enemies of the state?

For John's third year he lived at Holywell Manor, a new annexe to accommodate 40 members of Balliol; living was more comfortable there than in College, with running water in the rooms. In May 1936 something happened in Oxford which struck horror particularly into the hearts of those living at Holywell, and strikes horror still: a Canadian undergraduate of Balliol named Pat Moss, the son of a well-known attorney who had recently died, was knocked down by a car driving along Holywell Street, a narrow street close to Balliol. No policemen were near. The driver bundled Moss's unconscious body into the car, drove to a field beyond Cowley - about four miles away - threw him into a haystack, and set light to it. It was known that he had been alive when the fire was lit because in the autopsy some burnt hay was found in his gullet. Pat Moss was his mother's only child; she came over after his death but she was unable to persuade Balliol to hold an inquest. Neither the car nor the driver was found.

Michael Barton, with whom John had played tennis in Fleet when they were both fifteen, was at Oriel College. He and John met again because of their shared enthusiasm for cricket (Michael later acquired renown as a player for Surrey) and became friends. Michael remembers: '...we decided to go together on a four-week tour of the South of France, Rome and Florence in the spring of 1937, our last year at Oxford.

'John has left a fine photographic record of the trip, which causes me much pleasure when I look at it again. It was in the course of this expedition that he came to be known - at his own instance - as "The Practical Man" or in Italy "L'Uomo Pratico". He was proud of this sobriquet although it was not always appropriate. Two examples of this failure were provided by the occasion, when we were both listening to a speech by Mussolini from the balcony of the Palazzo Venezia (he had just returned triumphant from Tripoli), and John - riled by some anti-English references - exclaimed in a loud voice 'Abbasso il Duce!'. Luckily his words were drowned in a burst of applause from the crowd; otherwise we might have spent the second half of our holiday in an Italian gaol. And then when we disembarked from the train at Roquebrune he left our money, return tickets to London and his passport on the luggage rack.

'This made it difficult for us to run the villa in Roquebrune which we had rented from a friend of my parents. But we managed somehow until some funds arrived from England. Things seem to have been more honest in those days and eventually we got back the passport, the tickets and that part of the money which was in the form of a draft on the Bank of Naples.

'Cooking gave vent to John's practicality and I remember his delight at his invention of a savoury which he named "Croûte Usbornavitch" followed by the expression by now becoming familiar, "Practical Man Again!" It is true that it tasted rather like sardines on toast.

Michael Barton in 1965

'In the autumn of 1937 I went for a year to Cornell; but we kept in touch through letters. For some reason he began to address me also as "Practical" although in many ways, but not all, I was less practical than he was. So our missives would start off "Dear Practical" and end "Yours ever, Practical." '

Nicholas Monsarrat, John's friend and fellow-socialist, wrote in his autobiography *Life Is A Four-Letter Word*:
'I was nearest to Communism at this time, like nearly all my friends. We were anti-British Empire, anti-Big Business, anti-Religion: anti-fascist, especially at home; anti-war, anti-recruiting, anti-uniforms, anti-militarism, anti, anti all the things which disgraced the name of honour. All men in the services were bloody fools.'
Visually the 1937 May Day Demonstration was extraordinary, for the spectacle of its thousands of marchers, its cheerfulness, and for its colours - the variety of banners waving in the strong sunshine. 'Historic' was the adjective used by the *Daily Worker* in its report; the left-wing Press called it 'The Peace March' and described its atmosphere of fervour. Looking back on that day, knowing of the war facing everyone, it seems so poignant that there was optimism at all: it was the optimism born from having all but conquered the domestic scourge of unemployment, and the optimism of the young people there, in spite of, and because of, the reasons they were to fight for.

(May Day was established in 1889 in Paris as a festival of international solidarity of workers in the active struggle against capitalism. In the United Kingdom the First of May has been celebrated since 1900 as a National Labour Festival.)

The British Communist Party, who had organised the May Day marches since 1927, had never before had so large a membership. As the leader of the battle against Fascism and unemployment, the two poisons bedevilling working-class life at this time, its reputaion was good. Fewer men were out of work than at any date since December 1929, and these men had the confidence to be militant about pay and conditions. Two years earlier the party could not have trusted intellectuals, who were mostly right-wing; now, with socialism strengthening in the universities they were welcomed into the fold. Harry Pollitt, the leader of the British Communist Party, had appealed for volunteers to fight with the Republicans in Spain at the outbreak of the Civil War in 1936. The British Battalion was newly formed, but the Foreign Office made enlisting for it illegal. This resulted in recruitment going underground – giving it, for young idealists, just the romance it needed to maintain its momentum.

The Labour Party – not in harmony with the Communists at this time (over the issue of the Spanish Civil War) but determined to appear so for solidarity on this day – was also in a militant and determined mood. Attlee, who still used his First World War rank of Major in 1937, was present not only in his capacity as Leader of a popular Labour Party, but to show he objected to the policies that were leading us unavoidably into war.

On this gloriously sunny afternoon, 30,000 demonstrators walked from the Embankment to Hyde Park through streets which were decorated for the coronation of King George VI, to take place eleven days later. A large contingent of London busmen, striking for a $7\frac{1}{2}$ hour working day, led the march, cheerful and confident of their support. In step and keeping ranks, the drivers in spanking white coats and cap-tops, the conductors in blue uniforms, they marched holding their plain red banners for victory. Following them were 10,000 members of the London Communist Party: trade unionists, relatives of men fighting in Spain; Left Book Club members with branch banners and replicas of the book-choice covers, artists, writers, teachers; there were Indian communists bearing their portrait of Nehru; a contingent of students from Oxford, Cambridge and London Universities.

The busmen gave the occasion a festive note. People meant to enjoy the day, and they had dressed up for it. Nobody wore casual clothes – not that they existed for the working man (only the privileged, or Americans, had sports clothes.) James MacGibbon, a registered Communist, and his wife Jean, friends of the Usbornes and Watsons, were marching. Jean, wearing a grey coat and skirt and a red tie, pushed their baby Hamish in his pram. Jocelyn Herbert, 20-year-old daughter of A.P.Herbert – and like John to be a St Paul's Girls' School parent in the 1950s – wore a flowered dress and a hat. [I loved hearing Jocelyn say, in 1996: 'It was fun!' but felt a little sceptical at: 'We had more fun when we were young than you do now!'] John was with his Oxford friends. He left no diary entry, no notes…but the MI5 spies were active.

When the marchers arrived in Hyde Park, huge crowds – in the press photographs these show a sea of hats: homburgs, trilbies and flat caps – clustered round the platforms to hear Attlee and Pollitt, the two leaders; Herbert Morrison (conscientious objector in the First World war, in 1937 Labour MP for Hackney South), Fenner Brockway (First World War pacifist; at the time General Secretary of the International Labour Party) and Ted Willis (aged nineteen, secretly a Communist, working as a journalist on the *Daily Worker*). The busmen received a tremendous ovation. Harry Pollitt - a much-loved figure, just by his presence smoothing the tensions between the two parties - made a good, fighting speech. Then Attlee, described by Monsarrat as the 'slightly forlorn' leader of the Opposition, spoke. 'Both', he added, 'told us the news was bad.' Peace was not to be.

Chapter Three

'I sing the breakfast-table, and the hour
When Windrush young and old on healthy food
Their strength renew to face the daily round.
.... See at the groaning board
Expectant sits the mistress of the house
Scanning her letters, while the attendant Nurse
Speaks honeyed words to cat and dog in turn...
Now one by one the family appears,
The flow of talk runs on; light badinage
With jest and laughter; keen comparisons
Of Surrey's men with Sussex by the sea
In cricket prowess, or of Michael's Hobbs
With Bradman or Dulip, the loved of John,
The Master putting in a word for Grace.'

'The Breakfast Table' was written by John's Uncle Hubert in 1934, giving a good impression of his benign view of the breakfast ritual at Windrush during the holidays, and the gaggle of nine children, four of his own and five orphans, over whose heads Windrush kept its roof. It is one of a collection of verses entitled 'Windrush Rhymes'. Uncle Hubert published the first of these little navy-blue buckram-bound books in 1939 to celebrate the completion of a decade at Windrush. He recorded each family event: examination results, his wife's birthdays, the children's twenty-firsts, marriages, births, the deaths of ponies, dogs, cats (Jummy, the cat from Battle, had his epitaph in Latin: Ad Jummium) - even the selling for munitions-scrap of a beloved old car. Every visitor is mentioned, and many of their 'roofers' (thank-you letters, in verse, for weekends enjoyed) are included. To fill the gaps - usually to write about their aunt and uncle, and each other - the literary Usbornes contributed their own doggerel. The *Rhymes* were so popular with the family and the legions of friends that came to stay, that four books of them were published, the last in 1947, just after Uncle Hubert's death.

Uncle Hubert included other verses too: of a more sombre note - but some spiced with humour - they reflect his feelings of helplessness in the face of the escalating aggression of the dictators; and as a result of their hunger for power, the cruelty inflicted on children, especially. He expressed his appreciation of people working to relieve suffering; and in his own despair he offered solace to young people who felt unsure and isolated in their pacifist beliefs. This small part of his output is an older man's contribution - more frustrated than angry, more fatalistic, perhaps, than those of younger poets - to the political writing of the 1930s and the Second World War.

Windrush gave John a happy home. More than sixty years later, I try to imagine the feelings of my father, one upper-middle-class young man with a social conscience during that pre-war period in England. Perhaps there was something exciting, even gripping, about Hitler's onward march? Discussion, mostly at the table, took up a lot of John's time at Windrush. It was enjoyable and healthy. The misery of the lives of millions all over the country certainly didn't blight his youthful ebullience.

James MacGibbon, a long-standing friend of the family, wrote: 'My first visit to Windrush might have been a formidable experience. I was the 22-year-old newly married husband of Jean, old school-friend of Ursula's since they were at the Hall School, and already known at Windrush, while I had never before mingled with such a large family; and a first encounter with so many contemporaries all, unlike me, highly educated, could have been daunting - but not with the Usborne-Watson lot. They were all welcoming, prepared to accept a newcomer, on first meeting at least. John happened to be the first member of the family I talked to. In my memory the front door of Windrush was always open, winter and summer, and I was standing outside it that first evening, smelling the summer smells and listening to the birds long before the dinner gong sounded, feeling slightly shy. Then John appeared, tall, handsomely saturnine, olive-skinned. For something to say I deplored my inability to recognise bird-song. "Oh you needn't worry about that", he told me, "it's usually a blackbird". As John was a serious bird-watcher that cavalier comment won my heart.

'John had so many interests, so many gifts, perhaps he even suffered from having too many...however, this was an integral constituent of his charm. One of these interests he shared with us was being word-perfect with the lyrics of Cole Porter and Jerome Kern - a mark of the true scholar with the common touch. I remember his entertaining us one velvety-warm summer night when we lay on the banks of the Kennet gossiping and singing (it might have been after a late-night bathe) and exchanging all kinds of songs; Ursula engaged us with German folk tunes, Jean with French ones. Then John took over with the latest numbers from American musicals. He had a good light baritone voice and his singing of these popular numbers was moving and nostalgic. It is not beyond imagination to see him playing the lead in a musical play.'

Though a critical and grim one for Europe, for the Usbornes and Watsons, 1936 was a festive year. Henry, aged twenty-seven, now working as an oil combustion engineer in Droitwich, came down to marry, on 9 May, in the beautiful thirteenth-century parish church of St Michael's, Inkpen, his nineteen-year-old first cousin Pam. ('She was always my girlfriend,' he told me solemnly when he was eighty-five. He had courted her romantically: while he was training with the RAF Reserve, he flew low over Windrush to drop a note for her. He carried off the top of a tree, stuck to the tailplane. For that misdemeanor he was forbidden to fly again. Pam had wanted him to give it up anyway. Later, when he had two sons, he was grateful to her, because he realised that almost certainly he would have been killed in the Battle of Britain.) The family snaps of Pam as a teenager show a healthy girl with a thatch of thick short blonde hair, and the sun in her eyes; usually she was on horseback or holding a puppy. Pam had only ever had eyes for Henry; her parents tried to dissuade her, thinking of the genetic risk for her children, but they soon gave in.

There had always been an ulterior motive to Aunt Dorothy's encouragement to the children to bring school and university friends to stay: subtle match-making. (It had been done to her by her brother Charlie.) It was a sport for her, and Uncle Hubert left her to it. There were guests most weekends - her own Anglo-Indian friends, and 'a mob of young men and maidens', Dick remembered. Roland Alderson, a flying mate of Henry's, courting Jenny at the time, came down by aeroplane, landing in the football field.

It had become known locally that Windrush was a house belonging to the gentry, with its comings and goings of guests and its two grass tennis courts: gentry, though, with something suspicious about them, a little too self-sufficient. The mistress of the house did not attend the parish church on Sundays. For years Uncle Hubert had worked at home gathering signatures for the Peace Pledge Union. Spy-fever was making people very jumpy at the time; since a neighbour's tip-off to MI5 ('The lights are on all night!') his work for it began to be considered a front for communist activities, and a watch was kept on the house. Dick remembered a morning when the front doorbell rang and some men asked to check the books. It was a source of amusement for all the young pacifists, family and their guests.

For young left-wing visitors especially, during those tense years, the Watsons offered a refuge in an atmosphere tolerant and cheerful. That role was the life-blood of the household. These friends loved staying, and some, like James Currie, and the MacGibbons (James MacGibbon was already a communist) with their baby son Hamish, became absorbed into the family and were sheltered by it.

Tommy, John's eldest brother, married later than he wanted to; and not only because he had a difficult time finding work when he came down from Balliol in 1930. He eventually found a job in a Kent brewery, but soon tired of it. (He was to be unhappy in other fields - accountancy and merchant banking - until he joined the Board of Trade in 1939, starting his career as a civil servant.) The German language interested him; thanks to the contacts Ursula made through her studies, there were many young German visitors at Windrush. In 1932, a widower named Adolf Just, the founder of Jungborn, a famous sanatorium in a spa in the Harz Mountains, having had Ursula to stay, sent his youngest daughter to Windrush to learn English. Later that year Tommy, aged twenty-five, went to stay with the Justs - now living in Starnberg, Bavaria - and began to fall for Gerda, the third of the four daughters. She came to England in 1933, and found staying at Windrush 'heaven'. Aunt Dorothy liked her - that was important, Gerda said - and she took her under her wing. At her home Gerda had become the house-keeper for her family, looking after her ailing father and her depressive elder sister. Tommy was impatient - but he couldn't persuade her to leave Germany and marry him until old Herr Just died almost four years later.

The wedding was a grand affair in July, held in the church in Bad Harzburg, near the Jungborn, with much Teutonic jollification afterwards. John went over with his aunt and uncle and his cousin Ursula, and some of Tommy's friends.

The Just sisters' English guests, all of them left-wing, left a London astonished by the brutal jew-baiting in Stepney by Oswald Mosley's Fascist thugs. This little group had lost hope in both the League of Nations and in the Labour Party: neither seemed any longer in favour of peace. They had heard of the atrocious acts of violence Hitler was perpetrating in his concentration camps, and were curious to test the sensation of being among people who lived near these places but were apparently unaware of their true function.

In 1933 Victor Gollancz, a London Jew, published a document prepared by the World Committee for the Victims of German Fascism. Concentration camps were listed; it showed photographs, dates and signed statements documenting the violence. Anybody in Britain who had been at left-wing meetings would have known about this book. In 1936, all the while successfully publishing works by radical writers, Gollancz started the Left Book Club. It was phenomenally successful: its books reached, in three years, 57,000 people. The dust-jackets and the advertising had a striking house style, devised by a fellow socialist, the distinguished typographic designer Stanley Morison. Pictorial images were never used; solely strong magenta and black lettering on a searing lemon yellow.

Four days after Tommy and Gerda's wedding, the Spanish Civil War broke out. In Britain we had our drama too: at home, on 11 December, our king abdicated. His father, old George V, before he died in January, had warned Stanley Baldwin that Edward would cause trouble within the year.

On a skiing holiday in Wengen in January that year, John - in true upper-class fashion - had got talking in a hotel bar to a man who turned out to be a managing director of the Dunlop Rubber Company. He was offered a job when he came down from Oxford.

The obvious choice of work for a classicist with a third class degree was teaching, but there was an alternative: Sir John Reith, the director-general of the BBC, was recruiting Oxford and Cambridge graduates for his training school. From the end of May the new government of Neville Chamberlain was austere and uncultured, and so unimaginative that it was soon clear to Reith that it would not see the potential of broadcasting, especially as the obvious means of spreading calm and confidence in wartime. The BBC was under the aegis of the Postmaster-General in those days. Reith firmly believed that broadcasting should be a means of spreading culture - controversial or not - to the masses. But he had a cussed, difficult manner and almost without fail antagonised the politicians in his discussions with them. The producers in 1937 were forced to adopt a philistine attitude to all the contributors. Most scripts were cut cruelly, including those of the public figures and academics invited to speak. In 1937, Reith, who had managed to win the respect of Stanley Baldwin, could not adapt to the new government's tight control. In 1938 he would resign.

Although the technological development of recording was slow and the censor harsh, broadcasting offered great opportunities to young writers, playwrights, poets and musicians. The first television pictures had been transmitted a few months earlier from Alexandra Palace. (From when they first went out, John became an aficionado of Alastair Cooke's talks about America, broadcast at home first, and - from 1937 - from across the Atlantic. Cooke's start on the *Manchester Guardian*, his books, his voice, his style...all intrigued him for the rest of his life.

An Englishman (he took US citizenship in 1941), Cooke was an American influence that nurtured the seed in John.)

John had applied to the BBC persistently for several months before he left Oxford. However, his appearance at the May Day Peace March and other pacifist meetings had been noticed by MI5 and reported to the Ministry of Labour. Repeated letters of rejection from the BBC probably helped him later in making his decision to become a conscientious objector.

Predictably - in the light of the unfolding of his story - John left no words on his reasons for becoming a CO. For an undergraduate with a social conscience in the late 1930s, it was exciting to be a member of the Left Book Club. Attending the huge rallies - often like revivalist meetings, so intense was their fervour - raising money for medical aid in Spain and distributing leaflets made young people feel they were helping in the struggle against fascism.

Harry Pollitt, John Strachey, Aneurin Bevan, Ellen Wilkinson, and Victor Gollancz himself - all good orators - would have spoken at the Club meetings in Oxford. For ideological reasons many undergraduates - including John - wanted to join the Spanish Civil War, and would have, if the University administration had not cautioned them against it.

John and his cousin Michael, the youngest of the Watson children, held their pacifist beliefs right through the Second World War. None of the Usborne brothers except - occasionally - Tommy, had any desire to fight, and during the war, for what turned out to be a complex of reasons, they all avoided it. Nobody in their father's family had ever been on active service in war as far as they knew. Charles, their father - who had never practised it - saw a soldier's life as a romantic one.

After Janet's death, Windrush gave the Usbornes a very secure background; they were privileged, but equally responsible for their security was the complement of the personalities of their aunt and uncle. Aunt Dorothy, their father's sister - although the daughter of a Protestant vicar, had decided as a young woman that she preferred the doctrine of the Quakers, one of whose principles was a devotion to peace. She made the decision - and her husband accepted it - to send their three youngest children to a Quaker school, Sidcot, in Somerset. Aunt Dorothy was the fighter, always active, making decisions, organising the household; Uncle Hubert, aged 67 in 1937, took a more passive role. (However, he would have fought for his country if he had been in England during the First World War.) His aura - of a gentle man who was deeply concerned about the welfare of children - contributed to the natural make-up of Windrush.

There is no doubt that the pacifist views of the closest brother to John, Henry - held fiercely in the 1930s - would have strongly influenced him. (All his life John took Henry's views to heart.) Witnessing Mussolini's vainglory in Rome - I liked to think - would have fed the flames of John's pacifism; but Michael Barton assured me that it was well established by then. John had been dead set on joining the Peace March with the Oxford contingent on his return from France.

There being nothing worthwhile on Gabbitas-Thring's books, he had to fall back on the Dunlop man's offer. Henry and Pam, who were living in a suburb of Birmingham, encouraged him to give the industrial Midlands a try.

The family had teased John about his scatterbrained behaviour at the French border in April. On 12 September a masque was staged by the children in the drawing-room at Windrush for Aunt Dorothy's and Uncle Hubert's Silver Wedding anniversary. They all parodied themselves, with a family friend reading Tommy's verses from behind the old velvet curtains. Each of the first set of nine verses was 'the actual and the real'. John's 'real' went as follows:

'Who is this 'tiny', elongated streak,
With lovely clothes and dandy shoes that squeak?
Poor fellow, he is wondering where
He left his passport, girls and railway fare.'

John joined Dunlop at their Birmingham headquarters in the autumn. Almost his first move, after settling in as a lodger at the Bagworthy Hotel, was to join the Labour Party at their headquarters a short bike-ride away. At Dunlop he was to be trained in the Sales Department for six weeks before being sent out to India (that had been the carrot: an opportunity to visit his birthplace and his father's haunts in the Punjab). John's interest in Henry's work in industry, and the prospect of meeting and studying 'the common man', did not prepare him for a shock. Fort Dunlop, the factory in Erdington, was huge and sprawling and smelt of chemicals; his image of the perfect workman - hitherto his only experience was of the sawmill workers in Inkpen - didn't match up with the ones he met. He felt uncomfortable when they touched their caps to him. There were no left-wingers in his department, and nobody used his Christian name.

He soon realised that he was bored and unhappy in an atmosphere of commerce. With no difficulty he decided he was not being true to his principles: Dunlop was Big Business and it was feeding Rearmament; Birmingham's beefy red-faced company directors were all gun-runners to Hitler. He had to admit that he hated the place. The time came for a medical examination before going to India. When he failed it and learnt that the breathlessness he suffered occasionally was the result of an irregular heart condition, he decided that he would resign. So he was to be cheated by his health out of making a valid stand for pacifism! He would look for work in London again, and join his beautiful Paula.

In December they were skiing together at Wengen. Two Swiss girls whom Paula had met at Le Grand Verger and some Oxford friends of John's made up the party. With their ski-trousers they all wore neat cotton jackets cropped at the waist - nothing loose in those days. My father told me that all the men were in love with my mother.

Paula, now twenty, was living on her own in a room in Kensington. For two years she had been working as a manicurist and mannequin in a dress shop on Kensington Church Street. She took her work seriously and did it so well that some clients used to invite her to their receptions, and private boxes at the ballet. The proprietress of the shop, obviously seeing Paula as a live advertisement for her collection, allowed her to borrow hats for her evenings out, with the proviso that they were to be put back on their display stands in time for opening in the morning. (A Balliol friend of John's, John McNair - a small man with a long doleful face - remembered an early morning in his room in Onslow Gardens, standing in his pyjamas looking at the damage after a little party: on the arm of his only armchair he saw something he was unable to focus on for a few seconds... looking like some sort of tropical insect. It was a tiny black cocktail hat of Paula's, with a ridiculous little veil sticking out at the back. That one didn't get back to the shop in time.)

John knew the family was shaking its head over his infatuation with Paula. He enjoyed the couple they made, the way she made him dress, the way people watched them. A little of the good life didn't come amiss. And she was fancy free...

Derek Rawnsley, two years older than John, had wealthy parents living in Capri. After Oxford he set up in business at 44 Gordon Square, next door to the house where the Stephen sisters started the Bloomsbury movement. In May 1939 one of his ventures was described thus: '...the scheme of the founders of School Prints Ltd. is one whereby a group of schools agree to join together to see a collection of carefully selected colour prints over a period of years; circulating 150 pictures (mostly of Old Masters) around a group of 15 schools... each school can receive a new set of pictures every term for five years. The school receives 10 attractive frames at the outset into which each successive set of pictures fits.'

Thanks to John's brother Dick's introduction of him to Rawnsley, this little outfit, run for him by Rawnsley's friend Victor Bonham-Carter, kept John employed for about three months, until early in 1938. He familiarised himself with the ways of several public schools by talking to their bursars, taking orders for 'prints', and making deliveries. It was business, but thankfully he had no part in that side of it. The job was a pushover. (John knew that he had no flair for business - and he played up to it a little. 'He never foresaw the results of his actions,' Michael Barton told me. Henry, by contrast, he described as 'a keen man with a sixpence'.)

Living in London for the first time, with the job as a useful front, John was building up his network. There was warmth in the well-established orthodoxy of the London Left, even in its often open philistinism. John went to all the meetings he could and quickly found the vitality he'd been missing. He was enjoying listening to other people's anger and cynicism. Besides, being with Paula, meeting his friends and going to the marvellous concerts London had to offer did not allow him much time to sit on his own and write. He had discovered that he could write good short pieces with facility. For the moment, Rawnsley allowed him to be cheeky, to use his charm, to twist a few arms.

He was learning, too, to be more discreet. But he always loved gossip, Michael Barton said - 'at Oxford he discussed all his girlfriends. He was an open chap! I can see him now, one foot on the nearest chair, talking on the 'phone - you couldn't get him off it!'

A flat was found near to Paula's shop, in a dark, noisy little street called Strathmore Gardens. Recently I was imagining that John and Paula had their trysts there in the evenings, after he left Bloomsbury. (Pam, at the age of 79, laughed at the jigsaw that she saw I was trying to fit together - and made it simple for me: 'Ann! They lived together!') The aunt in Long Crendon was never to know of Paula's change of address.

Uncle Hubert and Aunt Dorothy, from their first meeting, did not approve of Paula as a mate for John; she was too stylish to be anything but extravagant and empty-headed. In spite of their liberal views it is likely they were snobbish about her Australian background; they may also have found her calculating. John would have no capital after his education finished. (Aunt Dorothy was always happier with young men than with young women; she could be rather fierce.) Although Paula particularly liked Jenny, the rebel of the Watson daughters, and Dick – who made her laugh – she was not at ease with this formidable family, large, clever - and fearsomely political. So that winter, she and John had no Windrush weekends; John may have met Uncle Hubert in town once or twice - but I suspect he avoided it. He did miss his home and the good blows on the Downs – after these two intense years he was never to have much love for London or city life.

Poor Paula! It took determination to withstand disapproval at Windrush. Was it worth bothering about? The fiancé of one of the Watson girls had just found his niche there. John's cousin Jenny - very much on his wave-length, anxious to get away from home, was engaged to a young Californian, a fellow student at the Euston Road Art School. Americans were popular at Windrush. A pattern was forming: except for those of Henry, Pam and her brother Michael, the girlfriends and boyfriends who became wives and husbands were all foreigners; two of the Watson girls would leave England. Ken Ross - to be the second American joining the family - was able to match the Usborne versifying talent. The over-educated Englishness of the Usborne children - and their hooked noses (inherited from both parents; John, the darkest, was often to be asked if he was Jewish) - brought out the tease in him. Jenny, ever since the 'invasion' when she was fourteen, had teased them herself, of course. Ken was cheered on as he wrote:

'Hic Haec Hoc
Salute the Usborne stock!
They all excelled
At their Latin and Greek,
Except for a slight
Engineering streak.
Did ever one see
Such a prominent beak?
Hic haec hoc.'

At the end of April 1938, (with a one-way passage, some say, paid by Uncle Hubert) Paula would be sailing for Sydney, to celebrate her twenty-first birthday with her mother. She hadn't been home now for more than four years. Hay, her mother, was a very shrewd woman. She had met John during a short social visit to London, and did not wholeheartedly approve: he was good-looking, but too intellectual and unruly to become a good provider for her daughter. John was telling himself that, happy as they were together, Paula wasn't suitable for him. He had begun to see that his ideologies, his plans, his work were of little interest to her. She didn't read; she didn't settle to anything. There was no chance for her of any skiing this winter. He planned that after the abortion - Paula had become pregnant about a month after they began to live together - he would end the relationship. Her birthday was perfectly timed.

But for Paula it was dawning, after an uninterrupted succession of admirers, that John was now all she had. Cousins living in Kew were her only nearby relations, and they had tactfully learnt to leave her alone. The bleak feelings of being an alien still struck her sometimes. She was aware of John's restlessness; her determination to hold him consumed her. It was a lonely time for her. John was concerned – and was as good to her as he could be; pregnant, though, she was petulant and clinging and wanted more attention than he could devote to her.

John saw Paula's ship off at Tilbury, and waved an old sheet to her from the dock. A few days later he was off to Norway to do the words for a photo-journalist friend, John Gabriel. The two of them had a story up their sleeves. *Picture Post*, the new Hulton magazine, was about to be launched, and they were both caught up in the chase to get a feature into it. The story, whatever it was, was not accepted. But for the rest of his life, John had enthusiastic memories of Norway. He thought its skiing had great potential.

In May a man by the name of Tew launched a new literary magazine, called *The World Says-* ('A Digest of the World's Reading'), costing the high price of a shilling a month. The tiny office was in Victoria House, Southampton Row. Mr Tew took John on as his sub-editor. It was a tough start, learning to type on a small magazine. His duties were to select articles from about fifty foreign periodicals; to sub-edit the translations, and to whip into shape the ten or so articles in English – a third of the contents. And to obtain permissions from each publisher, all the articles being in copyright. The subject matter was not political – for the most part light – and the range of topics was wide. *The Reader's Digest* had not yet been launched; the contents list of *The World Says-* for May 1938, seems only a little dated, reading almost exactly as that of the *Reader's Digest* today: 'On the Roof of the World', 'Insect Thieves', 'Industry's Best-Hated Benefactor'. It ran witty footnotes at the end of an article. The typographic cover-designs of those days – usually printed in no more than three colours on oatmealy paper – before the advent of the sophisticated reproduction of colour photography, look crisp, snappy and intelligent, in the style of Stanley Morison.

Two young men who had been at Eton and Oxford together, Philip Brownrigg and Paul Stobart, had been since March of that year the proprietors of *Synopsis* - England's first literary digest. (At about the same time Philip had, with Dick Usborne as prime mover, started another little magazine, called *London Week* - a minor echo of the *New Yorker*.) With *Synopsis* they did reasonably well for beginners, considering they published no advertisements. W.H.Smith and Menzies took sevenpence out of the retail price of a shilling per copy, sale or return. In October Tew asked them to take over *The World Says-* their younger rival, which was struggling to survive. Paul Stobart remembered a young man being handed over to them as part of the package; he and Philip both found him more agreeable than his boss. In their offices at 14 Burleigh Street, Covent Garden, still alongside Tew, John worked for them until late June of 1938 – as long as they could afford to pay him. Here he particularly enjoyed editing articles by his favourite American humorists. Later he used these early copies of *Synopsis* as reference books for his teaching and broadcasting.

Paula told the Sydney press that she was engaged to be married as soon as she arrived in Australia; immediately she was photographed, holding a small black and white terrier with one arm, looking elegant but severe in a tailored dress of the style of the Duchess of Windsor. The picture was published on the society page of the *Sydney Daily Telegraph* with the headline 'To Marry in England'. She cut her stay short by three weeks; those remaining eight or nine could not have been happy ones; she managed to hide from all her family that she was pregnant again. She was dying to get back to John.

John's siblings and cousins were horrified. They had forgiven him the first slip-up. Now they were saying, 'The silly fool!' People were beginning to call him 'Poor John'.

They were married on 24th August 1938, at Chelsea Register Office. Paula was visibly pregnant. Aunt Dorothy had not heard the gossip; she was heard asking the question of another guest. There were no pictures. My parents never explained the reason to me when I was a teenager, of course. They did tell me, giggling, that the party given for them afterwards in their Chelsea flat by Dick and his new American wife Monica - also pregnant - was a very happy one.

John and Paula spent their wedding night at Brown's Hotel; a few days later, after John's cousin Jenny's wedding, they went to County Sligo - whence Paula's paternal ancestors came - for a week at Lissadell House. The vast estate of Lissadell was established cruelly, with a fortune from plunder, by an Elizabethan soldier, Sir Paul Gore. Nowadays its romantic history is due mainly to W.B. Yeats and his friendship with the two beautiful grand-daughters of Gore's ruthless descendant Sir Robert Gore-Booth. The massive limestone house was built by him in the 1830s. Constance helped to plan the Easter Rising in 1916, and became the first woman MP for Sinn Fein, fighting against all her grandfather and his ancestors stood for; Eva was a poet. W.B. Yeats wrote a poem in their memory in 1927.

Lissadell was the family seat of Sir Robert's great-great-nephew, Colum Gore-Booth, John's Balliol friend; Colum had arranged for John and Paula to spend their honeymoon there. They wouldn't be bothered, he said, by anyone but the cook and the old butler. This butler, named Kilgallon, with a cast in his eye, dressed in a dusty suit with frogging, opened the enormous, creaking front doors of the porte-cochère to them. Ben Bulben's great crag loomed close by; at first the house felt haunted, but they quickly warmed to its atmosphere - and enjoyed playing the fool among its 'stage-sets'. They wandered in the beautiful estate and marvelled at the view south over the water; watched by Paula, John hit a golf ball out into Drumcliff Bay as a gesture of happiness; and they ate Sligo lobster. They were never to visit Ireland again.

John was, at the time, a fervent admirer of the prime minister of the Irish Free State, Eamon de Valera; and as a small boy at Summer Fields, Leonard Strong's Irish charm had made a great impression on him. If it had been possible, John would have swapped his Scottish blood with Paula's Irish. In spite of his fondness for his Scottish great-uncle Pat, he was unable to warm to the Scots until late in his life.

Before the week in Ireland Paula had her second abortion, done privately, as the first one had been. Nobody in the family knows why she and John made that decision.

They had started looking for a house outside London at the end of 1938. An Oxford friend who had enthused about the Chobham-Bagshot area drove them there one weekend. Neither of them knew Surrey at all. A 'For Sale' sign offered a plain, white-stucco'd, slate-roofed semi-detached Edwardian cottage, at the tail end of the tadpole-shaped village of Windlesham, about a mile from the A30. Its quarter-acre of garden had a ditch and a wooded lane for its western boundary. An outhouse would do for coal and bikes and tools. The garden had a lawn, two apple trees, and an old pear-tree. From the road, Kennel Lane, with a bit of greensward in between, its conifer hedge gave the place - my father used to say - a suburban appearance. They moved from London in the early spring of 1939, when I was a twinkle in his eye.

Paula Usborne in 1995

Early in 1940 Derek Rawnsley wrote an account of the founding of another of his enterprises: 'It all began in July, 1938, when Munich was threatening, and politicians were busy making the world unfit for human habitation.'

Over tea in his office, he and six friends decided that their only hope was in the common sense of ordinary people. '99 per cent of decent human beings don't want war. How could they unite to prevent it? What could we do?

> '...The objects of an organisation for Federation begin:- "to provide an organisation which would enable the ordinary citizen in all countries of the world to give practical effect to his desire for the rule of an international law based on individual liberty..."

> 'Munich came, and left the two founders, Charles Kimber and myself, more determined than ever.'

In the spring of 1939, praise from British pacifists for the book *Union Now* by an American journalist, Clarence K. Streit, gave Kimber and Rawnsley the boost they needed to found their movement, Federal Union. It struggled at first, but the support given to it by some distinguished liberal and socialist thinkers of the time brought it a membership of over 15,000 within a year. 225 branches opened all over Britain.

John was excited about the concept of Federal Union from the moment he first heard of it. Probably he first appeared on the scene when Derek Rawnsley suggested he edit a weekly newsletter for it. Having had good experience as an all-round worker on two magazines, and having kept in touch with Rawnsley all the while, he was able to propose the original format and plans for publication. It was to be his brainchild.

The first issue of *Federal Union News (FUN)*, printed on four sides of a folded octavo sheet, came out on 5 September, two days after Britain declared war on Germany. Public figures supporting the movement were listed proudly: Ernest Bevin, Lord Astor, the Bishop of Chichester, Sir Julian Huxley, Storm Jameson, Ralph Vaughan-Williams, Kingsley Martin and J.B.Priestley. In small type, below the heading of *F.U.NEWS*, is the line 'To unite all democratic peoples under one central government as a first step towards a World State.' Below the masthead are the first lines of the leader:'The Editor says: Please don't be disappointed with the size of this, our first number. I would ask you rather, if you can, to appreciate its very existence.'

A conference was held by the founders of Federal Union in Witney, Oxfordshire, later that month. Representatives from every active group were there. John had interested and recruited two of his brothers:Tommy, active in the Hampstead group, and Henry, representing Birmingham.

Tommy and Gerda were now living in Lawn Road, Hampstead, with Peter, their two-year old son. There was a Federal Union bookshop at 87 Heath Street; membership of Federal Union in Hampstead was growing fast. Tommy had been holding several evening meetings at the Everyman Theatre. Most people attending them were Jewish refugees from Hitler. Tommy - the family would remember his pipe and 'canary look' for this scenario - discussed with them the aspects of Federal Union relating to them, as refugees.

Henry and John both registered as conscientious objectors at the end of 1939. (Henry was a pacifist until Dunkirk; he knew then that the only solution was a military one.) At this time Henry was starting his reserved occupation: his company would shortly be making not only oil-fired heating but also wartime fire-extinguishers. Federalism was to become his obsession for the rest of his life. His faith in the Labour Party and in federal union - in the general sense - encouraged him to stand for his first seat in Parliament, an unwinnable one in Birmingham. He remembered, while talking to me in the autumn of 1995, that the leading people in Federal Union in 1939 were all squabbling, manoeuvring for their own particular supporters. A battle was being waged between pure pacifists and intellectuals. Henry - who had his own difference with Lancelot Hogben - 'didn't think much of it at all'. Rawnsley, always the entrepreneur, he said, was using FU to further his business School Prints.

Henry, the most practical of the five Usbornes, backed Federal Union because he thought 'it was good for the Labour Idea'. (Later - his eldest son Barnaby felt - he turned out not to be practical in politics. He never could accept the cut and thrust of it; he was too didactic, too persistent.) John, while working in that noisy office, finding his colleagues at their discussions faintly ridiculous, realised that he was a dilettante at heart; and that a career in journalism was his safest bet. He enjoyed publishing his own views in the newsletter, but was careful that his name as editor was never seen in it.

For the Christmas 1939 issue of *FUN*, John asked Bernard Shaw if he would be good enough to send a seasonal message to readers. The great man replied: 'Now that we are at war, any allusion to Christmas might land me in a concentration camp. Pray be careful.'

To keep his spirits up, in spare moments John indulged in writing some rhymes for *FUN*, under the pseudonym Telemachus. In Issue 15, at the end of December, with the title 'It Won't Work Because' he pokes fun at the movement:

'...Chieftains would sit at Westminster
And commissars at York,
And how would people pay for things
and how would people talk?

No, no! The time has come to fight
This hideous degradation,
The threat of vile encroachment on
Our self-determination!
So one and all, come let us call
This Federal Union fuss
Unthinkable and stinkable
And far be it from us!'

In a spring issue of *FUN*, the war giving him his opportunity, John wrote and signed an article entitled 'Instructions To Hate: a Federalist's Commentary':

'The poison is now trickling through again. Even before the Germans attacked Norway we noticed that the word "Germans" was being surreptitiously substituted for the word 'Nazis' in official Government statements. There were protests from those who were still tolerant, and retractions from inadvertent culprits. But now that the holocaust is a-smoke, very little effort is being maintained to distinguish between the Nazis and the German people...We are going to be asked to hate a great deal more violently when bombs are dropped in earnest in this country. Yes, Federal Unionists have a great and arduous duty in front of them.'

At Christmas there had been signs of strain: the movement was handicapped by a head office which was under-staffed, under-equipped and overworked. The money coming in weekly amounted to less than a quarter of the £200 needed to keep the whole British movement afloat.

Early on 10 May 1940 the Dutch and Belgians fell to Hitler. That night in London Chamberlain resigned as prime minister and Winston Churchill formed his National Government. Five weeks later the Fall of France killed any chance of the creation of the Anglo-French nucleus needed for a European federation.

The faith of thousands of Federal Unionists plummeted; the Union's finances were in a bad state. Staff were laid off; John, very relieved, was among them. Derek Rawnsley went into the RAF. He was killed soon afterwards.

'Of course I am a socialist,' John had told himself in a poem entitled 'Pin-Prick' for *FUN*. Being the dogsbody in a disorganised office had got him down. It had been an exceptionally cold, tiring winter. Running a home and a family in wartime, interrupted nights, commuting, with no breather since moving house, had left him constantly fatigued. He was thin, going bald rapidly like his brothers – and feeling, he wrote, 'a rather off-colour red'.

I had been born in November 1939. All my uncles were now proud fathers; I had four older boy-cousins. At Windrush, in the winter sunshine, we were all photographed together by Tommy's Leica – the boys sitting in a row, I swaddled at the end, on a rug laid on the gravel in front of the house.

Before he started work for Federal Union, John had persuaded his friend John McNair – now a budding playwright – to recommend an idea of his to the head of the Programme Division at the BBC. What about a series of talks on great men and their oddities – ranging from Alcibiades, via Swift to Beethoven, to W.G. Grace? John had already discussed this with the head of the radio department at the London Press Exchange, and to be prepared he had had his voice recorded. 'If you do like the idea,' he wrote to George Barnes, 'and have no one particularly in mind to give the talks, I should thoroughly enjoy giving them myself. I think I can pride myself that I have the right voice and a knack for putting it over in the mellow, hesitant, fireside manner that seems to be in such demand these days.'

A voice test was organised for him. He was nervous. Barnes wrote a memo to a colleague: 'His idea has some merit and in spite of cheapness and facetiousness his script has possibilities for our lighter programmes.' The result of the test produced a memo: '"Mellow" isn't the right word – sharp, staccato, more.' Once again, rejection.

A short spring led to a May of cloudless skies and blazing sunshine – called by some 'Hitler's weather'. In early August the Luftwaffe – probably 1000 planes per day – concentrated its attacks on Kent and on British convoys in the Channel. Mollie Panter-Downes in her 'Letter from London' for the *New Yorker*, wrote: 'This is the time of year when people ordinarily pack their bags and go off to pick up a tan which will last the winter; this year most of them are staying put in their homes while the homes are still there to stay put in.' In mid-August the Battle of Britain started in earnest. London had been waiting; its turn came with a 'nuisance raid' on the twenty-fifth. On 7 September, in bright sunshine, just after five o'clock in the afternoon, 250 German bombers flew up the Thames, escorted by about 500 fighters. They bombed Woolwich Arsenal, a power station, a gasworks, the docks and the City. The fires they started lit up the sky spectacularly when dusk fell, making a huge marker for the hundreds more planes which came over during the night. After that first attack, the Blitz accelerated, and the bombings continued for most of the remaining days and nights of the month.

John worked as a journalist on the British Desk at Associated Press, the American news agency, for about three months. I can only guess that those months were July, August and September. Certainly he endured most of the Blitz, as a commuter from the home counties; on arrival in London every morning he learnt the horrors of the previous night's bombing. I remember him describing the planes droning above in that cloudless sky while he crossed the bridge to catch his train home from Waterloo.

AP's offices were at 20 Tudor Street, parallel to Fleet Street on its south side. Norman Badderly joined the agency a month or two earlier than John, and was also on the British Desk. He did not remember John. It being an American outfit, he explained to me, Christian names were used. He'd have remembered a colleague named Usborne. '20 Tudor Street was a ramshackle old building,' he wrote, 'made worse by the Traffic Department's habit of ripping up the wooden floors to wire up the machines. The news room was the whole of the open first floor. There was the American Desk, the British Desk and at the back the Photo Editor's Desk. There was a row of four telephone booths. The teleprinter operators were beside each desk. The noise was more than somewhat, teleprinters and typewriters crashing, 'phones ringing and, in times of stress, people shouting across the room.'

John worked the 8am - 4pm shift, six days a week. He was paid nine guineas, a good weekly wage in those days. His duties involved writing news reports of events outside Great Britain, brought in from AP offices all over the world, for the British national papers. No bylines were used, so it is impossible now to identify his reports.

Very soon after John joined, early in the Blitz, the offices were bombed. There were no casualties, but great damage was done, and subsequently fire broke out. John was out on an errand when it happened. The next day the Press Association gave refuge to the AP staff in their building on Fleet Street.

In September, when registration for military service became obligatory for men of John's age, he tried to get into one of the regiments favoured by pacifists, the Royal Army Medical Corps. Inevitably he failed the medical examination. At about that time he had the first physical collapse of his life, caused by hypertension, while at the AP offices. St Thomas's Hospital, just across the river, treated him then, as they were to do during these crises for the rest of his life. We know nothing of what happened - his high blood pressure would have brought on a severe attack of breathlessness, or a faint - but John was shaken enough to know that he must give up working full-time in journalism. The doctor told him he would be well again soon and no precautions need be taken. 'Why don't you find yourself a teaching job in the country?' he suggested, 'Something a little more restful.'

Food rationing had started. John was enjoying himself growing vegetables for the family at the top of the garden. For the first months of my life, Paula had had a nanny to help her, an Irishwoman called Bridie. Her mother insisted on it, and probably paid her wages. All our family pictures of babies taken that hot summer of 1940, the worst one of the war for England, show sunburnt ones - in this instance, my guests and me in my playpen on the lawn. Paula was happy in her role; she looks appealingly pretty and fragile, with a ribbon round her head, in tailored cotton dresses of a style that became very fashionable again in the 1990s. In one picture she and a friend, invited for tea, sit chatting in deckchairs while I sleep under a fringed canopy in my Silver Cross pram. It looks idyllic. It did to John, who took the photographs.

Chapter Four

Gabbitas Thring produced a job for John, filling in for a teacher who had gone into the Forces. The school was preparatory, based in Broadstairs, Kent; called Selwyn House. It had about fifty boys and seven or eight staff. During both world wars it was evacuated to the family home of the founder's wife, in Llanfyllin, an ancient market town in Montgomeryshire.

The house, called Llwyn, was above the town and hidden from it by tall trees. A huge, rather grim white mansion, tall and square - it was what the Welsh call 'cilhaul' ('with its back to the sun'). By tradition, there was a house on its site in 1710, when the family of a raffish lesser squire from Merioneth called Humffreys, with a fortune made illicitly, founded the Llwyn estate. A century later, John Dugdale, who had made money in cotton, bought the estate and changed the first simple baroque house for the worse, adding another storey to it, and building a new wing. He became the first squire of Llanfyllin. His descendants, the Dugdales John knew, eventually sold the house to the Montgomery Education Authority at the end of the Second World War. It was demolished in 1975. A few people believe it still haunts the town.

Selwyn House School had been founded in Broadstairs in 1906; the daughter of the founders, Joan, was married to John Green. They were now jointly head-master and headmistress. Joan's uncle and aunt, Major and Mrs Dugdale, had moved to a farmhouse on their estate while Llwyn was requisitioned as a school. They were in their late sixties then, stalwart people, well-liked in the town; he a military man, she the daughter of a Lord Chief Justice, they took their role as the town gentry seriously. Mrs Dugdale was doing war work in addition to her usual activities; she was a group leader of the WVS and through the church she was chairwoman of the Llanfyllin branch of the Women's Temperance Society. Their only son John was a captain in the Royal Welch Fusiliers.

John decided not to uproot his family but to try living in Wales on his own for the few remaining weeks before the Christmas holidays. Up there, out in the wilds, he felt very vulnerable with his pacifist convictions. (Public opinion that summer and autumn since Dunkirk had been hysterically against conscientious objectors.) Lonely and ill-at-ease when he arrived, he worried about having abandoned Paula and a ten-month-old baby to live under the battle-skies of the south-east. He came home for a weekend in mid-November, during the week of the bombing of Coventry and Hamburg. He wrote me a poem for my first birth-day. Here's the first verse of it:

'Of man's inhumanity to man
You know not yet, my yearling Ann:
Though man is madder now to man
Than he has ever been.'

With the three or four weekends he had before Christmas, I like to think that John took some walks in an attempt, for a few hours, to diffuse - by refreshing his circulation - his misgivings about the job ahead of him. Did he have enough patience for it? Did he like the boys enough? Everything was so slow. As for the adults, the Dugdales and the Greens would have appeared to him rigid and inward-looking - and typically Methodist, probably. I suspect he wanted to shock them out of their narrow provincialism. I'm certain that he struck out to meet local shop-keepers and farmers, to hear their views in their own words. If he disagreed he would have needed to stifle his iconoclastic tendencies, if he hoped to make friends there. Could he make friends of these people? Did he miss the sophisticated humour of the Fleet Street drinking holes? These were the Welsh Marches, his first experience of border country - and border people. (The old Tudor county of Montgomery is traditionally nonconformist.) Did he find Offa's Dyke? I'm sure he scrambled up the steep hill on the far bank of the river Cain to see the view. The landscape, with its small fields and chunky old oak trees certainly charmed him.

At least John knew he was doing some good war work by teaching. He taught his Latin classes in 'Room 15', one of the two principal rooms on the first floor, under one of the best rococo ceilings in Wales. Fronds of laurels and vines were interleaved in a huge oval with, in the corners, cartouches of musical instruments and fluttering pages of Handel's manuscript of the Messiah.

In January, after a convivial Christmas at Windrush, the three of us set off by train, in freezing weather, from Sunningdale all the way to the little market sta-tion at Llanfyllin, changing at three different junctions en route. We made a bedraggled trio, jostling in the smoky corridors with the noisy troops; my moth-er was cross, and feeling off-colour, being newly pregnant with my sister. The journey was no adventure to her; she would have preferred to stay behind, even with the greater danger of bombing in Surrey. She was by now attached to the pretty home she had made of Sandy Lane Cottage, and did not relish leaving Tommy, Gerda, and their boisterous little boys Peter and Julian occupying it. Gerda, being German-born, felt brittle and needed sympathy - she had had an uncomfortable time living cheek-by-jowl with naturally hostile Jewish refugees in Hampstead - and the whole family needed to shelter out of London while Tommy looked for a house.

Did the three of us, that February at Llwyn, play on the lawn in the snow? In her dementia at the end of her life, my mother's only memories of her stay in Wales were the way to pronounce 'Llanfyllin' (she did it with relish) - and that she loved the pretty little Georgian town. Knowing as I do that the people are friendly, I can picture her slow progress in the spring, with me toddling, down the beech avenue from Llwyn to the shops. I probably saw my first rainbow - held up to a window of our flat in the eaves - spanning a stretch of that lovely, lumpy, ancient countryside.

The only writing John did was in letters, now lost, to his closest friends, made at school and at university - all in the Forces - Morrice James, Michael Barton, John McNair, Bill Davies, John Gaye. Rather lonely correspondence, but apart from the chance to be humorous, it gave vent to his need to write; like poetry, it was relaxing for him - and allowed some reflection. One letter, however, was to have serious repercussions. Like most young people it would not have occurred to John that irreverent remarks about 'officialdom' might be taken seriously if they fell into the wrong hands. This was wartime.

Morrice James was a rating in the Navy, stationed in Devonport, John thought, when he wrote to him in the spring. He was replying to a letter which Morrice had written to him at the end of 1940. 'In my letter,' Morrice wrote to John's brother Dick in 1984, trying to explain what had probably happened, 'I had (no doubt with some priggishness) severely criticised the Navy for its various organisational shortcomings, including that of wasting its recruits' precious time.' Somehow this letter must have passed the censor.

'John's reply never reached me since by the time it arrived at Devonport I'd disappeared from the barrack room on transfer to the Royal Marines. In his reply John must have echoed, or quoted my strictures on the Navy, since the only serious charge that could possibly be levelled against him was that he had written to a naval rating in wartime in a manner likely to cause alarm and despondency'

On the envelope John had included no surname with the Selwyn House address; and - naturally to a friend - he signed only his Christian name at the end of the letter: John. In the summer it arrived back at the Llanfyllin post office; the postmistress, doing her job, sent it over to the only John she knew at Selwyn House, John Green. And that John showed it to Major John Dugdale. A day or two later, Dick had a call from Jim Hale, an old Balliol friend. 'I'm about to use up the MI5 petrol ration!' he said. 'Your young brother has got himself into a spot of trouble up in Wales.'

'I remember John telling me; Morrice James wrote, 'that at their farewell interview the Headmaster was all smiles until he delivered (almost as an afterthought) his carefully-prepared punch-line:- "Oh, by the way, I've given the police that seditious letter you wrote to a naval rating at Devonport. Goodbye."'

We could have scuttled home then and there, but we made sure we had a little holiday at Criccieth first. I know we all built sandcastles. Why was the Criccieth beach not out of bounds, as I think most beaches were, mined against invaders?

Tommy, Gerda, and their sons Peter and Julian left Sandy Lane Cottage for Windrush in a mad scramble. My mother wanted to be home in time to have her baby. Julie was born, two weeks late, on 31 August 1941, a healthy baby with a large brown birthmark under her left eye.

Apart from the happy event of Julie's birth, the four months after our return were uneasy and guilty ones for John. He and Paula had made a few good friends in Windlesham and Chobham, but on the whole the neighbours and local shopkeepers, ignorant of John's medical history, were not friendly. Feeling very exposed, as a 26-year-old male apparently doing nothing for the war effort, he suffered their disapproval as he took himself on walks round the village while he tried to decide on his future professional direction. Also, no doubt, he felt the need to distance himself from a crying baby, fussing helpers and an exhausted wife. With the stiff autumn breezes - remembering the beauty of Montgomeryshire - he wished for some vigorous hilly country to walk in; and wryly considered some new ironies.

Ironies made good subjects for triolets. On Easter Day that year, while staying at Windrush, John had walked with a brother or two along the valley of the White Horse. Here's the result:

I was Uffington's pride
When the Danes were the raiders
I'd a glossy white hide
I was Uffington's pride
But I might be a guide
To the Nazi invaders
I was Uffington's pride
When the Danes were the raiders.

John knew that for whatever job he would do, Windlesham with its sandy soil and unsympathetic people would have to be his base; he would have to make the best of it. He had decided that he wasn't cut out to be a farmer; however, cultivating flowers in the garden was beginning to absorb him. The garden had been a strong reason in the first place for putting a deposit on Sandy Lane Cottage; as soon as they moved down from London in 1939 he and Paula had thrown themselves into embellishing it by planting shrubs and bulbs. Friends who came down during wartime from London, to have a few days' break from the Blitz – or just for Sunday lunch – remember the garden as particularly pretty and peaceful, with the grizzled old pear tree and the two huge apple trees providing the focus.

The autumn was grim and melancholy. People anxiously waited for news from the USSR on their wirelesses. John was worrying about the way the money given to them by Uncle Hubert as a wedding present was diminishing (Paula had an eye for antiques 'going cheap'). The BBC had rejected him again. However, a spark had been ignited in May, by George Barnes, at that time Director of Talks. John had met Barnes at the green-camouflaged Broadcasting House during his Easter holidays from Selwyn House, the school in Wales. He then put in writing to Barnes the ideas he had offered him. His letter inspired the following inter-office memo: 'I don't think this callow youth is likely to be of use to this Department. His suggestions for programmes are useless. On the other hand, he has a background and he has tremendous enthusiasm, and if high blood pressure continues to keep him out of the Forces it might be worth your while to see him.'

It would have encouraged John to know that his enthusiasm had been appreciated. For about five years there was no more direct communication between him and the BBC; he would waste no more of his energy, nor would he subject himself to any more disappointment. There was (and it remains) a hazard to being an Usborne: as it happened – John never knew it – his file card had been misfiled, put under 'O' for Osborne in the index; moreover, his brother Dick – before he joined the SOE in 1940 – had been broadcasting book-reviews (with his card correctly filed) and their voices, to producers and secretaries alike, were indistinguishable. Nobody bothered to clear up the confusion.

The people of Russia had fascinated John ever since his early ideological stirrings at Bradfield. Being a historian by instinct and an incurable romantic, it was always intoxicating for him to think of the numerous ethnic groups living as

Russians in that vast land mass. Like many young poets and writers of the time, with knowledge of pre-Revolution Russian literature, he could not bring himself to embrace Communism fully; the Soviet version was now belligerent.

From the mid-1930s until this hour, when Churchill's concern for 'the Russians who defend their homes' was expressed in his broadcast on the first day of the German attack, the British - if they knew anything about them at all - were full of prejudices about 'the Soviets'. Anybody showing an interest in their plight was suspected of being a communist sympathiser. John, in his Llanfyllin letter to Morrice James - to be buried in MI5 files - may have fantasised affectionately about a poor kulak who was unaware of the imminent danger to Mother Russia.

America also beckoned to John, as it did to many men of his age. President Roosevelt, an aristocrat, producing enormous social recognition of the poor while struggling against capitalism, was largely responsible. His courage - even his big grin - captured the imagination of young intellectuals at the time. Were they politically naïve? Churchill had said that meeting Roosevelt was like opening your first bottle of champagne. It was an irony that no other political figure had had quite this effect before - to attract young idealists to a nation of huge-scale free enterprise. Penned in by a country at war, were they mistaking it for freedom?

While waiting for a train in the blackout, John kicked out in a few lines of verse - calling this rather bad poem 'The Railway and the Daffodil':

'...Red Earth with reality in a daffodil
No train no moon and a nazi bomber...I,
I, and the marxian synthesis. God
Take it, blast you! - ad nauseam. I'm free, I tell you.'

The man who was to set John on his truest path, however, was Walter Oakeshott. He had been noticed for his brilliant touch as an actor and publicist while he was a second-year undergraduate at Balliol College in 1924. Cyril Bailey was his tutor. Through him, Plato's teaching, a component of the Balliol ethos, endowed Oakeshott, an agnostic, with a sort of religious faith in Goodness and Beauty that - in spite of a tendency to depression - drove him all his life.

While he was a young master at Winchester College in the mid-1930s, Oakeshott was given leave to work on an investigation into unemployment for the Ministry of Labour; he wrote a report, 'Men Without Work', which caused a sensation. Privately, though, he was a scholar and a bibliophile. Throughout his life, while he was a teacher, sociologist or administrator, he worked at his own unusual studies and published books about them. He had identified in the library at Winchester College the original manuscript of Malory's 'Morte d'Arthur'. He had a passion for Renaissance maps, and would later recognise the handwriting of Sir Walter Raleigh on one in the British Museum's collection.

Oakeshott was only thirty-five when he was appointed High Master of St Paul's, the London public school, in July 1938. The Munich Crisis in August had forced Maurice Tyson, the deputy of the outgoing High Master, to make a quick decision: to continue planning for another school year in the event of war, or to close the school. The latter would - almost certainly - mean that it would close for ever. He chose to keep it open.

Other public schools at this stage had their plans for wartime. Within his first few days, in January 1939 (he had been committed to teaching at Winchester until Christmas 1938), Walter Oakeshott talked to the school governors and the London County Council. He realised that the Governors had not met, nor were intending to meet, to plan a programme for the school if the war came; no extra money was put aside; in addition the buildings in Hammersmith were to be requisitioned by the government as headquarters of the 21st Army Group. (One of the governors was Cyril Bailey, an old Pauline; at Oakeshott's cry for help he immediately persuaded the clerk of the Mercers' Company - which owned and subsidised St Paul's - to make emergency plans.) Without wasting a moment, Oakeshott made his own plan of action: to find - by the end of the summer term - premises outside London to adapt as a schoolhouse for up to 600 boys, with lodgings for them, the masters and their families.

Oakeshott and Tyson decided on a huge Jacobean-style Victorian house near Crowthorne, Berkshire, called Easthampstead Park. Oakeshott charmed the owners, the eccentric young Marquess of Downshire and his stepmother, suggesting to them that their mansion and its beautiful park would be appreciated more by Paulines than by East End urchins. Wellington College was four miles away; its headmaster, a friend of Oakeshott's, agreed to lend its playing fields, gymnasium and science laboratories.

In February 1939 Oakeshott wrote to the parents using his diplomatic flair again: taking the school to the country would be an exciting opportunity; it was vital that, though uprooted, St Paul's should preserve its traditional spirit; its reputation - as a London day-school with a rich vein of Jewish boys contributing to its remarkable academic record - should not suffer from the evacuation.

The migration from London started with masters and their wives arriving in August. They were to prepare for the assigning of billets in the town for the expected first batch of 350 boys from both St Paul's and Colet Court, the junior school. Planning for a possible closing-down of the railways, Oakeshott had decided that each boy at Easthampstead should use a bicycle, to cover the daily ten-mile ride between billet, lesson and playing field; in March he had staged a rehearsal for their thirty-mile bicycle journey from West London.

During the first few days of September, when the newspaper placards were announcing Hitler's invasion of Poland, 150 boys - many on bicycles - arrived at Easthampstead. Masters and boys worked like beavers converting the mansion into a schoolhouse, building trestle tables, bookshelves and bicycle racks; in preparation for the air-raids trenches were dug and sandbags filled. Land was dug up on the estate for a Home Farm, and potatoes sown.

Within weeks the intake of boys rose to 570. Oakeshott's faith in the success of the operation inspired everyone. He was likely, all in the space of an hour, to be in the woods with a plumber discussing the construction there of school latrines, then pedalling hard to arrive at the mansion in time to teach a Latin lesson. 'I amaze myself,' he said, 'by enjoying it all prodigiously.'

By the end of 1941 Oakeshott had St Paul's running as smoothly as a school in peacetime. 'Life at Crowthorne has many drawbacks,' wrote George Young in *The Pauline*, 'but it offers Paulines at least one compensating benefit. Who, in pre-war days in Hammersmith, could have foreseen that he would one day walk to St Paul's School across a cornfield, or have his sandwiches extracted from his saddlebag by jackdaws?' The Junior Training Corps, however, had left something to be desired. An Old Pauline, a small, pompous, strutting man named Bernard Law Montgomery, who ran the 21st Army Group, had come down from London in the summer to give an inspection. According to a boy called John Thorn, the cadets didn't impress him, nor he them.

Since he became High Master Oakeshott had, through the Balliol network - in the form of Cyril Bailey - kept track of John's movements. (They had already met; probably in 1939 Oakeshott had offered John a post, long before he considered a career in teaching.) He knew John had an English degree, still quite a rare qualification in those days; he knew of the misdemeanour in Wales, and that his irregular health was making him available.

There were other schools close to Windlesham but it was fortunate for John that St Paul's had evacuated to a site nearby. He started teaching there at the end of November 1941. For his sixteen-mile 'commute' he bought himself a second-hand motor-bike. Paula remembered him arriving home in the blackout, wearing a leather flying helmet (purloined from Henry's collection in the cloakroom at Windrush) with the chin straps dangling, wheeling the bike up the garden path, exhausted after his cold ride.

The United States were coming into the war; the Japanese bombed Pearl Harbor at the end of John's first week. Oakeshott had been teaching some history himself, informally, and had visited each class to explain Wavell's North African campaigns; he felt strongly that the boys should be aware of the events of the war and discuss them as they happened. When he called John over to Easthampstead - to urge him to join his depleted staff, they naturally discussed the news; John enthused about Roosevelt and his career. An admirer of American culture himself, Oakeshott suggested John should teach a course on American History.

As he had had experience of preparatory school teaching John was made a form master of Middle Third, the form of ten and eleven-year old boys. At that level he was to teach English, French and Latin. He may have felt apprehensive about the rest, which was to be English at School Certificate level. (Until English teaching in public schools ceased being a natural extension of the Classics - at the beginning of the 1930s - it remained rather austere.) To Oakeshott the lack of imagination in the preparation of the English syllabus was glaring. By his own attitude in his teaching of it and by his recruiting of younger men he had already eased the severe atmosphere by the time John arrived. Oakeshott saw John's youth (he was his junior by ten years), his love of English poetry and his feeling for history as part of the reform he hoped to make. Encouraging him was easy because Oakeshott shared these interests himself. He recognised in John a man whose enthusiasms would guide him as a teacher.

In a talk entitled 'Putting It Across' which he broadcast on the Home Service more than twelve years later, John mused about the impression he made on the boys during his first English lessons early in 1942: 'Of course, having become pretty illiterate in Fleet Street I was at first very much more concerned with my own education than theirs; everything I was obliged to read and teach from seemed utterly enthralling and in my wide-eyed excitement I suppose I sort of bubbled over at my pupils, and that way they were able to get a bit of my infection.'

John Thorn - who became Headmaster of Repton, and later Winchester, was seventeen in 1942 and in his last year at St Paul's. He is remembered by his class-mates as a sophisticated boy; he was aware at the time that with many members of the staff away in the Forces, much of its talent was missing. Fifty-one years later, from his point of view as a teacher - and knowing that John acquired more skill in the ensuing years - he recalled him: 'He was tall and elegant and stood to teach, holding the book out in front. He was not a born teacher and he did not, in for-mal classroom work, stir our imaginations much. He read too much from books, so there was little give and take in his lessons. For some reason he taught us Irish history.' Richard Mayne, now a writer and broadcaster, was a year younger, at School Certificate level. At this particular lesson with John, a joint session of his and Thorn's two classes, Mayne recognised the rebel in him - and saw the subject of that Penguin book, Sean O'Faóláin's biography of Eamon de Valera, as excit-ing: 'John wore the first suede shoes I'd ever seen...a young intellectual, a writer, a thinker, a man of the world.' François Duchêne, writer and journalist, Mayne's contemporary, said, 'I associate him with a climate of debate in class. His name leaves a perfume of wide open intellectual spaces and new horizons... he was peripheral in that he did not stand on the narrow causeway to exams.'

John felt tremendously cheered to become a part of this extraordinary, sprawl-ing, liberally-minded community. At last he could drop his guard - and become one of what would be considered in Windlesham a bunch of eccentrics. Indeed, some were. Erik Sthyr, the Art master, told me: 'The High Master collected some interesting newcomers to the staff. There were, for example, two retired head-masters, one of whom (H.N.P. Sloman) was rumoured to have worried the board of governors with his somewhat adventurous night-life. This, incidentally, was a rumour that seeped out and added considerably to the prestige which he enjoyed in the Pauline mind.'

Of Danish extraction, Erik Sthyr was five years older than John. He had taught at the school from 1931, when he was twenty-two. When John met him he had just been invalided out of the Army. Their imperfect health, among other topics, created a bond. John's Balliol friend Colum Gore-Booth had gone on to the Slade School of Fine Arts, where Erik too had been a student. (Colum was probably the first painter John saw at work since he had watched Edward Burra as a child.) The style of Paul Nash - which Colum unwittingly adopted - was a distinctive one for young painters in their day; for John, the literary man, Nash's pacifist state-ments in painting had kindled an interest in contemporary art.

The exhibitions Erik mounted at the school resuscitated in John an interest in the process of painting which had been dormant, like his reading, in his 'illiterate' years. Among St Paul's alumni were several painters who had made names for themselves, including Claude Rogers, John Armstrong and Duncan Grant. Two more of them - Paul Nash and Eric Kennington - had been made Official War Artists. Erik Sthyr exhibited in London himself, through the Royal Society of British Artists, the AIA and the London Group. For the boys, this gave him glam-our; and they loved his woolly ties, his unpredictable temper, the provocative way he taught. Le Corbusier was his idol ('one of the biggest mistakes of my life!' he told me), and his own town-planning on the blackboard, for London suburbs after the war, is remembered by his old pupils. Like John, he didn't hold his enthusi-asms back from the boys.

Erik Sthyr in 1994

'Not everyone', Erik told me, 'was in sympathy with the rather easy-going atmosphere that prevailed; in fact, there was a small, tough opposition camp that deplored the liberal approach. One colleague - let us call him 'X' - carried around with him a curiously diversified set of dislikes which no one was left in any doubt about. First of all, there was the whole concept of general culture, dismissed rather contemptuously as 'cultch'. The function of schools was to provide instruction; facts, techniques, good examination results - these were what mattered, and attention was paid to them with almost ferocious efficiency. Liberals were inevitably referred to with a certain amount of scorn, as were prison reformers, small countries, Scoutmasters and, somewhat inconsequentially, people who drank cocoa. Ball games came in for rough treatment; as for the Classics, they were merely cultural junk from the past.

Erik's description led him to remember a late afternoon at Easthampstead:

'When everyone seemed to have gone home and the building appeared to be empty. John and I happened to meet on the stairs and wandered down into the common room. The only occupant was 'X', who was standing by one of the French windows reading *The Times*. Perched on the back of a sofa was a Scoutmaster's wide-brimmed hat.

'John and I exchanged glances. Neither of us had been a Boy Scout; nor were we given to horseplay. Nevertheless, the temptation was overwhelming. That tantalising piece of headgear suddenly seemed to take on a new identity - it became a symbol.

'In short, we set upon him. It wasn't very difficult to jostle him on to the sofa and thereafter for John to jam the hat tightly down over his head, after which the Boy Scout salute followed. It must have been the incongruity of the situation that caused both of us to collapse. 'X' - it must be said - took this slightly surrealistic episode in good part. A few moments later, the door opened and the High Master came in. Always the soul of discretion, he merely smiled apologetically, and left with a book he had mislaid.'

Out of a staff of about forty, for the most part John's closest colleagues were - as Erik Sthyr described them with affection - the 'soppy humanists'. However, quite soon in 1942 he would have planned and discussed his curriculum with Eynon Smith, to become a legend of St Paul's war years. Though he was revered by the boys, he was not popular among the staff. His authoritarian style, strong prejudices and eccentricity were cut short by his death from a flying bomb in 1944. Apart from the Classics he was engaged for, he taught the Eighth Form (St Paul's name for the Sixth Form) a general course he devised himself - current affairs, medicine, law, psychology. He ran the class; called 'Modern Special', it was the post-School Certificate year for boys specialising in English and History. He had most of his pupils eating out of his hand, enthralling them one minute and insulting them the next. The terrifying Frank Parker, who taught French (Erik's and John's victim in the Common Room) and Eynon Smith shared a house.

Leslie Matthews, an Old Pauline in his late sixties, with a boxer's flattened nose, was the Surmaster (deputy headmaster). He had been teaching at the school since 1895. He taught Classics, and coached Boxing, helping to maintain St Paul's good reputation for that sport. Oakeshott knew him through Balliol; John's father had been his contemporary there in the 1890s. George Bean - an immensely tall man - was not only a learned Greek scholar, but President of the school tennis club. Robin Mathewson, a Bradfieldian, another young Oakeshott protégé, also taught Classics. Tony Richards, an old Etonian, three times married, liberal, elegant, musical, was - when John arrived - head of English; and yet another young Oakeshott protégé was Arnold Monk-Jones, 'Monkey', who taught Classics to the lower forms. He and John, both keen amateur naturalists, became good friends. George Young, who loved cricket, coached the Colts' Rugby XV, and taught English. Alan Cook taught the Colet Court forms; a reasonable and humorous man, he gave the best years of his life to St Paul's. There were three communists - now a respectable persuasion - on the staff when John arrived: George Rude, a Marxist historian; Sam Barnett, a biologist, and Humphrey Higgins, who taught Russian.

The Music Department of the school was not a strong one. However, John was happy to find himself among some keen amateur musicians. Here was the first opportunity he had had - since his childhood duets with his cousin Michael and sing-songs at Windrush - to play the piano in a group. (I know that some of the fun he had at St Paul's rubbed off later in the rounds and canons - Tallis's Canon was a favourite - which he taught Julie and me. He played his beloved mahogany descant recorder and we played the Bakelite treble ones he'd bought for us.) Henry Wilson, an old Balliol friend of Walter Oakeshott, ran the Music Department, but he could give St Paul's only two days a week, between his duties as a church organist; he started a choral society and sometimes put on chamber recitals in the lunch hour, but his heart was with his London commitments. (He spent most of his money collecting paintings; he had picked up cheaply a Dufy, a Renoir and a Van Gogh.) Oakeshott, who had a good bass voice himself, was delighted that amateur chamber, singing and record-playing groups were proliferating among the boys and masters.

The journalist Edward Behr - in 'Modern Special' in 1942 - remembered John, once into his stride: 'When he took over the class, one was not conscious of being in school, of being "taught", of being involved in a "learning process".

> 'Rather, I am aware, after all these years, of a mood he created: we listened to a story-teller, a witty conversationalist who did not simply bask in the passive appreciation of others but stimulated his audience, encouraging us to participate in a debate that was never portentous, never moralistic, never dull.

> 'He made us feel, at the close of an hour, that we had been equal partners in an amusing, witty exchange of ideas that may have digressed completely from the subjects he was supposed to teach. But his skill was such that we were, in fact, learning all the time.'

Chris Arnold, who later became an architect in the United States, was a pupil in the American History class in January 1942. He remembers John saying that it would be good for the class to know something about its great new ally. 'Even at the time, I thought this was rather an imaginative idea. He introduced me to events, names and places which, later on, became much more familiar.'

Michael Summerskill - Dame Edith's son, and a marine lawyer - wrote: 'he was the first person who taught me the wonders of the USA, both its excitement and its details, as I sat enthralled at the news of Roosevelt's New Deal.'

'All I recall,' wrote historian Geoffrey Best, 'is a presence rather exceptionally stately and gentlemanly - a serious-minded man, evidently intellectual, suggestive (as were not many of them) of interesting things going on outside the school walls; never violent, never trivial; and his lessons (whatever they were!) looked forward to.'

'I remember him then', wrote John Tyrer, who became a diplomat, to whom John was tutor in addition to teacher, 'as tall, pale, a trifle saturnine but gentle and always calm. I suspected that he had health problems, perhaps quite wrongly; I certainly had them myself and this perception drew me to him... his grave manner and bearing was all that it should have been as a teacher on the threshold of his career.'

'Looking back I am amazed at how rambunctious and oddly-sorted we were,' wrote Seamus Flannery, a yacht designer and film-maker, 'and how lucky that a teacher such as John Usborne, wise to the real world, was better able to get through to us than the traditional other masters.'

John was teased, of course, for his grave demeanour. 'We often had him caught after class with his motor bike spluttering to a stop,' Flannery remembered. 'We would flood the fuel lines and the carburettor with petrol, and then turn the tap off on the fuel line. Hence there was enough for the bike to start, and for us to see him off with a big cheer, but then 500 yards down the hill... He was fun.'

Three Jewish brothers by the name of Shaffer, twins and a younger brother, had 'irrupted'- to quote François Duchêne - into the school in 1941. Peter and Tony Shaffer, Edward Behr, John Thorn, Martin Froy, Chris Arnold, Richard Mayne, all occupied the same room, with their teaching shared by John and Eynon Smith.

I wonder whether, during the war, John's preoccupations with world federalism affected his American history teaching? He had been responsible for starting his brother Henry on his lifelong crusade for World Government. In 1942 Henry sailed to New York in a convoy - to his wife's intense fear - on an unofficial mission regarding Federal Union. He was convinced that Britain's only way forward was to give up sovereignty and join a European state; that a world state, eventually, was 'the only way to avert Armageddon'.

Nine years on, in his new, chatty broadcasting style, John was to muse on those solemn years for a BBC talk 'Walking Abroad':'I had chosen meanwhile the hair-shirt of a schoolmaster: in other words my wife was faced with the prospect of having me about the house with no money in my pockets for three and a half months every year, with no car to escape in. No wonder I lost little time in becoming a bird-watcher.'

He'd been a bird-watcher for years! Hugh Whistler had taught him his first bird facts when the family lived in Battle; as a teenager John had looked for specimens for the bird-census in the meadows of the Pang at Bradfield. I imagine - having been given by him a copy of it for my tenth birthday - that when John was twelve, Hugh showed him, reverently, his newly published copy of *The Charm of Birds* by Lord Grey of Fallodon.

Windlesham had something to redeem it. During those difficult months at the end of 1941, while walking in the local nursery gardens, John had enjoyed getting his ear for birdsong in again, and looking for newly arrived migrants. Did he see a chiffchaff who had decided not to go south? Did he, as Lord Grey did, see a mistlethrush on a mountain ash tree? Did he leave Paula to Julie's night-time cries and go out to listen to owls?

Ludwig Koch's birdsong recordings, with Julian Huxley as narrator, were first transmitted on the BBC Home Service in 1936. A passionate admirer of those programmes, John longed for some recording equipment of his own. He is remembered by his post-war colleagues and pupils for his handiness with tape recorders. (In the late 1950s he used to go walking with field-glasses, and his tape-recorder under his arm on too short a strap; his trousers, also too short, embarrassed me.) He appealed to Oakeshott to obtain some recording equipment for St Paul's, but the Mercers' Company wouldn't pay. At Easthampstead the boys had the opportunity to join the new Natural History section of the Field Club; starting on Thursday afternoons in the autumn term of 1942, George Young, Arnold Monk-Jones and John gave talks - illustrated with lantern-slides and 78 rpm records of Koch's birdsong - to show boys how to learn some country lore. It was a happy collaboration. On a Sunday in November they led the first expedition for boys to seek out the birds of the Crowthorne district.

On hot days, lessons were given under the trees in the Park. John Gillespie (later to be a teacher), was with his classmates Geoffrey Best, John Tyrer, Michael

Summerskill and John Thompson in a pilot group in 1943, taking Higher Certificate English for the first time; he remembered the shocked astonishment of the class when John indicated that he thought Milton was a much over-rated poet.

The wartime summers at Easthampstead bring to mind Richenda Stubbs, a young staff wife and mother of a small girl, whose husband was away in the Army. The 'boys' clearly remember how pretty she was. Trained as a nurse, she had started working in the sanatorium, but soon took over as the school's nutritionist. John, boasting in her hearing one autumn about his glut of Blenheim Orange and Allington Pippin apples, made a quick sale: Richenda said she'd take the lot, and - using the school petrol allowance - she drove over to collect them. Her teas, put on for sporting events, were renowned, and earned glowing mentions in *The Pauline*. One was for a doubles tennis match in May 1942 in which John played with George Bean - and two other staff pairs - against a school team. John and George, the only staff winners, beat Parsons and Roper, Smallman and Kellett.

John was on a course at Dartington at the end of August 1943. Away from routine, and recovering from the month's events - the Allies had conquered the last Axis defences in the Mediterranean, and the British had bombed Hamburg - he celebrated with a poem the Devon landscape and the curlew, a bird which evoked for him the downs near Windrush. 'The Curlew and the Goldfinch' was dedicated to Julie on her second birthday:

> '...
> Round the lane's curve
> The curlew's croon rested a half-bar, a nerve
> String quivered out of turn:
> There grew a blueness in the bending sky. I churn
> Carelessly and noisily a dwindled puddle,
> Crunch the gritty sediment and muddle
> Devon soil in Devon rain. The noise dies
> As the bird
> On a cadenza stops because it heard...
> Not me... not me, but the cries
> The joyous, twittering cries of another bird
> Restlessly bouncing from bramble to briar
> Coming up behind me chip-twittering
> With busy inconsequence, never sitting
> On a briar but it must wish to flit
> To a better perch which t'will quit
> As soon as it can chirrup another catch to it.'

To think that I was unaware, then, of the violent deaths of my father's friends! His prep-school mate William Rhodes-Moorhouse, and a new local friend, Dick Reynell, both shot down in the Battle of Britain; John Gabriel torpedoed in the Atlantic in 1941 en route to Egypt to work in Intelligence; Bill Davies, his Balliol friend, killed in the Battle of the Java Sea in 1942; John Gaye, his Bradfield friend, killed by a sniper in France a few weeks after D-Day; and his neighbour Dick Seth-Smith killed while testing a plane.

For the war years I have a few memories of my own. The earliest - probably when I was three - is of being handed my silver christening mug filled with Ribena, to drink as I sat in the sun at the foot of our pear tree. The others pertain to the war: of being tucked up in a makeshift bed under the stairs; standing one night with my parents at the front door watching a V1 bomb, as its engine cut out, silently falling out of the sky - to land in Bagshot, two miles away. I distinctly remember - it would have happened that same year, 1942 - a British plane, perhaps caught by a buzz-bomb, burning in a field a few hundred yards away. There were sheets of flame, and people running up the road.

A tall, dark German prisoner-of-war named Horst used to tidy our garden sometimes. Julie and I were told to be kind to him because he was far from home and lonely. We must have irritated him, watching him as he weeded. One day our curiosity got the better of us: 'Horse,' I asked, 'why do you have a middle parting?' I can remember my father's laughter.

There is a batch of photographs showing us all with our adored orange and white English setter, Dinah. In 1945 she had a litter of eight puppies of which five died. We gave away Pluto - named after the wartime code name for the Pipe Line Under The Ocean - to a Bradfield master, and for a while kept Bolshie and Serena. When the puppies were tiny they were kept in the outhouse; they often managed to escape in spite of old planks propped against the foot of the door.

★ ★ ★ ★ ★ ★ ★

Having now cancelled from his mind his youthful image of himself as a county farmer, John was finding the science of farming a consuming interest - thanks to the experience he had gained of organising a small market garden with some of his pupils. Then he was introduced, through his friend Ralph Gabriel, to what became his own agricultural speciality in the growing of maize. Ralph, two years older than John, was the son of a farmer in Chobham, four miles from Windlesham. His two elder brothers, Kit and John, knew Tommy and Dick Usborne at Charterhouse. John met Ralph, an electrical engineer, at the beginning of the war. He was a bachelor then and came home for his weekends; he had a reserved occupation designing radio transmitters for the RAF, with a company called Gambrell, in Wandsworth.

In 1943, John heard from Ralph that his father had been given a little seed of a new strain of maize which was said to be specially suited to the English climate. (As a twenty-two-year-old John had eaten corn-on-the-cob at a Mayfair dinner party and had been curious about it ever since.) He had already seen the strain, Golden Standard, grown by a Dutchman called Kortlang at Grey Friars Farm on the Surrey Hog's Back. He dropped a broad hint via Ralph and was sent a matchbox with about three dozen seeds. He planted them, well composted, in a square patch in our garden. There was an astonishing growth. He was hooked; maize became one of his many passions. About it he wrote in the preface of his book *Corn on the Cob*, published in 1956: 'To me there is no food plant I enjoy staring at more. It is tall, graceful, sturdy, luxuriant of foliage, efficient in reproduction, prolific, many-sided in use, delicious to man and beast. But above all it is miraculous. To me, as to many millions who can grow nothing else, it symbolizes the interdependence of man and the soil.'

In 1945 John persuaded Ralph and John Halloran, a cousin of Paula's working at the Australian Air Force HQ in London, to become partners in a maize-growing enterprise. John had been lent a two-acre field in Chobham. They spent the long weekend of VE Day planting by hand 33,000 seeds. 'The next fortnight was the most heartrending time,' John wrote in an article for *Synopsis* in 1946,

> 'We had been forewarned about the love of birds for the young shoots of maize, and had ordered fourteen of those modern scarecrows which go off bang every twenty minutes or so. Not only did ten of these fourteen fail to arrive, but the four that did function made no difference at all, because Bisley Ranges were only three miles off and the local birds plainly had very little fear of big bangs.

Ralph Gabriel in 1995

'Germination was slow and very patchy, whereas the couch and knotweed were recovering with rampant vitality.' The three men battled with the weeds and wireworm weekend after weekend, using their hands and a two-wheeled Lend-Lease hoe. The resulting growth was so patchy that they were forced to transplant to a cleaner quarter-acre. The transplanting and subsequent hoeing, 'de-sideshooting', top dressing, and decobbing produced a good crop of 3000 saleable cobs. Naafi red tape prevented the sale of the whole field to the American Forces University at Shrivenham. A Soho barrow-man took two sackfuls for £15, and the rest went to Covent Garden market.'

Ralph Gabriel continued to partner John in his maize cultivation for another year or so, until he bought his own farm. Behind Sandy Lane Cottage there was an acre of glebe-land, rank with weeds and the dreaded couch-grass. John persuaded our vicar, John Archibald - in return for a bushel of cobs - to let him cultivate it. He did, and for the next 15 years paid rent to an absent owner. 'The field' provided John with his fresh air at weekends, and on weekday evenings in spring and summer. Visitors would usually find him digging out couch-grass there. Besides corn, he grew and experimented with buckwheat and many other grains and vegetables; and he raised hens in a portable aluminium hen-run with a dome at one end.

Good neighbours and friends living nearby at 'Cooper's Green', were a large family called Dawkins, with four children. Charlie was a stockbroker and did the journey up and down to London all through the war. Our fathers would take us for walks in the 'nurseries' to play our favourite game there: hide-and- seek in and out of the arches cut in a massively high - or so it seemed to us - yew hedge. Charlie and John played cricket with the village team for amusement and relaxation. John's love for the game found expression more than once in poetry:

Go in the deep field, Charlie, and stay there on the over:
Ears on the rod-reel warblers and all eyes,
With nerves and sinews wired for Merlin hover
For chasing and for pouncing Bradmanwise.

Warm is the day in June and gay the daisies
Mower-defying near the boundary sward.
Once again the cricket game amazes
Never, as now, though, half as much adored.
Charlie, bowl from the Rectory and next over.
Delightful limbering battle. Swing that arm
And leap that plantain, paean as you cover
Half a pitch length in projecting dear alarm.

When there was hope about the war, and the British victories - over Rommel at El Alamein in November 1942, and six months later the final one in Africa over both the Germans and the Italians - a happy domestic life was all the happier. The summers then, for me, still seem idyllic. A verse from a poem called 'The Owl' expresses John's contentment of his household:

'While Paula bakes her cakes at midnight,
Ann has dreams of Julie's tears.
While I examine Housman's rhythms,
The Barn Owl jeers.'

Windlesham life suited us all at this time, in spite of John's irrepressible urges to shock the stuffier neighbours. Occasionally he and Paula were persuaded by our vicar to take the village Sunday School together; John even wrote a prayer for it. On other Sunday mornings, on the spur of the moment (Paula probably had a little grumble), my parents would take Julie and me to the local pub, the

Half Moon - where they would play shove-ha'penny with friends. We were parked on a bench outside with some lemonade. Very soon we felt cold, hungry and cross; forgotten too - which we usually were!

From his first days at St Paul's, finding Walter Oakeshott's and Erik Sthyr's teaching styles emphasising discussion, John was as keen as they to bring in visitors to lecture. Through his own friends and his experience as a journalist, he had good contacts with the literary world. The boys themselves were avid for a chance to forget Shakespeare and Milton for an hour or two and hear about current writing. To start with, he drew on a treasure-trove of distinguished OPs: Laurence Binyon the poet, Ernest Raymond the novelist, Leonard Woolf the publisher, Max Beloff the historian. Victor Gollancz came down to speak about the Left Book Club. John's old Summer Fields English teacher L.A.G. Strong gave a recital of his poetry, and spoke to the Eighth Form on 'The Modern Novel'; Cyril Bailey, in his seventies, spoke on Roman Religion; Rex Warner on Allegory.

As was usual in the school holidays, John worked as the Press Officer and Educational Adviser to the Iron and Steel Federation, a supplementary job he had for most of the war and for four or five years after it. Most days he went up to the headquarters in Tothill Street, Westminster. It was a job that stimulated his teaching. His colleagues at St Paul's all knew and accepted that he had interests outside the school which he would never give up; yet the school was his mainstay.

Chapter Five

The need for reforms was exercising the minds of educational theorists in Britain from 1941, and Walter Oakeshott was a major participant. He was determined in his drive to educate 'the ordinary boy' having seen first-hand the terrible effect of years of unemployment on the morale of ill-educated men. The success of St Paul's evacuation from London, and the school's growth since, had won over his Governors. They now supported him in his vision - that the school should open its doors wider, and provision should be made for boys who would go in for practical careers after the war.

In his own reserved occupation as a headmaster, Oakeshott felt guilty, among boys who would soon be going off to the war, some to their deaths. In 1943 - quixotically and without explanation to his staff - he acquired a berth for himself with a merchant convoy sailing to North America during the spring term. He had persuaded the Admiralty that in exchange for the berth, he would write a report on the conditions for convoy crews for the Ministry of War Transport. He felt strongly, with young men in the Forces open to such great dangers, that he would be a better schoolmaster if he were to see for himself the experience of a seventeen-year-old cadet in the Merchant Navy.

He had never crossed the Atlantic before and was sick for the whole fortnight spent on board. He was treated boorishly by the commodore of the merchant ships, who knew he was there to snoop. From research he had done a year earlier for his government report 'A Plan for Youth', Oakeshott knew of conditions in the equivalent American and Norwegian ships, so was able to compare; and, unsurprisingly, he reported on slum-like conditions. Equally foreseeably, his findings were never published.

From Nova Scotia he travelled to New York, intent on some detective work at the Pierpont Morgan Library for what was to be his most absorbing private study, of the artists of the Winchester Bible. After seven years spent familiarising himself with all existing fragments from photographs, Oakeshott was sure that the work on the 'Morgan Leaf', a twelfth century illuminated fragment in the Library, was by the same hand as a miniature in the archives at Winchester. As it happened, the Library's most priceless treasures had been evacuated to the Middle West. Nevertheless - and needing some cheer after the rejection of his Report - Oakeshott enjoyed himself in New York, being fussed over by some cousins, and fêted for a recently published book.

On Oakeshott's return, John was enthusiastic about his plan to forge links in the United States to benefit St Paul's. John knew he needed his own experience of the country to be able to develop the scope of his teaching about it. (During his last year at St Paul's, Oakeshott probably looked into exchange teaching programmes with John in mind.) A year later Oakeshott invited down to the school, and charmed, the black-eyed and beetle-browed American Ambassador in London, John Winant. There were speeches; the school sang the 'Battle Hymn of the Republic', and Winant was presented with a first edition of Erasmus's *Epigrams*.

Very cold weather and coal and food rationing made the wartime winters grim. The news of the huge British raids on Berlin, five times heavier than the heaviest on London, in November 1943, satisfied the British. 'The Battle of Berlin', said Sir Arthur Harris, chief of RAF Bomber Command, 'will continue... until the heart of Nazi Germany ceases to beat.' I picture my 26-year-old father, chugging home in his Red Baron helmet, his gloom giving way to some verse:

> The snag about riding a motor-bike now
> That I'm old and without adipose
> Is the buffets I take from the weather and how
> It attacks both the knees and the nose...'

John enjoyed teaching his fourteen-year-olds to write verse. Gordon Derrick remembers having to write 'a parody of *Hiawatha*, your father starting us off with the first line '5x is a form of idlers...''

Dennis Bertuzzi-Amanda told me: 'I still have some exercise books in my loft with your father's comments. I managed to meet his standards reasonably well with prose but what he had to say about my efforts at poetry are best left unsaid! He opened my eyes to Shakespeare but failed miserably, I'm afraid, on Chaucer.' Another 1944 fifth-former, Edgar Hawkes, sent me a report on him by John: 'Although his emotions and his imagination are moved with the greatest difficulty, he is a very careful and conscientious worker...'

Hitler's flying bombs and rockets tested the nerves. In 1945 the spring term started at St Paul's on Tuesday 23 January. Christmas had been colder than for 54 years, and snow was to lie thick on the ground until February. John, now thirty, felt jaded and run down. In winter he was bad at shaking off colds, and mouth ulcers would plague him. The overdraft seemed to have taken root: why couldn't he make ends meet?

I knew quite early that my mother was extravagant: I remember feeling indignant about a mauve crêpe suit with a toque to match for which she had carefully saved the family's clothes coupons. Mrs Rallings, the dressmaker in the village, worked regularly for her. Her work had to be good - my mother's knowledge of the fashion business made her an exacting client. I'll never know how she got hold of the materials: Julie's and my party dresses were usually made of embroidered organdie and they were always exquisite; it was a special moment for us all to see them laid out on my parents' bed, freshly ironed by our charwoman Mrs Peckham, ready for a birthday-party. Once, though, independently of each other, Julie and I refused to wear two hand-smocked dresses my mother had ordered for us at great expense. We thought them too elaborate for everyday. We weren't chastised; I suppose she felt guilty.

Throughout the war the Usbornes and Watsons and their spouses visited Windrush as often as they could. Although it was now only the spiritual home to the four Usborne brothers, for their sister Margaret, a single professional girl, it remained her base. As the writers Ralph and Frances Partridge provided a haven for their London friends at Ham Spray, a mile or two from Windrush, so did Uncle Hubert and Aunt Dorothy hold open house at Windrush as a respite from the bombs falling on London. There were fresh eggs for breakfast, and the chance to relax and have some fun; family friends of all ages were staying. That was the way 'The Aunt' liked it. Nanny was there to take charge of the children. The wartime cuisine of Windrush was usually rabbit, with Harris's vegetables (he grew them not only in the kitchen garden but on what had once been the lawn. 'The Aunt' had had it ploughed up to provide for the needy of Inkpen). And there was always a good tea: scones with blackcurrant jam and cakes made by Gladys, Harris's daughter. As for drink, the men drank beer. Quaker tenets forbade alcohol for the girls...except for a taste of sherry, when a visitor arriving prompted The Aunt to send one of the men over to 'The Olive Branch' for a bottle. Some precious old Hock was served very seldom, for special friends who came to dinner.

Julie and I were beside ourselves with excitement at the prospect of a stay at Windrush. We loved the journey: coming into Reading, where we changed trains, we read out 'Huntley and Palmers' from the big letters on the biscuit factory; Daddy pointed out the frightening dark prison and mentioned somebody called Wilde. Approaching Kintbury the bends of the river Kennet would appear - and disappear - alongside the line, and we would recognise picnic places; then the train's noise would change to a tinny drumming, and we would see the cress beds by the station as Daddy let down the leather window strap to open the door from the outside; and there, waiting for us as we jumped down on to the wooden platform, with her head on one side, smiling, would be Aunt Dorothy.

Once arrived, we ran off and became tomboys. At Windrush our mothers didn't nag us; but they were never far away when we wanted them. We children all ate together at a large scrubbed oak table presided over by Nanny; we were allowed to get over-excited and forget our manners sometimes; there was always a younger child to show off to. Uncle Hubert always seemed to be nearby as we played in that big, wild garden. He was a benign presence; he loved to watch us running about or climbing in and out of the empty stone fishpond. A portly figure with his toes turned out, he stood by the front door in his old tweed suit with baggy knees, waistcoat and chain, a trilby shading his eyes (Margaret confirmed that this was not only his photographed pose). Aunt Dorothy would call him: 'Man dear!' - a common Anglo-Indian wife's endearment for her husband - and he would disappear into the house for a few minutes.

Uncle Hubert still did a little work as Chairman and Honorary Treasurer of the Save the Children Fund. During the war, the organisation took an important role in bringing refugee children to Britain; and after - repeating the post-war work it had done in the 1920s - it helped to build refugee villages in Europe for displaced orphans.

But as we, privileged ones, were born, he wrote poems for each of us, the offspring of his daughters and son, and of his nephews. In June 1945 there were twelve children, the two oldest aged seven. (As they were written, all poems - by Uncle Hubert, the three Usbornes, and friends - were put up on the wall of the men's cloakroom.) When she was pregnant for the second time, in the autumn of 1940, Dick sent his American wife Monica home to New Mexico with her toddler David, because he knew he was to be posted to the Middle East; when she gave birth to Karen in March 1941 Uncle Hubert amused himself writing for her a poem peppered with little Americanisms; it began:

'Telegram from Albuquerque
"Born a daughter, fine and perky"
Like her mother I should guess
Full of charm and liveliness...'

Six months later, for Julie:

'You must fit yourself quickly
To cope with the boys,
Be possessive and prickly
If they covet your toys...'

In September 1942, for Christine, Tommy and Gerda's third child:

'With all that plethora of boys
There was, I own, just too much noise
For one who peace at times enjoys,
And now there's you, Christine!'

With his poem in June 1945 for Pippin, his fourth granddaughter, he celebrated the Peace Pledge Union (which he had espoused since its founding)
because they had the same initials:

'Blow the bugle, beat the drum,
Europe's free and Peace has come
Make an overwhelming noise.
All triumphant girls and boys
And to her initials true
Greet our darling P.P.U.'

In 1945 Tommy transferred from the Ministry of Economic Warfare to the
Treasury. (He was our most lovable uncle, because we knew him best - and we
knew that in Daddy's opinion he was a bit of a crank. He was usually engaged on
some odd learned study in his spare time; I remember my father laughing as he
told my mother that one of them was Danish slang.) Helped by a loan from
Margaret, in 1943 Tommy and Gerda had bought a house in Weybridge. (It was
cheap because it was close to Vickers-Armstrong's aircraft factory, an area highly
susceptible to bombing.) They loved it and nurtured it, and never again moved.
Tommy worked fanatically growing vegetables for his family during the war. His
garden, dominated by tall pine trees, with an air-raid shelter full of frogs, had a
slightly creepy atmosphere. It was better for hide-and-seek than our own. Peter
and Julian, our cousins, dug seven-foot tunnels under those trees and sat in them,
playing 'war-hero' games. Gerda suffered terror for them but Tommy didn't turn
a hair: it was important to him that as a boy he had survived some equally dangerous games. Ten miles from Windlesham, Weybridge was the right distance away
for bicycling expeditions planned by Tommy and my father when we were all
children, meeting for picnics at 'The Clump' on Chobham Common. At the end

of that year, Peter, aged eight, would be the first Usborne of his generation to start at the Oxford prep school, Summer Fields.

Henry and Pam and their three children lived in Tanworth-in-Arden, Warwickshire. They seemed out on a limb, up in the Midlands. Henry, since the age of twenty-three, had had his own firm in Droitwich, Nu-Way Heating Plants Ltd; from its founding in 1932 he ran it very successfully as a co-operative. His achievement, while in business, in maintaining his ideals as a pacifist (he had been an elected member of the Council of Federal Union since 1938) made the family very proud of him. He had an aura of importance to the rest of us in Surrey. Who had handed down to him his business acumen? None of the others had it. And now he was a Member of Parliament! 'I never intended to become a politician,' he said in his election address in 1945, 'but my convictions have compelled me to offer to become one.' His first seat was Acocks Green, Birmingham - won, to his great surprise, when Attlee's Labour government had its landslide victory that July.

Dick was in Egypt and Lebanon with the Special Operations Executive from 1940 until 1944, away from his wife and children - but having an enjoyable war. One day in June 1941 he was at the other end of a Cairo swimming pool from General Sir Archibald Wavell; hours later the general told 'the SOE boys' that the Germans had invaded Russia. Dick arrived home in 1944 with the rank of Major. A few weeks later Monica and his two children arrived home from the USA. They all, plus Grumpy, a bulldog bought from the Dogs' Home, lived through the last of the doodlebugs in a flat in Battersea. They then moved to the Walton end of Weybridge, two miles from Tommy's family. In 1945 Dick was taken on as an editorial dogsbody by a magazine called *Lilliput*, a 5"x8" digest expertly stuffed with good writing, good illustrations and good photography. From *Lilliput* Dick went on to be assistant editor on a weekly paper called *The Leader*. He had the most fun of his career on small magazines, he told me. The post-war paper shortages changed them for ever.

Margaret was twenty-seven in 1945; unmarried, but a fond and cheerful playmate to all the children staying at Windrush. She had trained as a nurse at Newbury Hospital after Cambridge, but was recruited in 1941 into Intelligence, her colleagues calling her by her school and Newnham nickname MUZZ, helping to break German codes in Hut 6 at Bletchley Park. After the war, she lived in what seemed to the Usborne children a very bohemian flat in the Adelphi, which vibrated every time Big Ben chimed. She started a job at the House of Commons that she was to do for seven years, as secretary to the Labour MP for Plaistow, Frederick Elwyn Jones. He later became Lord Chancellor in James Callaghan's government.

★ ★ ★ ★ ★ ★ ★

Wiggly Lane was the Windrush name for the last lap of the two-mile walk to the Downs. The great hump-backed chalk ridge of them could be seen from the bedroom windows at Windrush then, and they had a certain drama; these days they are obscured by trees. Our fathers used to lead us children, in a great troop, to climb to the Gibbet, the seventeenth-century wooden scaffold standing at the highest point,

975 feet. (Charles II was visiting Nell Gwynn at Combe Manor, in Hampshire - on the other side of the Downs from Inkpen - in 1676, at the time that a young thatcher from Inkpen and his mistress, a married woman from Combe, drowned her children in a local pond. These two were hanged, watched by a throng of villagers, from a gibbet that was erected for the purpose on the boundary of the two counties.) The slope is tremendously steep. I remember the harebells, inches from my face, as I scrambled up. The view was better every time I turned and stood still to get my breath. And the thrill of arriving at the top, feeling the force of the breeze, craning up at the terrifying gibbet... and a view on both sides!

Savernake Forest, visited from Windrush when I was about six, was the nearest thing to Fairyland I had ever seen. I have now, over fifty years later, a gorgeous Pisanello vision of its rich detail. I remember the magic of my first sight of wild strawberries, growing beside the track, and my father's intense delight in showing them to me.

Much darker, and distinctly unfriendly, was the Rough, the dense pinewood a few hundred yards from Windrush. Birds called nightjars were there after our bedtime, we heard. It smelt of foxes, strong and musty. Getting lost in it was my constant fear. My father and his brothers would enjoy scaring us with stories of the spirits that lived in the Rough. It frightened my boy cousins too - something they are now admitting to.

* * * * * * *

In May 1945, the month of the German surrender, the High Master of St Paul's was responsible for an occasion which was a fitting finale to the school's years in Crowthorne. It gratified his well-known liking for the powerful effect of Greek tragedy, and of one play in particular. He was producer - coaching the boys with Classics teachers Tony Richards, Pat Cotter and John - of a performance of the *Oresteia* by Aeschylus. Twenty-one years had elapsed since Oakeshott had acted in the play with the Balliol Players. In this wartime version, performed in the open air at dusk in front of the Mansion, black-out material added to the sinister aspect of the Furies as they chanted. Antony Jay, just fifteen, played Cassandra, to great acclaim.

Oakeshott was obliged to fight the War Office tooth and nail to have the Hammersmith building restored to the school in time for the autumn term. Masters and boys arrived in September to tackle the immense job of re-converting the gloomy old building to a school, to be ready for 1 October.

John left no comments on the ending of the war; neither on the Atomic Bomb, the start of the Cold War with Russia - nor on events in Britain. In his near-Marxism in the 1930s he had battled for his point of view; during six years of war he had continued battling, to keep himself and his family going, suffering bombs and shortages like everyone else, and crippling restrictions to his freedom. Recognising difficulties ahead for Britain, and feeling depressed and trapped by the impoverished state of Europe, he wanted to get away from it.

He dreaded the start of a change of routine which would mean more strain, bad city air, and less time pottering in his field. Undoubtedly, he felt at this point - with the war over and his glow of achievement at his successful maize-growing - that conformity, in the form of a job in London, was about to get the better of him; he would be sucked into it, never to extricate himself. In April 1951, five and a half years later, he broadcast a wry fifteen-minute talk on the BBC Home Service entitled 'More Eccentrics Needed'. It reflects immaturity in his determination to shock; and to me – his restlessness. He was no longer supporting totalitarianism. (The wit keeps it light; it's that, I would guess, which sold it to the producers.) Luckily, from the inner strength he had developed as a result of being ragged by three older brothers, he was always able to laugh at himself and his prejudices:

> 'I have a "thing" about bowler hats. I suppose, when I was an infant, I knew an ogre who wore one. I'm not in the least bit sorry about it, but I thought it best to warn you, in case you or your nearest and dearest wear them. D'you remember the owl – it was some time last year – that used to attack men on their way to catch the morning train? He only went for certain people – people who wore bowler hats, and he used to knock them off. I could have offered a home to that bird. Catching a train to the office in a bowler hat is a thing done by thousands of good, clever, hardworking people. But I can't help it; a bowler and a suburban railway line symbolise for me something which depresses me, and that something is slavish conformity.'

John got rid of his old black motor-bike. The mode of his 46-mile round trip to London varied over his future seventeen years at St Paul's. (He could not afford to buy a car until 1958.) If the Aldershot and District coach was running on the A30 so soon after the war, that was his first. It had a stop a few minutes' walk from the school. Leaving Sandy Lane Cottage, he enjoyed the walk to the stop on 'the main road'. Local trains to Waterloo were not convenient for Hammersmith; and as he had said, he would have shied away from waiting on the platform with bowler-hatted stockbrokers. Later, to earn a lift up with his neighbour Robert Simpson, a chartered accountant who had multiple sclerosis, John was the reluctant chauffeur of Robert's big Triumph; a Windlesham man who worked in the same firm did the return drive.

He hated the travelling he had to do, both routes being full of eyesores – a word he used often. He never could accept suburbia. In writing about it later, he employed some rare sarcasm. (I used to go up to St Paul's Girls' School in the Simpson car with him on Monday mornings in the 1950s, and when I became a little queasy during the ugliest stretches, he saw me as a fellow suburbia-hater.) The bus took the old Great West Road, before the M4 was built; Robert Simpson's car went the 'back way', not quite as ugly, through Chertsey, Sunbury, Twickenham and Richmond, before the M3 was built.

John's premonition that the travelling would affect his health was proved right; and his frustration at the wasting of his precious time compounded his exhaustion. 'I'm often taken to task by my better adjusted friends for being an escapist,' he said in 1950 when broadcasting about his love of the land, 'not facing the world, not coming to terms with it. But if the world's what they seem to think it is, then I don't like it and I'll take every opportunity to escape from it.

> 'I wish I could be glib enough to give as my reason for living in the country the fact that I'm a countryman born and bred. No, I live in the country because, quite simply – I hanker more for the country, when I'm

living in town, than I hanker for the town when I'm living in the country. (Happy is the man who knows how to bargain with his hankers.) It probably has a lot to do with my notions of freedom and slavery. At any rate, I live in the country. Did I say live? I am domiciled in a country cottage, and I live - I live for a few blissful hours during weekends and summer evenings...in a field.'

Paul Longland, also a lover of the country, was to become a good friend. He had joined St Paul's in 1944 to teach Senior History in the absence of the revered Phillip Whitting. He became form-master of 6a, the History Sixth, which gave him the responsibility of some clever boys, among whom were Geoffrey Best ('my star turn'), Kenneth Baker, Michael Summerskill, Greville Janner and John Thompson. A small wiry man, Paul was keen on boxing, for which St Paul's was well-known in that decade. Both Paul and John had elder brothers who were socialists and in the public eye; Paul's was Jack Longland, the educational administrator, mountaineer - and a broadcaster familiar to millions as the questionmaster of 'My Word'. For both, wild places, huge continents, and birds held a fascination; later their mutual enthusiasm for the warmth and humanity of American people strengthened their bond.

Paul Longland in 1994

'He was not an intellectual', Paul said of John. Because of the nature of his teaching, Paul told me, John always got on well with both masters and boys. He was popular for his good nature, he said, 'I never saw him in a temper'. Paul remembered him as a sportsman, 'the cricketer of those years'; and - for the rest of his career at St Paul's – as a master who had one foot outside the school. 'We all regarded him as being in with the theatre and journalism.' (Paul and John fell out only once: Alec and Eric Bedser, the famous cricketing twins, were invited to the school to speak to the boys as a promotion exercise by Coca-Cola.'I was dead against it,' Paul said, 'but John was intrigued. I'm in no doubt that he would have been good at writing advertising copy.')

★ ★ ★ ★ ★ ★ ★

John now wanted to examine the United States in the light of the severely anti-American climate prevailing in Britain. Through the English Speaking Union, an opportunity to go there came up at last: he was one of 74 English teachers chosen out of several hundred for a post-war exchange programme for the academic year of 1946. 'Social Studies' was to be his subject, at Hamburg Junior High School, in a suburb of Buffalo, an industrial town on Lake Erie in the Northwest corner of New York State. Lester T. Hannan would be crossing the Atlantic the other way to take John's Current Affairs classes at St Paul's.

July 1946 was abnormally hot, and the maize and tomatoes, grown together by John and Ralph Gabriel in 'the field', ripened very quickly. It had been a growing season full of suspense. They had decided to experiment with symbiosis – they had heard that tomatoes thrived in the company of maize. May had produced corn stalks as big as stakes, and the tomatoes grew well. In June, neither grew more than two inches. 'It was unspeakable. A record showed that every day of that month it rained for at least half an hour, that the hours of sunshine were negligible and that mean temperature was about 45 degrees Fahrenheit.'

In writing about that summer afterwards for his book *Corn on the Cob* John showed, characteristically, that he had relished the drama and the element of risk. No warnings from Paula that he was overdoing it were heeded at the time. That term, in addition to preparing boys for exams and writing reports, John probably had taken cricket coaching. But in the field where he was growing his crops 'docks and couch, mares-tail and spurry were fighting hard'. After supper on weekdays, while Julie and I were being put to bed, he'd rush out of the house to push the old Planet hoe along those rows. He was now intoxicated by market-gardening after two successful growing seasons, and by the frisson the greengrocers' orders gave him. By the day of my parents' sailing to the United States, he was in a state of feverish excitement. Some last-minute lowdown on orders for tomatoes and the first cobs was written to Ralph only an hour before he and Paula left for Southampton. His postscript said: 'If you want to buy a farm remember us as partners. We're both dead serious about this. I'll find the money somehow. I must get on the land.'

Julie and I were being looked after at Sandy Lane Cottage by our grandmother, who had now sold most of her property in Australia and was based in a flat in Kew. My mother planned to spend one term only in Hamburg with my father, and return to us in the New Year.

They disembarked in Montreal. English friends in Great Neck, Long Island, had invited them to stay, and they did, perforce, for three weeks. John arrived with pneumonia. The friends, Lu and Mary Kirkby, told me that their doctor – who

SANDY LANE COTTAGE,

WINDLESHAM,

SURREY.

BAGSHOT 349.
Friday morning

Dear Ralph,

A few addenda to my letter.

I promised the Rector we would let
him have some tomatoes as rent. I don't
see the need to supply him just yet. I
should wait till the glut and give him
a basket full.

All the fixtures for the Planet are
in my old haversack which hangs on the
right of the entrance to the outhouse.
They're all wiped overwith an oily rag.

Let the family have a few little
cobs whenever you're over. The kids have
aqui acquireda taste for them and I know
my motherinlaw is fond of them. Very Very
soon the garden ones will be ready.

My typing is very bad, but we're off in
about an hour and I have a huge lump in
my throat and visibility is rather poor.

Au revoir and good luck. Don't forget
the kids.

Letter to Ralph Gabriel, 9 August 1946

lived in the same apartment building, would check on John three times a day. He warned him that, with his heart defect, he would be in grave danger if he did not rest by staying still in bed. (Nowadays, no doctor could force a patient to rest; a person with John's physical abnormality would have a heart bypass operation soon after diagnosis.) I know that Paula's casual attitude to John's illness shocked that kind doctor. Fresh from dark and deprived England, and dazzled by the Fifth Avenue department stores, she was restless at John's bedside, and an irritable and impatient nurse to him.

He rested, and recovered in time for their journey upstate. Arriving in Hamburg, they were given a warm welcome by some very curious people. 'British Exchange Teacher and Wife Amazed at Number of Automobiles' said a headline in the local newspaper. 'Mr. and Mrs. Usborne of London Hope to See Increased Anglo-American Friendship'; 'as Britain's unofficial ambassadors to Hamburg, they are democratic, cultured, observant and, best of all, anxious to learn more and more about America, her people, her customs.'

They had lodgings in Hamburg with a woman of whom they both became fond, Mildred Francis, at 260 Maple Avenue. During Paula's stay of one term, she and John made fast friends of two couples with whom they corresponded for years afterwards. Jack Moore and his wife Bee, in their sixties and childless, took Paula under their wing, cosseted her and gave her a taste of the American way of life of which they were proud. She loved them both for their affection. Bee recognised my mother's flair and in those three months she introduced her to the best in American furnishing ideas. Bee's present of a spiral-bound engagement calendar with superb scenic photographs was looked forward to every Christmas for about fifteen years (and then it didn't appear, and we heard no news of the Moores thereafter). For my mother its American sophistication brightened our house.

Nan and Jim Eells were my parents' age; Jim was a colleague at the High School. I remember him on a visit to England a few years later; he was skinny and insect-like, and made us laugh. I found a menu for The Twin Pines Dining Room, Hamburg, among Paula's things after her death. I picture the Eellses and the Usbornes, for a dollar twenty-five each, having a raucous evening dining there on Chicken Fricassee with Biscuits and four glasses of milk. Snapshots were taken on a sunless December Sunday while the four of them were walking along a railway line, heading into a local quarry. Their faces were pinched with cold. John, the silhouette of his head grotesquely small against the snow in that old leather flying helmet, grits his teeth against the biting wind.

John had been warned that his 9th Grade pupils were 'a pretty unruly bunch', and that they were children of either German or Irish origin 'not exactly pro-British...the lion's den wasn't in it.' His view of their appearance was that of an Englishman newly arrived from a country still suffering seriously from the habit of war; war-scarred people, including children, were the people he had lived among for six years. No doubt he felt unsure of how to enjoy himself. The concept of 'a teenager' was not then known. Initially he was shocked at the children's frivolity, their lack of culture, but it didn't take long for him to be charmed by their puppyish friendliness, especially that of the girls. Here he recounts his first class in a talk broadcast for the BBC in March 1950:

'The bell rang, the door burst open and in poured the thirty-five boys and girls who were to be my special charge for the next ten months. It seemed to me that about half of them had their shirts hanging outside their trousers - and that they weren't the sort of shirt I'd dream of wearing even at a fancy dress affair. You have never seen such patterns or such glaring colours. One very fat boy I remember wore a light pink blouse with blue cocktail glasses printed all over it. Not one boy wore a coat. Their trousers, or pants as they called them, were of many designs and cuts, but the commonest were a rather tight-fitting overall trouser (which they called Jeans) with the most peculiar lace-up effect behind.

'The girls, the bobby-soxers, wore blue jeans like the boys and they contrived to look good in them. The effect all round was one of studied informality, possibly achieved by the almost universal sloppy-joe, by the almost universal brown and white saddle-shoe, and the neat little bobby-socks.

'But you'll be wanting to know how these young popinjays behaved that first lesson. Well, they behaved perfectly. Not a sound. I began to imagine in my folly that I was holding them spellbound. For nearly a fortnight this exemplary behaviour went on. But I'm very irritable about chewing gum, however discreetly it's managed. These children are most indiscreet. I'm sure it was my irritation about this that gave them the cue to be irritated with me. They fidgeted. The boys made eyes at the girls or passed notes around. When I caught anyone misbehaving, there were loud expostulations of innocence: 'But, Holy Cow, Mr Usborne, I wasn't doing nothin''. Once, when I got really livid with a little dead-ender and shouted barnyard orders at him to stand up on the chair, he strolled up to me and addressed me thus: 'Say, lookee here, you god-damned Britishers throw your weight about too much, see?'

'I was almost in despair for a while. Though my pupils were never unfriendly to me out of school - quite the reverse - in school we were on the very worst terms, and I knew that since there was no frightening them into good behaviour and good work, I had to re-establish friendly relations before hoping to teach them anything. How on earth was it to be done? I think it'll surprise you to know that the answer came from them.

'It appeared that they really did want to learn World Geography. After all they had to pass an exam in it in June. But my teaching was so vague: there wasn't anything to get hold of, to learn and memorise. Yes: 'memorise': that was the word: it holds the clue to American High School education. I hated it but that was what they wanted. They were using a charming but firm bit of blackmail on me. 'You teach our way or else...!'

Eight years later, John recollected his frustration at his American pupils' ignorance of geography: 'I am saying that the U.K. is far smaller than the U.S. They take it silently, but obviously without perception. 'Why' I say, 'England and Wales would slip into New York State and still feel a draught'; none of them so much as smiles. I swear to myself between grinding teeth that if I teach the little blighters nothing else for a year I'll teach them the U.K.'s smaller than the U.S.'

The comments and criticisms of this 'British Educator' on the American grade system were written up very seriously for the local paper. He was critical of the large classes, and the grouping of pupils according to age rather than ability. With diplomacy he was quick to add that American children displayed a more definite zest for living and were more energetic than their English counterparts. 'Of course, this may be partly due to the fact that children get more to eat in the United States.' 'There is a more carefree, happy atmosphere in the American schools, I believe. I like the American child very much and I am also happy in my association with my colleagues, whom I have found to be tolerant and understanding.'

From early in his stay John was asked to speak publicly in Hamburg and Buffalo on many aspects of the British way of life. His audience, all first or second generation Polish, German, Irish, French, Southern Black and Japanese refugees, were greedy for his views, and greedy for hints and praise for their private enterprises. He was much in demand - but for insultingly low fees. But: 'God, how I need them!' he wrote to Ralph. 'Prices are worse and worse. These Republicans are up to no good, I'm sure, and woe betide England when this country has its inevitable depression. Politicians are crazy here.' As an educational ambassador, he was learning when to use discretion. At the beginning of November, he spoke to a group of Buffalo Republicans after the results of Congressional elections gave their party control of the House of Representatives and the Senate. 'I told them frankly Britain was not pleased and why. I joked about it and they were most magnanimous about my animadversions. We discussed for about $2\frac{1}{2}$ hours and I was surprised and mighty proud to find these Americans 100% curious of everything British except our Class Distinctions. They agreed that we could make Socialism work because we had a good Civil Service recruited on sound lines. They envied our stability and the monarchy which symbolises it (I have to modify my republicanism here). They admired our police system and the fundamental honesty of our people; and by the end of the evening I had a lump in my throat and tears in my eyes for dear old England.'

Soon after they arrived, John went out to introduce himself to local farmers. He couldn't have been kept away. His reasons would have been: Geography was a subject he had been imported to teach; he needed material for articles he had promised to British publications; and he missed feeling the earth on his hands. To Ralph he enthused: 'I had to address the Young Cooperative Dairyman's League on "Rural England". I talked on British Farming and used *The Countryman* (a small English digest for which he was writing), your letter, and our experiences last year. They appeared to lap it up and asked a multitude of intelligent questions. Up here, American farmers, especially the young ones, are a bloody fine lot. The land is rich and so are they. They are better educated than their English counterparts and most progressive. I talked to several who farmed their own 100-acre or so Dairy Farms single-handed at the age of about 24, and despite very hard work they seem to have time to meet in the evenings to educate themselves and have fun. They are far the best Americans I've met so far.'

Paula said her goodbyes before the Christmas vacation. She and John went down to New York to be with the Kirkbys and their three children. This time John was well, but naturally, tired. 'My dollars are running out very rapidly,' he told Ralph. 'I'll have to make every cent I can out of speaking and writing... prices are crazy, utterly nuts!' Paula was delivered to her ship on the morning of New Year's Day. They and the Kirkbys had seen the New Year in at the Casino Russe on 157th and West 56th Streets. Paula and Mary, both petite women, each wore her 'little black dress'. Lu, their host, a Wall Street broker, in the fashion of the day, a double-breasted suit with his hair slicked back, looked like a hoodlum taking time off; John wistful, balding, wearing a bow-tie. They all enjoyed the luxury, beaming up from their banquettes for the photographer.

Back on his own in Hamburg for the deadest time of year in the Northern United States, missing his family, John thought of our garden - and missed the sight of birds. In his first broadcast for the BBC, a talk called 'American Birdsong', transmitted three months after his return home, he said:

'Not only do we have the blackbird, the thrush, the robin and the wren - and several others - but at least one of them is liable to be singing in one's garden on all but the bitterest days. But there you'd be more likely to hear nothing at all. It's a queer sensation, I can tell you. That was my most memorable impression of a North American winter. There was snow, of course: there were blizzards. But there was an unimaginable silence in all nature.

'The first great moment for me was late in March, when - in the thick of a snowladen Barbary bush - I noticed a dark brown bird of thrush size with a dark head and a dark red breast, obviously in a sad state of suspended animation because of the bitter weather. So this was the American robin. I wondered what could have induced the early New England settlers to call this huge thing a robin. But to my American friends it was what the cuckoo or the skylark's song is to us. My landlady was most excited. The snow was at least six inches deep outside, the thermometer showed five or six below freezing. But for her the winter was over, because the robin was back.

'...it was already mid-April and still quiet of bird-song. How I pined for the willow-wren's ripple, and the warming cuckoo.' He had read about the spring arrival of the American warblers: 'They were a fortnight late according to my several books. But when they did come, it was a deluge. I was living only a few miles from a bottle-neck of two of the Great Lakes, which provided passage for those small birds which couldn't risk flying over the broad lakes into their Canadian breeding grounds. So the great migration passed almost, it seemed, through the garden. It was a great show for the visiting Englishman.

'There are dozens of kinds. Almost every time I looked out of the window into the fruit trees I seemed to get a new one; there were black and white striped ones, bright yellow ones, pink and brown ones, hooded ones, masked ones. They were far more lovely than our warblers. But they were not very able singers. There is no song of the American woods to touch the nightingale's, the blackcap's, the woodwren's, the woodlark's - or even the thrush's and blackbird's.'

He went on to describe two American songbirds, the bobolink and the Baltimore oriole; and his first sighting of a bluebird. In May, with his field glasses and a pocket handbook to American birds, he walked, relishing the heat of early summer. He went over fields, through vineyards and woods, into the bed of a great gorge in the foothills of the Allegheny Mountains. He almost stepped on his first American plover, the kildeer, and watched it 'play possum' to lead him away from its nest.

John made notes continuously and excitedly, to be used for articles and broadcasts. *The Countryman* wanted an article on a 'truck farm' (market garden), so he arranged to join in some beet-planting with Polish women and Jamaican men and a German foreman. 'Lovely to get on my knees in the good earth again.' Feeling well and more at ease, on 17 April he wrote to congratulate Ralph on his engagement: 'Do congratulate Irene from me: she deserves it, I can tell you, getting an old bachelor like you off the shelf.'

'Round Easter I had an interesting steel tour of Cleveland and Chicago by plane. The big bosses are rampant anti-Union men and their attitude is dangerously militant. They make no attempt to understand Labour. One man said to me: 'These men actually demand to see our books.' Now I don't see what right they have to examine the firm's books. Communism they see round every corner. Childish race.' [Not only right-wing politicians have their prejudices, evidently. John had his own too. Surely at the height of the Cold War some paranoia regarding communism was to be forgiven?]

'I'm worn out with typing and MUST have a cup of tea - from a nauseating 'tea-bag'. Do you want me to get anything for you in this country? Steel fishing-rod? Pen? Seeds for your father? What-have-you? Write occasionally, Yours ever, John.'

Chapter Six

'Girl unpredictable, delectable,' John wrote,
Girl variable in moods, adorable
Always. You take more knowing
Than Cleopatra or Karenina,
And, I should say, once known are more, far more
Complete to love and labour for than she
Or she. I do not know.

A decade have I loved you, seen you change,
Permute and show unfacetable gems.
Through all I stand thumb poised
To press each light to stay a-shine to form
A tidy constellation...'

'After three days on a ship,' a nightwatchman on the S.S. Columbia once told the writer V.S. Naipaul, 'everyone is faithless.' While sailing home to her daughters, Paula had a shipboard romance with a young American company director. John's and Paula's friends Ralph Gabriel and Helen Simpson, who had been asked by John to meet her at Southampton, watched Paula as she came, starry-eyed, down the gangway on the American's arm.

Julie and I were excited to have Mummy back - and the yellow dungarees she had brought home for us. The teachers in Hamburg had sent with her a tea-chest full of toys, including the first party balloons ever to be seen in Windlesham. We had had exciting food parcels from them already. I remember the single helpings of cereal in cartons lined in greaseproof paper with doors you opened to pour in the milk, and bubble gum in wrappers with cartoons on them... even the brown paper smelt good, of vanilla.

Paula's discontent had been growing. 'John was always her whipping-boy' a neighbour remembered. Perhaps the stay in America, with its home comforts, had tipped the balance.

Our home was well-run. Paula's friends admired her decorative talents. But not having had the chance to acquire a skill, nothing she did absorbed her for long. She wasn't resourceful, so needed entertaining. More and more she felt excluded from the relaxations John enjoyed, pursuits that were often solitary: reading, listening to music, walking, birdwatching. None of them interested her. For his work he read constantly, of course; there was less time now for his role of Scott Fitzgerald to my mother's Zelda, so evident in their first years together from the loving inscriptions in the books he gave her.

As a family we did less and less together. When Julie and I were small, we had walked *en famille* to Fromow's nurseries, to look at the carthorses and to play hide and seek in the tall hedge, but the walks I remember best were with my father, after his return from Hamburg. Having just seen our first film, *Song of The South*, I remember – as we skipped along – singing, to his distraction, 'Zippety Doo Dah'. Miss Smyly had taken us and the Simpson boys to Northumberland to see the Roman wall and I had to tell him about 'the remains'.

In 1945, aged twenty-eight, Paula had written to Vivian Spong (at the time a major in the Royal Tank Corps in India) - who as a 21-year-old subaltern had wooed her during her first year in England, 1934 - to say that rather than John, he was the man she should have married. She had made no effort to hide from friends her irritation with John before their departure for the United States.

Not being a practical man, John himself was content with the status quo. The household to him was as harmonious as he had portrayed it in his poem of 1944 'The Owl'. To him Paula was forever beautiful and fragile; he always forgave her her naughtiness and extravagance. He truly loved her, indulged her, and tried to earn enough money to please her. Being seduced by all things Irish, for him she had a streak of Irish wilfulness. She wheedled. ('You have to twist them round your little finger to get what you want!' she once said to me, about husbands in general.) John was well trained to remember all anniversaries, but that was no difficulty; he was sentimental and could always find an excuse to write poetry. Like his brothers, he was an honourable man: it was important to him, once he had chosen his wife, to love and cherish her. But of them all – and my uncles' wives were none of them fragile – I think he was the only true softie... an inveterate dreamer.

John loved romantic love; in literature the subject always intrigued him. He had written poetry for Paula often, and in spite of his fury when he learnt of her affair, he continued to do so for a year or two afterwards. ('Girl Unpredictable' was written for their wedding anniversary a month later.) For a long time he was unable to see why she was unhappy.

Paula left America - where houses were centrally heated in winter - arriving in England in early January 1947, during a violent blizzard. There was worse to come of that notoriously protracted winter. The extreme cold and heavy snow - in some places lying in drifts for four months - was to paralyse the country, and be the ultimate disaster for Attlee's government. Telling the population to tighten its belts again was the last straw. Food rationing was continuing, almost two years after the war. Coal miners stayed away from the pits as a protest against their working conditions, with the result that steel works closed down. Nobody escaped the long daily power cuts.

But my mother and her friends were all young and healthy, and they stuck it out together. At Sandy Lane Cottage she and Julie and I huddled round a paraffin stove. (For years my parents' most hated chore was the cold bicycle ride to the ironmonger's to get the can refilled.) Although in Hamburg my father was living close to the breadline under American inflation, there was enough money in the bank at home for my mother, Julie and me to be comfortable. My seven-year-old's letters to my father during that winter - my spelling roughly checked by my mother - show that, apart from missing him, our home, as usual, was happy: 'The ice came today and it is frozen cold. There are little iceicels over the grass and plants. The birds are singing as much as they can but they are so cold, poor things. Julie is next to me doing her colouring and Mummy is sitting on a chair lengthening my school coat.'

Paula's American visited her regularly, though I don't remember him. (I imagine her at the top of the steps, in a New Look outfit made by Mrs Rallings, opening our front door to him.) Robert and Helen Simpson and another local couple were invited over to meet him. Paula was glowing: they could see that she had no intention of finishing the relationship. They began to fear for John, Julie and me. On a sunny spring day Helen was given lunch in London by the American: he wanted to know whether there was any future for him with Paula. He learnt that Paula's husband loved her very much. The man didn't appear in Windlesham again. Poor Helen! Paula never forgave her.

John sailed home on an American troopship. He arrived back with a few days to spare for the writing of his report for the Iron and Steel Federation, before Ralph Gabriel and Irene Allen's wedding on 9 August 1947. John was Ralph's best man, and Julie one of the three bridesmaids. To look at the happy photographs one would never guess Britain was suffering a severe economic crisis. The summer was a beautiful one, luckily; people badly needed sunshine and warmth after a winter of freeze and a spring of floods. The coal industry had been nationalised in January, but it had made no improvement; by the late summer the country was at its most impoverished. Attlee told the Commons, 'We are engaged in another Battle of Britain.' In June Ernest Bevin, our Foreign Secretary, had accepted Marshall Aid, money promised by the United States to any government willing to resist Communism. In July Stalin rejected the principle of the plan, seeing it as 'dollar-enslavement'; and the deadlock caused the suffering of all Europe to continue.

Before St Paul's claimed John again, Julie and I went with him to Windrush for a weekend organised in honour of the Aunt's 60th birthday. She and Uncle Hubert watched a great gathering of the family: apart from the adults there were seventeen children - six of them new to us, the progeny of Ursula and Jenny (the older two of the three Watson daughters), who were returning to England for the first time since before the war. Margaret's opening 'Song' was sung by the grown-ups to the tune of 'I do like to be beside the seaside':

'Oh! we do have some jolly jinks at Inkpen,
We've put the kids to bed and so we're free.
We've cast off the cares of parenthood - hood - hood,
And we'll murder any child that isn't good - good - good;
Oh! we do have some jolly jinks at Inkpen,
We've put the kids to bed and so we're free.
Draw the corks and mix the drinks,
Here we are to join the jinks,
The jinks at Inkpen, near Newbury.'

Margaret was chief planner of the weekend's entertainments. There were Sports for everybody: for adults a paperchase and a cricket match to take part in, a hockey match to watch; for us children - already occupied queueing for the hired slide, and jumping off a haystack into the chaff - there were special events on the lawn: an egg and spoon race, a sack race, an obstacle race. (We had been allowed a glimpse of a trestle table piled high with prizes before these began. The judges made sure we all got at least one.) Our parents cheered us on rowdily from behind the ribbon.

The high points of that great reunion, described in verse by Tommy, Dick, John and Margaret, take up about thirty pages of the last little blue volume of the *Windrush Rhymes*. After the weekend – making sure he slipped in some American expletives, and allusions to Baseball – John wrote about the Inkpen cricket match, to which Windrush had contributed five men. The war was over and he was playing cricket again. What fun!

Uncle Hubert died of a stroke a month later, aged seventy- seven. His body lay on his bed while Edwards's, the sawmill across the road, made his coffin. An era had ended.

★ ★ ★ ★ ★ ★ ★

Before he sailed for home John had written to a lady producer at the BBC offering recordings he had made himself, of 'certain aspects of American High School life which might be of interest to English listeners'. If she got her reply off to him sharply, he told her, he could write the talk on the ship. No answer came, not because of his cheek, but because his file couldn't be found. It was under 'O', not 'U'. Eventually Mary P. Ussher offered the idea to the Director of Talks, who rejected it. John wrote again from home, suggesting a talk on the American farming methods which he wanted to try out in England. He offered Douglas Allan (the producer in the Schools Department who had recorded John's pupils in 1944) the school recordings. Allan suggested, kindly, that he try 'Children's Hour'.

John's best idea had been accepted by Douglas Allan before the American trip: his talk on American birdsong, accompanied by recordings promised by Cornell University. In September 1947, the script having been in the files for about three months, some inter-office memos started flying between producers, expressing guilt that a year had elapsed with no slot planned for the talk. Eventually the Third Programme agreed to broadcast it. Meanwhile, Cornell's delay in dispatching the birdsong recordings was frustrating progress. After the recording, a month later, John was thanked by a producer of Home Service Talks, 'Tex' Rickard, for his 'patience and co-operation during the long, and I fear, tedious weeks of preparation...' At last, on Saturday 31 January 1948, late in the evening, the 20-minute talk was broadcast on the Third Programme.

Transmitter failures ruined it. They caused two breaks, one of three minutes and the second of a minute and a half. After the talk an apology was broadcast – but not immediately, so that very few people still had their radios on to hear it. In spite of some harsh criticisms from the well-known ornithologists James Fisher and L. Hugh Newman, the BBC had several requests for a repeat. John nagged – and the talk was adapted for 'Children's Hour' and broadcast on 28 March.

Teaching absorbed most of John's time and energy, but now it was one of many commitments. More money had to be earned (St Paul's paid its junior masters six pounds a week in 1947) and writing was the only means he knew. On the Common Room telephone at St Paul's he plagued the BBC producers with talk ideas; for the English Speaking Union, who had been involved in the Ministry of Education's exchange programme of teachers to the United States, he was editing a book on those teachers' experiences; and for the literary digest *Synopsis* he was writing about his first months at the American High School.

★ ★ ★ ★ ★ ★ ★ ★

Dr R.L.(Jimmy)James, who had taught Classics at St Paul's before the war, had become High Master at the start of John's absent year. He was liked by his staff because he usually left each member to teach in his own way. In the gloomy dried-blood-coloured Victorian building in West Kensington, John had to settle back into his old role in Room 2, a dark, sombre classroom - north-facing as all the classrooms were - to the left of the entrance, on the ground floor. To many of the younger boys the school was austere, intellectually and morally. John felt it too; he was struck by the melancholy of the Gothic pinnacles on the roof, the gargoyles, and the forbidding echo of the place after the modern schoolhouse he had left in Hamburg. David Wiggins (now Wykeham Professor of Logic at Oxford University) felt overwhelmed, as a fourteen-year-old, by the size of the school and the drabness of the surroundings. Wartime rubble still sat in odd corners, and some broken window-panes had not yet been replaced.

The musicologist Stanley Sadie remembered - as one of an Eighth Form general period - John explaining, as if to a group of his own colleagues, the differences in attitude and outlook between American and British teaching. '...I recall his talking, in those days just after the end of the war, about peace in the future, about the need to renounce sovereignty and join in a European state and ultimately a world state, as the only hope of averting total catastrophe in the future. It was, in those times of narrow nationalism, visionary, and the vision he imparted is one that captivated me at the time and has influenced me ever since.' (David Wiggins, a senior boy in the same class three years later, 'had an impression of someone benign'... but this benign man uttered 'words of warning about Britain shutting itself out from consideration of European community matters'. It was May 1950, and the Schumann Plan had just been proposed by France: to create a European Federation under a single authority to control French and German iron and steel production; and to make it open to other European states.) John's near-Communist, young man's views were being supplanted by those of his brother Henry: ideas no less ideological, but with wider, more generous horizons. As a teacher, John felt obliged to show the scenario from different angles - to develop in his pupils some healthy scepticism.

He had learnt that the boys responded only if he enjoyed himself as he taught. But he knew, and said it often, that it was essential 'to conserve energy'. He knew his own pace; in both teaching and writing he learnt to watch himself for signs of boredom: 'Yes, I confess the fire of inspiration goes out in a hurry with me,' he once said over the air. 'I'll write about anything for 2,000 words and enjoy it all - so long as the autoreversible ribbon on my vintage typewriter does autoreverse...'

Sometime during that autumn term of 1947, through Douglas Allan, John was able to arrange a visit to the BBC for a fifth form English class. The boys gathered round a microphone, and, taking the parts, recorded a play; about Louis XVI and Marie Antoinette's flight from Versailles during the French Revolution, John had written it especially for radio. A thirteen-year-old, John Wood, was the

Narrator. He wrote to me recently: 'Today that may sound commonplace, but in 1947 it was electrifying and very advanced. Being taught by your father was fun, which was almost unique in those days... he stimulated our minds wonderfully.' Peter Kraushar - coeval with Wood, felt the same: 'My interest in the law stems from a day he arranged for us at Quarter Sessions, and another at a rent tribunal.'

Guy Burn, aged 34, tall, dark and pipe-smoking, took over as Head of the Art Department when Erik Sthyr followed Oakeshott to Winchester in 1946. Guy had been a student at the Slade, a couple of years behind Erik. In Paris before the war, he met and married a French girl, Anne; they had a son. During the war Guy's good French sent him to Algiers as an interpreter of aerial photographs at the Allied Force Headquarters. In 1944 he was with the French Colonial Army in Italy (where he did 76 drawings, now all in the Imperial War Museum's collection); and for the last months of the war, in France. He was awarded the Croix de Guerre.

Over the sixteen years Guy and John were both teaching at St Paul's they were close; during lunch breaks a familiar sight in the Common Room was the two of them laughing together. (John was fond of Anne too; he called her accent 'pure Yvonne Arnaud'). Both of them felt strongly that it was important to have one foot outside teaching. Guy was nonchalant about his school responsibility; he was thought to be a 'skiver' and something of a rebel. As a working painter, and at the school a one-man department without much of a voice, he felt that the curriculum at St Paul's was too much geared to university scholarships. The few boys who showed interest in art, he believed, were under so much pressure that they were unable to give it the attention it deserved.

Friendship with Guy helped to maintain John's fighting spirit. It also kept him aware of style. Bryan Govett, to whom John was both personal tutor and English teacher from 1947, wrote:

> 'I recall John Usborne as tall and elegant. He dressed in light colours, unusual for the time, and I have the impression of a pale grey suit and pale blue socks. I thought of these colours as American and 'progressive'... I thought of him as progressive in other ways. I remember him trying to develop our linguistic skills by handing us newspaper cartoons and getting us to explain the joke to other members of the class. I don't think other masters got us to do things in that way: even languages were taught as dead languages, a fact I still regret.'

★ ★ ★ ★ ★ ★ ★

At the end of the 1940s John was teaching English, Latin, Geography and Current Affairs. American History had been his way into Current Affairs, six years earlier. America was becoming his corner of the market at St Paul's. For example, he made use of his brother Henry's experience to illustrate Geography lessons. In 1932, when he was newly graduated from Cambridge, Henry had visited the United States with a motive. He found - being manufactured in Springfield, Illinois - an oil-fired heating burner called the 'Nu-Way'. He was to become the British agent for it. 'Going into business was what you did,' he told me in his eighties. That year also saw the establishing of the Tennessee Valley Authority, Roosevelt's brainchild: this was a government agency set up to control the floods and improve the navigation of the huge Tennessee River and its tributaries. The TVA improved the living standards of farmers severely affected by the Depression by producing electrical power over a vast area. Henry, as an engineer, was awed by the massive programme of the building of dams and hydro-electricity generating stations - and as a socialist he was inspired by Roosevelt's determined social responsibility to the region, in the face of tough opposition from private enterprise.

Henry Usborne in 1994

An undergraduate then, John's interest in the TVA was fired by Henry's reports. It was to become one of the most virile subjects of his Geography teaching. As for all his pet subjects, his journalist's ear was cocked for original material. According to Rex Brown, a senior boy in 1947 who became an engineer for BP, he was 'full of it' after his year in the United States. In a Fifth Form Geography lesson at the time, Stephen Charkham listened to 'his impassioned advocacy of the TVA and its role in creating employment at the end of the Depression.'

The character of his English Literature classes was also forming: they had a strong emphasis on poetry; and he was having success with his verse-writing instruction. Tony Richards, with whom John had a good rapport, had been his head of department since John arrived at the school in 1941, and he was to remain his head until he retired in the mid-1950s. More and more, John was establishing his own method of teaching within the framework of the School Certificate syllabus. To be able to teach on subjects he enjoyed wherever possible, he took courses only to that level. He was never ambitious to teach high levels - for him too close to the grind of specialisation. However, the senior boys, while specialising, were obliged to take one general period a day. (A tradition of Winchester College - introduced to St Paul's by Walter Oakeshott – it was called 'Transitus'.) Teaching these gave John opportunities to speak on any subject which inspired him.

Alan Amos, now a solicitor, told me that in 1947 John took over as master in charge of tennis at St Paul's while he, Amos, was Secretary. St Paul's was well-known for its boxing and rugger, but in spite of its tennis team beating Eton in 1942, the game was still considered a minor sport – as it was at all public schools (except perhaps Millfield) – until the late 1950s. Over the years – he was President until he left the school in 1963 – John encouraged the boys in the club to work towards raising the profile of St Paul's as a tennis-playing school. (Of the public schools it is now pre-eminent at the game.) He was keen to incorporate tennis into the sports syllabus.

John's classroom, according to A.G.Robson, 'exuded an air of informality and the relative comfort of home base'. Two other sixth form English pupils of John's in 1950 remember, in that atmosphere, his encouragement of their creative abilities. Dennis Napier, now a publisher, told me that John introduced the class to George Orwell's comments on the writing of English, from his essay 'Literature and Politics'. 'It was all about keeping the text simple,' he recalled, 'using Anglo-Saxon words rather than those derived from Latin and Greek, using the active rather than the passive voice. As I was a classicist, I took all this very much to heart.' (Hilary Haydon, SPS 1945-50, had an essay returned by John with the word 'perspiration' crossed out and 'sweat' substituted.) Ian Robinson, a writer and publisher, told me: 'John Usborne really taught me how to write (and how to read, too), and directed me to books that he thought would be (and were) helpful to me, made me think about what I was writing, and why; and showed me, without ever being too directive, how to solve the problems I came up against. The fact that I'm still writing I owe entirely to his advice, wisdom, and humane approach to literature, quite apart from his kindness and thoughtfulness towards a rather gauche and ignorant boy.'

Of the same era, David Ross, author and journalist, remembers John's relaxed teaching style. 'He used to point out,' Ross said, 'with his usual small, relaxed gestures of the hands and wrists, that literature was not to be confused with other than the achievement of art – at the highest level'.

Guy Burn remembers John as not being interested in sport. He abhorred boxing; doing duty on a football field wasn't his idea of fun. That, though, was during the winter terms (and before he took over from Pat Cotter as Master in charge of Tennis in 1947). In summer he came into his own as a cricketer. Playing for the staff in matches against the boys, he is remembered with amusement.

William Cruickshank, 'Crookers', teaching Classics and History to the Eighth Form, told me: 'When I knew that John was to be playing, I made a firm point of watching. He had a unique style of batting – when he made up his mind to hit the ball, he would, as the bowler ran up, wind himself up in a leisurely, almost lazy way, and as the ball reached him he absolutely exploded with the bat and his whole body. I may be only imagining that one hit went clear over the rooftops of the school, but I'm sure it wasn't far off it. I recall one fantastic innings against the School First XI – a 6, 8 fours, and a single, and out!'

* * * * * * *

The commuting was loathsome and drudgery ever-present, but the school and its stimulus were very necessary. The last years of the 1940s were gratifying for John as a teacher, but unhappy domestically. Since the summer of his return from America Paula gradually started a succession of minor illnesses. (One of her many doctors at the time held the theory that she had contracted polio after a cold swim in Lake Erie.) She was sickly for a long time. Taken together, I suppose those illnesses made up a mental breakdown.

Breakfast is a chaotic meal in most households, I know. I remember being angry that, because my mother was 'ill', she stopped getting up to see us off to school. She had never liked rising early; now she had an excuse: she was 'resting' – languishing in bed with the gas fire on. Urged by my father, we went upstairs to say goodbye to her (why couldn't WE have a fire in our room?); I remember being unwilling: I wanted to punish her because she had been responsible for our gloomy breakfast. Julie and I missed her morning ritual of giving us each a spoonful of our malt syrup, Virol. The kitchen seemed bleak without her. My father would be preoccupied, reading as he munched or fiddling with his Radiostoleum tonic, anxious to get away. He tried, absent-mindedly, to make up for our mother's non-appearance. 'You must be good girls while Mummy is ill' he'd say. I wasn't deceived – he was cross with her himself, and suffering from divided loyalties. I felt he was weak because he didn't admit this to me.

That year, 1948, we acquired a dog – a springer spaniel – who helped to keep the family together through the bad years. Micky's head and ears were black except for a white streak widening from his brow to encompass his muzzle, and he had black 'freckles' round his black nose. The rest of him was uneven black and white. Locally he was considered 'a character'. With the sparse traffic in our area then he was free to roam about the village all the twelve years of his life. We never worried about him; when he spent days away we knew he was chasing a bitch on heat.

Julie and I both have our anecdotes about him. Left to guard us for an evening, Micky would lie on the landing outside our bedroom, front paws dangling over the top stair, snuffling every now and again in his boredom. Once he licked away – on the party wall he was sprawling against – a small section of the embossed white pattern on a new wallpaper which was my mother's pride and joy. The new patch she carefully appliquéd over that spot never stuck properly. It always made us laugh. Often Micky came home smelling pungent, with his legs and feathers stained orange from chasing water-rats in the lurid ferric mud of a local stream; my father used to send him to his basket with a melodramatic pointing of his finger and shouts of 'Aaaah!' and 'Stinker!'. Over the months of one winter, on the evenings my parents went out, he gnawed steadily at the tough wooden side stakes of his basket so that it was reduced to barely more than a flat disc; the jagged points his teeth had left hurt the underside of his tail as he sat stiffly, cowed by my father's admonitions. He put up with Julie's and my games. We hitched his jowls up under his teeth 'to make him smile' for a box Brownie portrait.

During our recorder sessions with my father at the end of the 1950s, Micky – if he was at home – disliked being left out, so he would sit in our verandah with us; Julie and I giggled, finding it difficult to concentrate, knowing that at any moment his nose would lift and he would start howling. During our Sunday lunch, he would be close by, waiting to be fed; the smell of our joint must have been tantalising to him, because he would go half-way up the stairs to look down, ears dangling, over the banisters at our food on the table. Then he'd howl to order, knowing he'd be rewarded later with some good scraps.

In the summer of 1948, when I was eight and Julie six, Miss Smyly, now in her mid-seventies, closed down her little primary school of six children. She had taught us all superbly; we were lucky to have had so good a start. For the next year I went to a school called 'Timberdown' in Camberley. In retrospect the eight miles' travelling with schoolmates on the top of a double-decker bus, and joining the Brownies, were the best things about it. I longed to swim at the big public swimming-pool next to the school, but never did; we were warned that such places bred the virus of 'infantile paralysis'. There was a TB scare too: around the back door of Sandy Lane Cottage that summer the revolting smell of boiled milk pervaded the air.

About that time - in my own consciousness - I ceased being a child. One day after breakfast my mother put her head in our oven and turned on the gas. I clearly remember the tension in our sitting-room, the sunshine streaming through the window, when her limp figure in a dressing-gown was stretched out on the sofa, with my father and two doctors leaning over her. I watched unnoticed; they had their backs to me, trying to prevent my mother from swallowing her tongue. Nobody sent me out of the room.

I am now the only person alive who is sure my mother tried to kill herself. Friends remember her long illness. It lasted two years, perhaps a little longer; the period of tip-toeing round the house 'being quiet' seemed never-ending to Julie and me. My mother was a patient in what she called a 'mental home' in Pinner, Middlesex, several times; each time she came home she would have a 'relapse', and was bundled back again.

If my father had lived longer, I like to think he would have been open about that time with us; my mother never talked about it and retreated at the end of her life into Alzheimer's disease.) Henry, as always, was a good elder brother to him and at the time they discussed the situation whenever they could meet. I know my father did not confide in any of his colleagues at St Paul's. Certainly his teaching and writing were a refuge. I can't remember how, practically, we managed without my mother - except for a hated month when Julie and I boarded at our convent school in Sunninghill.

How did he pay our fees? Hustling for work with the BBC went on, in spite of repeated rejection of his ideas. A Home Service Talks producer received an elaborate letter from him in January 1948 suggesting a verse-writing competition. It was to be called 'Puzzle The Poets', and would employ the talents of A. P. Herbert, Ted Kavanagh and 'Sagittarius'. After six months of a group of producers batting the idea around, its rejection infuriated him. He recorded two short talks about teaching at Hamburg High School, neither of which was broadcast. (One of them, a pet story, was an account of a girl bringing an earthworm into the classroom. As she sat playing with it at her desk, John threatened to make her swallow it if it wasn't put out of the window within a few minutes. It wasn't, and the girl ate the worm.)

Growing corn on the cob, he was convinced, was a subject that could be spun into a light-hearted talk. (He was again growing it successfully; friends, neighbours, ourselves and our chickens had stripped more than 400 cobs in 1948.) He carried it off finally, after many attempts, in September 1952. The talk was a celebration of our first corn roast party, given in August 1948 in our field; the company being – give or take a few chickens – the same consumers: 'Rip the burning parts off the ear,' he said with relish, 'and roll the fleshy, edible bit in butter before it gets too cool. Then the crowning moment. Throw all restraint to the winds and get cracking. It's quite dark by now except at the perimeter of the fire. No one will see your oily sticky face: no one will mind your hands being black: no one will hear the gross sounds of your dental rendings. And if they do, what of it? The hair is now down.'

Harman Grisewood, then Controller of the Third Programme, was sent by John a batch of – to him – humorous ideas, such as 'What The Greeks Did To Me' and 'I'm An Illiteracy Neurotic'. (John learnt the hard way that some of these smacked too much of a public school education.) May Jenkyn of 'Children's Hour' was sent a talk on Henry David Thoreau, with suggestions for sound effects suitable for creating an atmosphere of Massachusetts woodland: 'I can give an imitation of the White Fronted Goose as Thoreau said an Indian taught him to do. The woodchuck's whipping noise is easy. The snake's squeak can be faked from the record of the Spring Peeper frog.' She made John revise the script, and pronounced his revision 'very delightful now' to a colleague. It was again rejected. Not until March 1962 did John succeed in broadcasting a talk on Thoreau.

Thoreau and Thomas Jefferson were John's two favourite men in American History. Thoreau's life and writing had been an inspiration to him since 1933, when Cyril Bailey had introduced him to *Walden*; the young refugee from 'the resignation' of nineteenth-century urban life was a subject which could always be relied upon to give John ideas for a broadcast, an article, or a lecture. In 1950 the St Paul's Field Club heard him lecture on Thoreau, during which he used recordings – from his Cornell University Ornithology Laboratory and Ludwig Koch collections – of American birds, woodchucks, frogs and toads. Having worked with sound engineers, John was now becoming adept with tape recorders himself. Bringing in Ted Gawne (a new member of the history staff), the classics master Arnold Monk-Jones and John between them kept alive the tradition – started at Crowthorne – of natural history talks during Friday lunch-hours. They were always well attended.

Money was short and he had to escape from the house. Fromow's Nurseries employed John as a labourer to hoe shrubs for a fortnight in August 1949. The work was back-breaking, with most of the time a dour foreman watching the schoolteacher for signs of strain; but an Irish hand called Bill supplied some good lines, and John saw a corncrake for the second time in his life. He made a talk out of the experience, filed away to be broadcast on New Year's Day 1952.

★ ★ ★ ★ ★ ★ ★

From Windrush Aunt Dorothy had moved to Ryall, a hamlet overlooking Marshwood Vale, in the south-west of Dorset. Nanny was with her still, now in her eighties. Aunt Dorothy had promised her sister May that she would provide a home for her spinster daughter Agnes, and she would do that (with the addition of her cows and chickens) for the rest of her life. One of Agnes's four brothers farmed near Axminster, and he had persuaded the trio to come to Dorset. Aunt Dorothy bought her house, a solid slate-roofed white stucco'd villa, for the panorama from its windows: on the far side of the deep valley a patchwork of

Clockwise: Simla, 1906; the engagement of Janet Muriel Lefroy, aged 28, to Charles Frederick Usborne, aged 32. Janet was six feet three inches, Charlie five feet seven.

Janet with John, aged nine months, in Dalhousie

John's birthplace, 'Peterboro', in Dalhousie, the house in the Himalayan foothills which the Usbornes rented from April until October, while Charles was Deputy Commissioner in Hissar, in the Punjabi plains.

Clockwise: Hugh Whistler, a great friend to the Usborne family, and hero to each of the children, in 1914. He retired from the Imperial Indian Police in 1926. A noted ornithologist, he was to publish the classic *A Popular Handbook of Indian Birds* in 1928.

Taken by Hugh Whistler on deck as he, the Usborne family and the children's nurse sailed home from India in April 1916. The elder three – from left to right Dick, Tommy, Henry – had been told to hold on to John, aged 20 months, to make sure he didn't go over the side.

A portrait study taken in Battle in 1919. John aged 4, Dick 8, Henry 9, Tommy 10.

Dear Mummy.

I love shool. We did have some work Yesterday, and hardly anyone could read, exept me and morhouse. I was going to play footer yesterday. But there was not a noufe footBoots. I sleep in upper south. nothing els to say.

Love faom
John.

Clockwise: John's first letter home from Summer Fields School, Oxford, written in September 1922, just before his eighth birthday.

Four new boys at Summer Fields in 1922: left to right, John Usborne, Christopher Ede, Adrian Enthoven and Erroll Bruce.

Leonard Strong, better known as the author L.A.G. Strong, aged 32 in 1928. He taught English at Summer Fields for 12 years. Light relief for his pupils, in a rigorous Classics syllabus, was his talk of the Dublin music-halls, and his talent for telling stories. (Photo courtesy of Summer Fields School.).

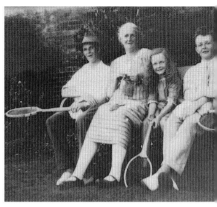

Top left: the family with their spaniel Gerry in the garden at 2 Upper Lake, Senlac Hill, Battle, 1923. Back row, Tommy, Dick, Henry, Margaret; seated, John, Janet.

Top right: Henry, Janet (knitting), Margaret, Dick by the family tennis court, Battle, 1924; a snap by John, aged ten.

Centre: Summer Fields gym group in 1928. John stands to the left of the instructor, Sergeant Morley.

Bottom: the combined Usborne and Watson families in 1929, just after the move to Windrush, Inkpen, Berkshire. Front row from left to right: Michael (half obscured), John, Pam, Uncle Hubert, Margaret with Juggins; back row: Dick with ferret, Henry, Jenny, Aunt Dorothy, Ursula, Tommy with Buzzy. Buzzy barks at the ferret.

John in the lines at Tidworth, at Bradfield College's O.T.C. summer camp, 1931.

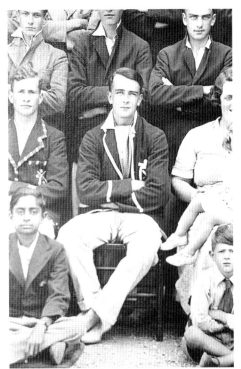

John in 1933, aged 17, as Head of Army House, Bradfield.

Overlooking the Arno, Florence.
John photographed by Michael Barton in April 1937

Portrait study of Paula Halloran, aged 19, 1935.

Above:
John and Paula (centre), with friends, Wengen, Switzerland, January 1938.

Left:
The family sprawls on the lawn. Nanny approaches with a message. Windrush, 1938.

Bottom left:
John with me, aged six months, May 1940.

Bottom right:
John and his daughters during his first corn harvest, Windlesham, 1944.

Above left: John with our English setter Dinah and her puppies Bolshie and Serena, 1944.

Centre: The family on our veranda steps, Sandy Lane Cottage, 1943.

Left: Autumn in upstate New York, 1946. Time off for John from his job as an exchange teacher at Hamburg High School. With a female colleague, Jack and Bee Moore and Paula.

Above right: 1946, New Year's Eve at the Casino Russe, New York. Mary Kirkby, John, Lu Kirkby, Paula.

Above: Fruit-picking camp at Henry and Pam's house, Totterdown, in the Vale of Evesham. 1957. John is standing, back row.

Right: Micky, our springer spaniel.

Bottom left: St Paul's School photograph, 1959. Masters' row, left to right: Ted Gawne, S.M. Haskell, John Usborne, Jack Moakes, Brian Hayes.

Right: John on the balustrade of a Costa Brava hotel, while on holiday with Paula, August 1962

Bottom right: John at Woodberry Forest in 1964.

ancient pasture, ancient hedges and one or two farmhouses, a wooded ridge in the near background, and Black Down and the Hardy memorial forming the distant horizon. She loved to watch the mists roll in from the sea.

Travelling by the Royal Blue coach, changing at Bournemouth, my father took Julie and me down to Ryall for a week in our Easter holidays, the first visit for all of us. My father sat writing in a small wooden pavilion which Aunt Dorothy called the 'chicken-house' - kept warm by a paraffin-stove - at the far end of the garden; or he disappeared to bird-watch. (He preferred to sleep also in the chicken-house.) Julie and I didn't see much of him, but we didn't mind. We collected eggs, laid by Agnes's hens under the hedges; we picked wild daffodils and primroses; we went - helping her, we thought - on errands with Aunt Dorothy in DMO, her little car, going too fast along those high-banked lanes. Otherwise we were allowed to run wild. For a treat Agnes would wring a chicken's neck and we'd have it boiled for supper with her special parsley sauce. We loved playing Mah-jong with our great-aunt in the evenings in her cosy drawing-room. Her sheepdog Boffin was stretched out on a rug; familiar things reminded us of Windrush: the scrubbed surface of the oak table, the faded brown velvet curtains and the bronze boy getting a thorn out of his foot.

At the end of August we joined our cousins, two uncles and two aunts for a camping holiday in a field inland of the famous cliff, the Golden Cap, two miles from Ryall. John, as usual, had writing commitments - a photo shows him in shorts, hair wind-blown, sitting in an old Windrush canvas chair with notepad and books spread out on an old table-flap on his knees. We children enjoyed ourselves damming the stream, looking for fossils, and swimming when the weather was warm; but on a cool day we look - in Tommy's snaps - like gypsy children, tousle-haired and pinched, as we huddle on the grass round a large portable radio, listening to 'Children's Hour'.

★ ★ ★ ★ ★ ★ ★

Three years of staying-power were paying off: Patrick Harvey, the producer who was to nurture and encourage John probably more than any other, offered him a series for the 8.50a.m. slot on the Home Service, called 'John Usborne Talking'. Just as John loved to do in his teaching, he would talk - but with a script - about anything that interested him. After he had been signed up, Harvey wrote to him: 'I'm sure there's a talk - an evening talk - in your 'American Exchange', but can we leave it in abeyance until you've had at least one morning canter?'

Writing his scripts, in the winter months, now consumed all John's spare time. He paid a penance; for the sacrifice of family life that it involved, Paula furiously resented it. And as yet there was no evidence of a higher income. He confided to Richard Keen, a young producer, that working at his typewriter on Christmas Day in 1949 caused 'the near-perdition of my marriage'.

He would fire his ideas off to the producers as soon as they formed: on Christmas Day 1950 he wrote to Marguerite Scott suggesting a vehicle for his American frog recordings, to his chagrin still not heard by English listeners: 'So many of the frog choruses reminded me of cocktail parties and football crowds and whist drives, that I thought it the very thing for a BBC Legpull. May I bring them up one day and play them to you?' He received a kind - but slightly stuffy - letter of rejection.

95

John had known from an early age through his prep-school friend Ben Nicolson, something of Ben's father, the writer and diplomat Harold Nicolson. (Invited by Ben, John stayed at Long Barn - the Nicolson home before Sissinghurst - several times during the 1920s.) He grew up to admire, like all his brothers, Harold Nicolson's witty and stylish writing. Nicolson had published two books about manners; articles by him often popped up in periodicals both in Britain and the United States. The success of these gave John an idea, permission to have some fun: an opportunity to use the knowledge a well-connected background endowed him with. Apart from his BBC work that winter of 1949, he was planning - with his sister Margaret - *A Dictionary of Etiquette*, 'on the Emily Post model'. This prompted another idea. Euphoric, he wrote in longhand a postcard to Patrick Harvey, describing their plans, and suggesting a talk on the subject. Harvey, answering him formally, hinted that the dictionary wasn't being taken seriously enough; that his sense of humour was too strong. John retracted, and the idea wilted.

'...I'm supposed to be well-brought up, I'm bourgeois and, by Gad, sir, I'm British, and I have certain snobberies and hypocrisies which I cannot - and don't particularly want to - get out of my system.' John's amusement while planning the abortive dictionary was siphoned off and used in 'On Writing About Good Manners', the second of the series of three morning talks (all broadcast in March 1950). It tickled him to have carte blanche to sound off on the radio: 'I am one of the worst-mannered men my wife has known; I have inherited a perfectly fiendish delight in shocking shockable people. What a glorious opportunity a book about Manners was going to afford me of shocking just the very people I've always loved shocking, namely, the genteel, the respectable, the snobs, the people, in fact, who are perfectly certain they know the difference between good and bad manners, what is done and what most definitely is simply not done.'

'Lovely stuff!' pronounced Michael Bell of the Home Service Talks Department. The series was a success. The first talk of the three was called 'American Children Are Irresistible'. The material was full of good detail about his American teaching experience; and about Teenage, a concept that then had no name - all the things about American youth that intrigued British people so much at the time. With the last, into his stride, he confided to the listeners his love of pottering in his field, his need for it as an antidote to the intensity of teaching, and his determination never to be bored with his freedom.

For weeks of work, even 50 years ago, the fees were low: fifteen guineas for each talk. John complained that he had to stay the nights preceding the broadcasts in town (he stayed with the Burns) and needed expenses. He was paid 27 shillings and sixpence per night plus eight and sixpence bus fare.

In the climate of the McCarthy witchhunts of liberals at the end of the 1940s in the United States, John wrote a script entitled 'How To Like Americans'. (Patrick Harvey said, when he accepted it, 'I like this piece. It's going to make, thank God, a quite unusual broadcast.') 'I find myself', John read out in June, 'at the ripe old age of 35, liking Americans. I like them, in fact, quite as easily as I like my own people: which means that for me they've ceased being Americans and begun to be just people.

'Americans couldn't be as bad as all that. How bad were they? Well, in the first place, I decided, they were rich; they had dollars. We were poor.

And that was very bad of them. But what are riches: what is money? Filthy lucre: the root of all evil. No civilised man worries about money. So no civilised man should envy the Americans. Feeling better already. Next. Americans have no manners. They have loud voices and loud ties and talk to me in buses before being introduced. I recall a little girl on a country bus near Buffalo interrupting my routine study of the Air Edition of *The Times*. 'Hi Mister,' she said, 'your necktie's kinda cute.' Who's in charge of this brat, I thought and went on reading. The brat didn't know when she wasn't wanted. 'Like a stick of bubble-gum?' she asked me. 'No thank you,' I said, 'I don't use the stuff actually. Very kind of you all the same.'

'The Cuckoo, A Skit For Springtime' was dashed off for Richard Keen, and it was broadcast a month after the last of the series of three. John's new hearty style, worrying a few, was discussed in inter-office memos. Patrick Harvey – in charge of the morning talk 'space' – complained to Marguerite Scott, an editor for 'Woman's Hour', about the torrent of ideas coming at him from John. (However, his entertaining letters usually managed to stop short of exasperating them.) 'Your Child's Homework and How To Do It' amused Harvey, and he quoted John to Marguerite Scott: 'We schoolmasters at day-schools can almost classify homework, elder brothers, elder sisters, younger sisters, fathers, mothers, co-operative and genuine.'

Chapter Seven

John's six talks in 1950 had made the BBC value him as a regular. His producers began to trust him with their own themes. He was asked to write a script for a series called 'The Man's Point of View'. He did – calling it 'How To Argue':

> 'I spent a large part of my boyhood and most of my late adolescence arguing with my three elder brothers. One of them is arguing still – in the House of Commons – we always said he would – the rest of us try arguing with our wives. We've been trying for years. It's no good. What's the use? Women won't play fair.'

Inspired by one of his own kitchen arguments with Paula – over the use of four saucepans versus a pressure-cooker – he was to play out the scenario with an actress. He made the scene funny, of course; but knowing John and his obsessions – in this case the pressure cooker, brought from America ostensibly for Paula – to me it seems uncomfortably personal.

He still did not always strike the right note. Marguerite Scott rejected the script because it 'looked like high pressure advertising of pressure-cookers'. She was right.

I remember my father's bared teeth when he was exasperated. He wasn't peaceful to live with. Entirely without talent as a domestic handyman, he was constantly fizzing with ideas for his own schemes. It came as a surprise to him that this should madden my mother. There were rows, always started by her, always about the lack of money. These days he was neglecting the family for the typewriter, he knew.

Friends – who didn't have to live with him – loved him for his charm, humanity and sense of fun. Helen Simpson was dusting one morning when John appeared, canvassing for the local elections. 'Have you voted?' he asked her. Helen replied, 'Well, John, I think...' 'The trouble with you, Helen,' John said, 'is that you don't think.'

He knew he was eccentric – but that was not solely to blame. Coming from Australia, Paula was more conventional, even, than most of the local middle-class wives; in Windlesham, when John upset an old blimp, she felt vulnerable. He could avoid these people on weekdays; she could not, nor did she want to.

Called affectionately 'the professor' by his local non-academic friends – for his glasses, bald head and preoccupied expression – John was not seen so benevolently by the political figures in our very reactionary village. These were usually people running their own small businesses, like Mrs Boyce the fishmonger and Bill Thomson, a market-gardener. Both were town councillors. In their eyes John was a suspicious character, no less an irritant than he had been in the early years of the war.

Despite the somewhat strained relations which were to develop between John and some Windlesham people, he had played cricket for the village team since

1939, the year he and Paula moved there. Politics were no impediment to a keen player. Cricket was essential to his summer weekends at home.

Micky, our dog, used to run out to John while he fielded in Windlesham cricket matches. 'I personally get more laughs playing village cricket than anything else I do,' he confided in 'The Funny Side of Life'. 'I don't find first-class cricket at all funny because all the players are so skilful and serious about it. In fact any game that has to be taken seriously bores me and ceases to be a game. But when human beings get fun out of their mistakes as we in our village team do out of cricket, there you have humour in its purest and most innocent form. How often do I wish A.G.Macdonell were alive today and could spend his summer Saturdays with me. I feel our whole team might almost have walked out of the pages of that classic chapter in 'England Their England', and I'm sure thousands of village cricketers who have read this feel the same.'

Gordon Derrick was an eighth-former at St Paul's in 1949. Specialising in science, he was in one of John's General period classes devoted to the arts and literary subjects. Individual masters would present their favourite works; John introduced the class to that chapter by A.G.Macdonell. 'It says a lot for cricket, I think,' he wrote in a magazine article, 'that it has always attracted more fine writers than any other game, and that almost every one of them finds the humour of the game not the least important of its blessings.'

Cricket had to be forfeited during the summer holidays; they – and, if possible, the Easter ones - were for getting away. John did not trust himself to be kicking his heels in Windlesham. Even small bird-watching sorties to 'the nurseries' became less frequent. However, one local friend, a young bachelor, enjoyed John's sense of humour and sought it out, rather to the disapproval of his father. Mark was the son of Douglas Paterson, the founder and headmaster of Woodcote House, a boys' preparatory school near to us. With his school's reputation to think of, Mark's father had long been wary of John's rebellious streak. Mark remembers, as a boy in 1939, hearing the gossip about the arrival of a Conscientious Objector in Windlesham.

Mark used to walk over the playing fields and down Sandy Lane of an evening, after teaching at Woodcote House, to see us all and to talk a little shop with John. He did this regularly until 1950 when he married. Julie and I found his floppy straight hair and wry grin rather glamorous; I suppose our little girls' chatter made him laugh, accustomed as he was to listening all day to little boys. The atmosphere lightened when he dropped in. I would emerge from my room when I heard his voice down below. I remember the two men standing over our fire guffawing at Latin jingles – and Tom Lehrer and Danny Kaye records playing on the gramophone.

Mark became involved in one of John's schemes: they would be partners in a popcorn business, growing the stuff from maize they would import cheaply from the Baltic countries; the corn would be popped and sugar-coated in our kitchen at Sandy Lane Cottage. 'Woodcote House was going to hand over all its spare property for growing popcorn!' Mark told me. Needless to say – to Paula's relief – the project died a natural death.

The expressions 'What a crackpot!' and 'For crying out loud!' would accompany John's guffaws and bared teeth at home. His knowledge of American speech and culture was always kept topped up by his reading and research. American humour - and French, central European, Cockney, Jewish, and Shakespearean versions - consumed him during the Christmas holidays of 1950-1. He was to broadcast six 15-minute talks on Humour, with actors participating, to go out weekly in February and March 1951. The idea had grown out of a chat with Dick Keen, the producer of Forces Educational Broadcasts. FEB had a subject - planned in series of six talks each - for each weekday: citizenship, Plain English, current affairs, literature and music - with a producer assigned to each.

What a coup - for John a gift from God. (And the scripts could be adapted later for articles.) The first talk, 'The Funny Side of Life', started with a domestic anecdote about a prank Julie played on him. 'We have two priceless gifts,' he said, 'that probably have nothing to do with the brain, namely hope and a sense of humour, and I wouldn't be at all surprised if they were the same thing.' His other topics were Farce, Caricature, Looking Silly, Forces Humour, and American Humour.

For the dialogues in all six talks - he often took part himself - John had a team of superb actors. I've heard that they enjoyed themselves. They were all radio regulars - in those days a smaller and more specialised corps than now. Jill Balcon (the wife of Cecil Day-Lewis and mother of Daniel), playing Olivia to Ernest Jay's Malvolio, remembered a few moments of extreme panic during their broadcast, when Jay's script fell apart, and four of them rushed to retrieve it and put it back in order. Deryck Guyler (who had made radio history with the first Liverpool accent heard on the air, as the gormless Frisby Dyke in *ITMA*) read from *Three Men in a Boat*; Jack Train played his own *ITMA* character Colonel Chinstrap; Betty Hardy, famous for her dialects, played Mrs Gamp; Norman Shelley, with a voice familiar on 'Children's Hour' as the Magician in *Toytown*, took the part of a squadron leader from a play by Terence Rattigan.

That year John did 13 broadcasts, more than in any subsequent year. He gave two morning talks for the Home Service; for 'Woman's Hour' he was now doing film reviews - and talks, usually about teaching children; and for 'Children's Hour' he set and judged a poetry-writing competition.

The BBC paid him 17 guineas only for each of the Humour talks, two guineas for the broadcast and 15 for the research. Now with a literary agent - Jean LeRoy of Pearn, Pollinger and Higham - he was no less impecunious. A spin-off (he would have winced at that expression; he often winced at his daughters' colloquialisms) of the talk on American humour was some reviewing of books on humour for the *Spectator*, which he did twice that year, and again in 1953. In the first he wrote disparagingly about the lack of subtlety of 'The Humor School of American Writers'. '...I saw it all coming. I couldn't raise so much as an exclamatory ha. "That's funny!" my authors shouted. "Laugh!" *The Treasury of Humorous Quotations*, an English publication, earned his praise because it allowed him to compare English and American wit. 'The title is wrong,' he wrote, 'the quotations are seldom humorous but very often witty.' 'Most readers for a laugh prefer humour to wit,' he said in another review, 'because the belly-laugh is easier, more satisfying and better for the digestion than the cranial type. But since humour is always erratic and usually subjective, a good humorist always adds wit as a stiffener.'

John always enjoyed teaching about writing humorously as a means to writing well. However, he was well aware that it was dangerous to be dogmatic about humour. From America, his favourite examples of good comic writing were James Thurber's fables, Robert Benchley's Shaggy Dog stories, and the verse of Ogden Nash.

Teddy Hodgkin, the younger brother of Thomas Hodgkin, Dick Usborne's contemporary at Balliol, had joined the *Spectator* when he returned from Palestine at the end of the war. He was part of an intake of new young writers to the journal at that time, and it was he who introduced Dick to it. Others who were contributing then were James Pope-Hennessy, Harold Nicolson and Goronwy Rees. Dick started writing book reviews and setting literary competitions.

Surprisingly, John's and Dick's paths never crossed at the *Spectator*, although they did the same sort of writing for it. (Nor did they meet at the BBC, where Dick Keen was producer to both brothers.) John's and his sister Margaret's paths there ran parallel in the early 1950s. In the company of such names as L.A.G.Strong (John's old prep-school English teacher), Marghanita Laski and Katherine Whitehorn, they were all three engaged in literary sport. As setters of the well-known competitions (John's total - over three years - was nine), they were thinking up outlandish themes for pastiche. There is a page in an issue of July 1951 on which Margaret is setting one - offering the standard prize of £5 ('which may be divided') 'for a limerick with rhymes conspicuous for their absence, c.f. The Old Man of Tralee (or Dundee) who was stung on the leg by a wasp." - and John is reporting the winners of another:'for an old English teacher's Poem of Revolt on 'doing' either "The Lady of Shalott" or "A Midsummer Night's Dream" for the forty-second time.' (On reading through these pages more than 47 years later, Dick commented: "Very schoolmasterly! John enjoying himself!") Margaret remembers, during a weekend at Sandy Lane Cottage, sorting through the entries with John for a competition he had set. They agreed on the winner, and Margaret couldn't admit yet that his name was her pseudonym.

(In the issue of 5 September 1952, mindful of the Lynmouth flood disaster in mid-August, John started his report on the entries for a competition for a four-line epitaph on an English drought.) 'The drought, whether actually dead or, as many insisted, only moribund, had left many with their muses, if not high, at least dry, and their wit, like the obsequies, wet. Some, more concerned with wit than grief or relief, made epigrams instead of epitaphs.'

His film reviews for 'Woman's Hour', on the other hand, did not exude enjoyment; they were forced, a little too breezy. He saw the films in London after school and was very late home; he cursed them - they were nothing but a chore. Before his first reviews (of, among others, *The Blue Veil* and *All About Eve*) he introduced himself by teasing the producers:'Good afternoon. This is an entirely new experience. I must confess to you that in the normal way I not only don't review films, but I hardly ever go to them. Bear with me if I seem at first a bit querulous and crusty.'

★ ★ ★ ★ ★ ★

For almost four years - since his return from Hamburg in 1947 -John had been pulling strings to get himself across the Atlantic again. His curiosity whetted by regular reading of *Farm Quarterly*, his favourite American magazine, he wanted to visit farms in the Southern states. Nowadays he was calling himself an agriculturalist; he knew he could do some good and profitable writing about the subject. Thanks to his brother Tommy, in the Ministry of Transport, a berth was found for him on a 2500-ton collier carrying anthracite to Newport News, Virginia in August 1951. The departure was a month late - in September - so that John missed four weeks of the autumn term.

It was to make good copy that he was a bad sailor and that it was the hurricane season. Two days out from Swansea he acquired his sea-legs and began to understand and be amused by the broad Scots of the crew. He was officially purser - in truth such a small ship had no need of a purser - but his actual job (including some typing for the Master and stitching of laundrybags) consisted of hammering the blisters in the ship's paintwork and chipping off the mouldy patches. John discovered during a violent twenty-four hour storm that the deck of the rickety old ship was a better place to be - terrifying as it was - than his cabin, where waves were shooting through a ventilator on to his bunk; or the engine room, with its din, stink and carpet of oil. Four weeks working his passage on a tramp-steamer produced two talks which had all the right ingredients - drama, humour and good atmosphere:

'I remember a Sunday. A loose, undisciplined Sassenach can hardly forget a Sunday on a Scottish ship. I was so bored with the deadness of everyone and everything, so bored with reading, writing, walking round and round the decks, eating boiled cabbage - and so appalled by the rigid Sabbatarianism that when suddenly during the late afternoon I caught sight of a school of porpoises making for the ship - vaulting, diving, flying, bouncing through and over the waves, and watched them shoot under the ship, race round it and do a succession of circus turns, giving themselves up to glorious, reckless, joyous revelry, I was in two minds as to whether I should leap overboard and share their wickedly unpresbyterian fun.'

By friendly agreement with the master, John disembarked at Boston, having promised to rejoin the ship at her coaling station a week later. He stayed a night in Harvard with his Hamburg friends Jim and Nan Eells and their baby, Bug. Overnight, sleepless, he travelled by Greyhound bus from New York to Newport News, Virginia, watching the dawn of a hot day break on the market-gardens of the Delaware Peninsula. He was soon to have his long-awaited first view of the South. Later that day, weary but happy, his pack on his back, the hot sun prickling his bald pate and his shoulders, he was walking in the farming country of Tidewater Virginia. Gaudy cicadas hopped and enormous butterflies fluttered as he kicked up the earth; he looked through his field-glasses at birds new to him. He saw his first peanut vine; '...large cloverish affair it was. Rotation crop, perhaps. I scrape the light grey soil. Talk of nodules. Here was the biggest nodule you ever saw. Familiar shape too. Have you guessed?'; and his first cotton bush: '... I pull a bit and it comes away beautifully, expanding as I pull, a glistening, snowy white, billowing stuff. I make a sketch of the leaf and the bud and write: 'Could be cotton...'

'That night I slept in a bag under the stars between a row of hybrid maize and a row of peanuts, sung to sleep by the massed choir of cicadas. I woke late to the hilarious flute-notes of a Mocking Bird from a telephone wire. As I stood up in my pyjamas three negro workers peered at me in amazement between the corn.'

He spent the next day looking over an experimental farm in the village of Holland, in an area calling itself the 'Peanut Capital of the World'. It being the week of the annual peanut harvest, he watched a plant pathologist testing the plants for ripeness; he picked cotton with black women and their children; he watched newborn piglets - bred for their succulent corn- and peanut-fed meat - having their umbilical cords cut and their eye-teeth clipped; he discussed the hybridising of maize with the head of the station. 'Somehow I felt the day had been auspicious', he wrote later on the experience, 'for peace and plenty for the second half of the Twentieth Century'.

Two talks and an article came out of the four days he spent in Virginia. 'Virginia Ride', a talk broadcast in February 1953, described the people he met as he hitch-hiked, and their quaint language. Monticello, the beautiful Georgian mansion built by Thomas Jefferson, had been proudly shown to him by a farmer who had been on his way to Charlottesville to buy a heifer. He drooled to his English listeners as he described hamburgers, peaches, and ice-cream soused in pecans and maple-syrup.

John's broadcasting technique was attracting praise, not only from listeners, but among BBC personnel. Patrick Harvey, introducing him in a memorandum to his Talks Chief Assistant in July, wrote: 'He travels whenever opportunity occurs (which seems to be much more than a schoolmaster could normally expect). He uses his voice with skill, incisively but without arrogance.' And each of his jour-nalistic styles - tailored for the *Spectator, The Countryman*, the *Geographical Magazine*, and *Everybody's* - was sure-footed. His standing at St Paul's was good too: Philip McGuinness, a young man newly graduated from Oxford who joined the staff in September, remembers: 'John was well-installed, extremely popular, agreeable, lively, outward-looking...'

Geoffrey Dearmer, well-known in poetry circles for his poems on the theme of the Great War, wrote articles and poetry in the early 1950s for *Collins*, a suc-cessful children's magazine. As one of the 'Children's Hour' editors, he encouraged John to set for the programme a poetry-writing competition, called 'Young Poets' Corner'; and helped it to be the considerable success that it was. 'YOU are a nation of poets, whether you like it or not,' John told his young listeners, 'and yet how many people at any one time have so much as tried to compose a line? We rattle off John Gilpin and Tiger, Tiger, Burning Bright and Once More Into The Breach, Dear Friends. But as for making up poetry or verse ourselves... Well, enough of that sort of thing, say I. Between now and July 10th you're going to write me some verse and enjoy it and feel jolly pleased with yourselves.'

He explained scansion, calling it the tumty-tumty rule. 'What do I mean by tumty-tumty? Well, in tumty language, Mary Had A Little Lamb becomes Tumty tumty tumty tum. But Mary and her lamb keep to the rule there... those tumty-tums MUST keep going smoothly and no monkey business with tumtiddletums and tumtiddletiddletums.' On 19 July he gave the results: 420 children had entered, to be split into two age groups. 'Wastepaper poets please take heart and don't stop writing poetry. Think of the terrible amount of tripe Wordsworth and Tennyson wrote in order to get the occasional gem which made the tripe worth while. And I can think of quite a lot of Shakespearean tripe too.'

The early 1950s was a fertile time for journalism for children: a new coloured newspaper called *Eagle* - thought up by a vicar in Lancashire - was launched. There was *Collins Magazine* for teenagers. My father was very enthusiastic about their high standard and subscribed to them both for Julie and me. *Collins* usually had a funny cover drawn by John Verney, and inside it was stuffed with good things: puzzles, competitions, lists of pen-friends to write to, advertisements for things to send away for; adventure stories by Captain W.E. Johns and John Pudney for boys, and homey ones by Pamela Brown for girls. I wanted the Noel Streatfeild serial *The Bell Family* never to end. I remember long mooning spells in my room gazing at its beautiful illustrations by Marcia Lane Foster.

The Festival of Britain, a government-sponsored event which opened in May 1951, was certainly a spur to children's creativity. My father's excitement about it was infectious: he took Julie and me to the South Bank to visit it at the beginning of our summer holidays, one wet and windy day. We marvelled at the Dome of Discovery, the largest circular-based aluminium dome in the world, with a diameter of 365 feet; all holding hands, we craned our necks looking at the top of the Skylon, the tall aluminium spike standing next to it. We watched the Emett Railway clicking and whirring at the Fun Fair in Battersea Park.

John's literary success rubbed off on some of his Paulines. Doggerel-writing, to his pleasure, became almost infectious among his fifth-formers. As a boy with his sister and brothers he had played verse-games at the table, and he liked his dinner guests at Sandy Lane Cottage to play them with him when suitably mellow. Tom Abell remembers still - after fifty years - four lines of a long page of John's verse. This page and three others were written in the mid-1940s to instil into his pupils some historical facts - and almost reached publication as 'A Verse History of The Tudors'. The lines Tom Abell remembered were from 'Henry the Seventh':

'This Henry began as a middle-class man:
A middle-class man was he.
His right to the throne was as good as my own,
He was one of the bourgeoisie.'

★ ★ ★ ★ ★ ★ ★

In the summer of 1951 my mother was ill again. The atmosphere had been bad at home. Julie disputes this, because she was younger, and, being at a local school, she saw my parents every day and was a part of their rhythm. In September I started my first term at St Paul's Girls' School; I was staying during the week as a paying guest with a colleague of my father's, Freddie Page, and his wife Doris. I liked school, and wrote enthusiastically about it to my father, care of Jim Eells in Boston. One Saturday evening in late October, when my father was home again, my parents were in the middle of one of their blazing weekend rows. (Perhaps my mother didn't want to hear about my father's American adventures...or did her pleasure at the Tories winning the Election annoy him?) I was disgruntled that five weeks had gone by and they had not yet given me time to tell them about my new school. I decided to run away, and did, then and there; I ran in the direction of the A30. My instinct was to go to London to live with the family of my best friend Jenny. Darkness had fallen as I panted up Snow's Ride, one of the bleakest of Windlesham roads, to its junction with the A30, about a mile from home. There, parked across the road, was a police car, and standing in the beam of its headlights with the policeman, a little knot of people stood with their bicycles: my thirteen-year-old friend Ann D'Arcy-Smith, her father, and, looking very anxious, my own father.

Home became quiet, and there was very little affection among us. I blamed my mother for making it an unhappy place. My father was unable to pretend it was otherwise. I became very withdrawn. I sat on the floor with my arm round the dog. Being with both my parents at once was difficult; it didn't seem right to me that they were together at all.

Like the mutual need a doctor and his patients have for each other, the vitality John could engender in his classes was like a mild drug, to cheer himself up. His pupils probably saw him at his best. Did he wish then that he had a son, I wonder? As a father he was good at thinking up plans for us, but rarely set aside time to be with us; he was too preoccupied and too often tired. Energy was saved not for his life at home, but for what he did away from it. At St Paul's he could choose his company. He was one of four masters, I'm told (the others being Jack Moakes, Jack Strawson and Rob Brown), who ran to the Common Room and back to complete *The Times Crossword* together during the morning break. Tom Gilbert told me that to him, as a boy, John looked elegant running between classrooms. Alan Cook, who was the deputy High Master, and an English teacher at the time, told me, in his nineties: 'I have many happy memories of John. It is no criticism to say they centre round the table in the old tuck shop after afternoon school at West Ken, where he would produce specimens of his latest horticulture experiment to our interest and amusement. We'd all have a good talk, and were sorry when he had to leave us for his drive home.'

In their extra-curricular activities at school – and to a degree in their form work – John's placing of trust in his pupils is a memory of him that many of them have. Discipline was never a thing he worried about. He enjoyed delegating; he reaped the rewards of the compliments he paid to the boys he found promising. He was an adviser on *The Debater*, to which both Paulinas and Paulines contributed. He enjoyed showing its readers how enjoyable he found writing; he published in it, under the pseudonym of 'Fotheringay', a cryptic verse; and he pulled out of the hat a short, dashing article on an experience which he knew would fascinate masters, Paulinas and Paulines alike: he pestered a friend of his, a BOAC pilot, to procure him a seat on the maiden flight to Rome of the Comet – our first jet-propelled 'airliner' – as a member of the press. The flight was so smooth, he told me, that he had stood a pencil on its end and it hadn't toppled. He lunched at the Casina Valadier in the Pincio; he had time to walk a little, along the Tiber; and – something which still produces a laugh from people who read the article – he arrived home in time to feed his chickens at five.

'He (John) did play a major rôle in shaping the atmosphere of a school and an epoch that I recall across the gulf of the years with enormous pleasure,' wrote

John Riddy, educationist, of his time as a boy in the last years of the 1940s. 'He was an important part of a background propitious to the production of a very talented generation - Oliver Sacks, Ian McColl, Dick Norman, Geoffrey Best, Valya Boss, Tony Cutler, Erik Korn, Greville Janner, David Rowland, Jonathan Miller and a dozen more passed through his hands - add Dick Lindenbaum and Mischa Nathani, now alas, I believe, dead on some Israeli battlefield.'

John Fuller, writer, poet, Oxford don - at St Paul's from 1950 until 1955 - told me: 'English had to go with Geography in the early '50s. "Intellectuals" were classicists; but scientists Jonathan Miller and Oliver Sacks were posing a threat to them... I expect John Usborne recognised me for the odious dilettante that I was, but I felt emanating from him an absolutely even-handed courtesy and consideration of the sort that one person should always give another in any formalised relationship, which is so often forgotten when grown-ups pull rank.'

'And there was so much sharing in fun, too.' John Fuller came down to Windlesham one summer Saturday in 1952 to film some scenes for a surrealist film he was making. He was using a contemporary, Gavin Brown, as his hero. The filming ended at Sandy Lane Cottage, 'where Gavin emerges from a large box on the Usborne verandah, where John is discovered, wearing a tasselled skull-cap and blank glasses. He bounces about, all knees and elbows, unfolding an enormous map in slow motion. Gavin fumes and despairs. We last see John running about and sticking knives and forks into his orchard grass.' (I was there too, aged thirteen. I already had crushes, from glimpses on the way to school, on both these boys. I remember thinking the antics of all three were very childish.)

'What he must have had to put up with that day! There was never the tiniest shadow of a hint of weary duty, knowingness or condescension towards our amateurish excitement. Possibly he even quite liked it.'

John could play the fool with those voluble scientists John Fuller mentions. Most of them were Jewish boys. He knew them of old, having taught them English as fifth-formers. In their senior years - 1950 and 1951 - he and Guy Burn both lectured to them on the literary and visual arts in their General periods. Jonathan Miller remembered how grown-up they all felt hearing about the Impressionists' mistresses! Erik Korn (ex-'Round Britain Quiz' competitor, now a literary critic and antiquarian bookseller) was secretary of the Chesterton Society - the very popular debating society (still going strong) - which met, while John was its chairman in 1951, in his classroom. Everybody at St Paul's at that time remembers, as does Guy Burn, how comic were Korn and Miller when they performed their double act, year after year, in the Colet Club Reviews; small, myopic, with a white face, Korn was the 'feed' to Miller, who was tall, scrawny, and anxious-looking, with a mop of red hair and an agonising stammer.

In my research I found an article written by the fifteen-year-old Miller in *The Debater*, the magazine G.K. Chesterton, as a Pauline, had founded. Called 'Did

Squeak And Gibber In The Streets', its theme is the comic situations his stammer caused. 'Transport is quite a problem for bus conductors and men in ticket offices are apt to get rude. I live at Swiss Cottage but I can't say that without swishing a lot. So I have to ask for Finchley Road which is one stop on. On really bad days it gets pretty dear with trips out to Watford and Harrow.'

Miller was strident in his criticism of the bullies among the staff. He described John as 'one of the few liberal refuges in the place'. Of all his teachers, the Christian names of John and Guy Burn were the only ones he knew. They kept in touch, for I remember in 1962 John laughing at an excited letter to him from Miller, posted in New York, where he, Peter Cook, Alan Bennett and Dudley Moore were performing *Beyond The Fringe*. The excitement was about the imminent birth of his first child.

John didn't like to be solemn for more than a few minutes. But this passage of his, from 'More Eccentrics Needed', a talk he gave in April 1951, is a solemn warning: 'Now I know only too well we must conform a great deal these days,' he said, 'We are enjoying the glorious privilege, as Lord David Cecil said the other day without a trace of irony in his voice, of living in a Welfare State... But I dislike, as I'm sure you do, being a tiny cog in a giant scheme, whether government or otherwise. I don't enjoy being controlled by some distant Leviathan in the interests of my Welfare. It makes me feel rebellious; but because I, like you, am a law-abiding citizen, I obediently invest a large part of my singular identity in the Plural State and wait for the glorious dividend. But I've still got some part of myself left uninvested, and, by golly, I'm going to make it clear to all that it's my part and no one else's. And being in need of support for this defiant attitude, I'm looking for others to do the same.'

★ ★ ★ ★ ★ ★ ★

At the end of 1951, Ralph Gabriel (engineer, farmer and wartime maize-growing mate of my father's) and his wife Irene asked my parents to dinner, to meet some London friends. Oliver Thomas was Welsh; he had been an air raid warden as a conscientious objector during the war. Now he was a producer of documentary films - for Shell, among other companies. His pretty red-blonde wife Milena was Jewish, a refugee from Czechoslovakia. It was a good party. Irene remembers that when farewells were being exchanged, Milena gave my father a big kiss, and told him to drop in after school for a cup of tea, 'Any day - we live just round the corner!'

Soon after, Milena and John both became godparents to the Gabriels' baby daughter, Anne. John began to drop in to the Thomases' house in Gratton Road after school; that was to become a regular event, two or three times a week. He found Milena affectionate and her household a jolly one. He got to know their small children, Charlie aged three and Jane, a year, and the au pair girl; and the family friends - often travelling in their work - who were mostly of the documentary-film-making fraternity of the time. There was a cosmopolitan note. It was, for John, the first London household unconnected to St Paul's that he had come across.

I can understand so well Milena's attraction for John. She has a quick feminine intelligence; 'pithy' was his adjective for her analyses of situations. She is warm and motherly too; young people love being with her and she basks in their affection. She's sexy still – she has a catlike face and she moves quickly and gracefully. Her appearance, in her eighties, is still youthful and elegant. Good health and her many interests keep her active. Her curiosity keeps her travelling.

In March 1938, Hitler, intent on achieving his plan to unite all German-speaking populations, defied the clauses of the Treaty of Versailles and annexed Austria; soon after, he took the German part of Czechoslovakia, the Sudetenland. The Nazis among the Sudeten Germans saw this as an opportunity to make an outcry about Czech 'persecution'. In this dangerous climate, Milena's mother, the daughter of a farmer, more intuitive than her lawyer father, had realised that their communist daughter had no future under Hitler. Milena was offered hospitality by an English family in Leicester. She queued for twenty-four hours outside the Gestapo to get exit visas for her brother and herself. They left Prague by train at the end of March 1939, when Hitler's tanks were all over the city. Milena, equipped by her mother with new clothes (even a black dress and a white apron in case she found a job as a waitress), expected her parents to follow soon after. For a long time their father waited for exit permits for them to go to Paris. He had just obtained them in June 1940 when France fell. So – as Milena's brother had predicted – they never did get out. They died, her mother in 1942 from a weak heart, and three years later her father, of grief, Milena is sure, in a concentration camp called Terezin.

Milena Thomas in 1995

My father was 37, Milena 36. Both were idealistic, their politics left-wing. Both were musical. Milena had worked in a girls' school in Oxford, and while there she had joined the city's Bach Choir. She had broadcast too: in 1941 the BBC heard about a nursery school she was running for Reading Council, and made a programme about it. She had left Prague with a Social Science degree from the Masaryk College for Health and Social Studies; the London School of Economics examining board were impressed by her, and awarded her a scholarship to take a course on Mental Health. In Cambridge, whence LSE was evacuated, she met Oliver, who was an undergraduate at Clare College.

Milena now laughs at me: although she doesn't remember hearing at the time of John's recent visit to Virginia, USA, I believe that his meeting with her was responsible for the verve of 'Alien Corn', a talk he broadcast in February 1952;

'It [the visit] was a whirlwind courtship, a four-day affair; and then I had to leave. At dawn of a day last September, as the sun shot its first rays at us from behind Fort Munroe, my ship took me slowly out of the old James River away from Virginia, away, through the great maw of Chesapeake Bay. The beaches began to glisten in the distance and the air cleared and woods and fields began to stand out and shimmer in the growing heat. Virginia's. Virginia's fields and woods.'

I feel that the Jewish people my father encountered – those garrulous Paulines and Milena, and his BBC producer Dick Keen, gave to his life an injection of vitality that he needed. He could relax with them. With Milena there was no need to conform. He was accepted for his eccentricity and teased about it, not looked at askance. Milena's earthiness and forthrightness made her refreshing – and rather exotic. Although she tells me, as she would have told him, that her race and religion have never been important to her, I know my father would have seen those qualities as Jewish traits. She was positive, at a time when people's horizons were widening again after fifteen years of sitting tight. She was cosmopolitan, speaking four languages. Like him she liked to shock, put rockets under sacred cows, think about people beyond the shores of England. She too was restless (her husband could get away; for his work he was obliged to travel to the Middle East); she had been used to travelling before the war and now longed for some freedom to explore again. She teased John, which he loved and knew he needed. She teased him about his prejudices... 'I'm bourgeois and, by Gad, sir, I'm British, and I have certain snobberies ...'

Milena appreciated John's sense of humour. She was a good listener. Paula, though she had been a good critic when she and John had been closer, could not compete with Milena's sophistication. America had become an obsession with John – and Paula always found obsessions unhealthy. Julie, aged nine then, remembers that the winter evenings, particularly, 'could be grim. He'd arrive home, fling himself, exhausted, into his chair, and correct papers; conversation at supper was a bit terse.' Julie, being unaware of her existence, did not know that he had just seen Milena. Paula had lost her patience for bearing the brunt of his fatigue at the end of the day. She, after her daytime of chores at home, wanted to dress up and go out to drink. He had to do what was always pressing: mark his papers and work on his journalism. Anyway, he didn't like the evening habitués at 'The Bee'.

In 1937, aged 22, John had walked the Ridgeway, the ancient route of the Celtic drovers which stretches from the Dorset coast through Wiltshire, Berkshire, and then crosses the Cotswolds. In September 1952, aged 38, feeling there were cobwebs in his hair, he walked part of it again with his old Balliol friend Colum Gore-Booth.

Two days' hard walking – a total of 40 miles from Streatley, Berkshire, to Marlborough, Wiltshire, staying overnight at a pub – indeed blew the cobwebs away. Painful feet in unsuitable footwear made them both feel old and decrepit;

but Micky, running on ahead, had never enjoyed himself more, chasing hares, putting up coveys of partridges and a Stone Curlew or two, cocking his leg irrev-erently on a sacred stone at Wayland's Smithy.

They laughed about it afterwards. The reality - according to John's synopsis for the proposed talk, sent to the BBC Talks Department, was slightly different: 'A lit-tle mugging up on the Ridge Way in the Hammersmith Library. Nothing but purple passages and maladroit quotes from Jefferies. After one hour's walk: 'Track peters out... council houses and main road. Chance for a pint at one of East Ilsley's nine pubs. Mocked by Lorry-men. Why walk to Marlborough? We're going there in the lorry and could take you all the way. Walkers, both sore and realising they're 15 years older than they were in 1937, are sorely tempted. But duty calls; we must enjoy a real holiday... Rains hard and we hope for a lift. No luck. Marvelling at the toughness of the Britons and wondering what the Saxons thought of British weather, we almost swim down the hill towards Swindon. We pass through Coate, Jefferies' birth-place. Dreary suburb now. Steam ourselves out by fire in a pub. Limp into Swindon after brief bus-ride. Train home.' And as a postscript: 'I can lay on the flora and fauna in a big way, if you like!'

I don't know when - probably in 1953 - the inevitable happened: Paula met a man who made a fuss of her and who made her feel happy about herself. Jim (I have never known his surname) was an employee in a Windlesham garage. He drove one of the two village taxis. 'The panel-basher' was the name the husband of one of Paula's friends called him behind Paula's back - a small punishment because she didn't introduce him to her old friends, keeping him firmly in the circle of her pub cronies. Julie and I met him, only once. We know they met at 'The Bee' through two of her friends.

I remember my mother poring over racing form in her paper, the *Daily Mail*, laid out on the kitchen table after she had cleared it of the breakfast dishes. (She was rather sullen, not expecting us to be interested.) Jim had obviously resusci-tated her interest in racing - a deep-seated one, sparked by her reverence of her father's love of it. In her early years in England in the mid-1930s she had been taken to race meetings by prosperous young men. I suppose it gave her a chance to dream of glamour and easier times.

Chapter Eight

John was exposed to poetry from the age of two, hearing his mother reading to his brothers at home in Battle. Their father gave his wife advice on what to read to their sons before he left them all to return to India in 1916. The boys - in that year aged 8, 7,6 and 2 - loved hearing their mother read, usually from Kipling's *Jungle Books*, or a story about a dog, called *Owd Bob*. For poetry, she read them *Hiawatha*, and maybe a few lines of their father's own verse for children.

Charles Usborne had set verse-writing competitions for children in *The Times of India* at the beginning of the century. John, in his turn, was dogged in his determination to organise a verse-writing competition for radio. His first idea was rejected. In July 1951, after the success of his 'Young Poets' Corner' broadcasts, Geoffrey Dearmer encouraged him to try again. He asked Patrick Harvey: 'Why not a discussion on verse-forms, clerihews, for instance, with members composing their own ambulando?' - and was rejected again; the idea finally died. One of John's competitions in the *Spectator* had been to write a triolet stanza - beginning:

'It's bound to stop now
That I've got my umbrella.'

'The crux of a triolet, once one has sensed its special function,' John wrote in his report on the entries, 'is in its fifth and sixth lines, "the turn", as it might be called, where, on a classic occasion, an intended ode was "turned" to a sonnet. It was Rose crossing the road, you remember, with something on her head which rhymed beautifully with what the ode turned to. For this reason I offered "umbrella" for the feminine rhyme in each alternative. There were very few good rhymes for it, and with a puckish sense of power I hoped to steer the real trioleteers down the select lyrical avenues which this word manifested. There was the further obstacle in the subject: a "native comment on English weather", which baulked several, including four who were for assuring Stella, Petronella et al. that even if the cow were a bull it was bound to stop now that they had their umbrella: and one even had his cow in the cellar, a rhyme I couldn't allow into the final rounds.' Oswald Clark was awarded second prize; his "turn" struck John as "sheer poetry":

'It's bound to stop now
That I've got my umbrella,
And we're wet anyhow.
It's bound to stop now
So clear is the Plough,
And so close to me Stella,
It's bound to stop now
That I've got my umbrella.'

Antony Jay, an old Pauline and television writer (of *Yes, Minister* fame), told me of a conversation he had with John at the school in the early 1950s. (While Jay was at Cambridge, he would come back to St Paul's in July to help out in the Classics Department for the last weeks of the term): 'John was very welcoming in the common room and I remember his telling me about the lavatory of - I think - his old family house near Newbury. Someone had put up a notice in verse... and such was the erudition of the guests that over the years translations of it appeared all over the lavatory wall in French, German, Italian, Latin, Greek, Persian, and Chinese.'

'The cistern to induce to work
Release the chain without a jerk;
And, kindly as you go outside,
Leave door and window open wide.'

I realised Antony Jay wasn't told that on the gents' lavatory wall at Windrush there were also many English versions of the notice, written in the styles of Chaucer, Shakespeare, Herrick, Browning, Rossetti and others; and that they and the foreign ones were mostly from the pens of Uncle Hubert and his nephews, rather than from those of their weekend guests.

'Most of John's work with us was introducing us to poetry,' wrote Peter Ceresole, a Pauline of the mid-1950s who is now a documentary television producer. 'He once took us through a chunk of Chaucer - was it *The Nun's* or *The Priest's Tale?* - starring Chaunticleer and Pertelote, and he used the new pronunciation which made it that bit harder to understand, but a lot more fun. He took all the parts, sitting on his desk or walking up and down in front of the class, always with a bit of five o'clock shadow, a very modern man enjoying his material.'

Ian Davies wrote: 'I remember your father intensely disliked Longfellow's *Hiawatha* [he had loved it at his mother's knee, but from his teens, writing his own poetry, its facile rhythm grew to irritate him]; he once set us on the task of writing as much verse as we could in that metre, on the subject of school lunch - in the ten minutes or so left before the class actually broke for lunch. He intended of course to prove that anyone could churn out that kind of thing, and, as far as the metre was concerned, I guess he was successful.'

'To this day,' wrote Dennis Bertuzzi-Amanda, 'if I find I am writing anything more than a shopping list, I find myself, sometimes quite consciously, asking myself: "What would Mr Usborne think of this?"'

Poetry, sweetcorn, cricket, America...could always generate excitement in John. Obviously, each new subject for his journalism demanded enthusiasm. He would later re-infect himself for his teaching. He enjoyed, and he enjoyed the boys' response to it - particularly in his current affairs and geography teaching - distilling from his 'bank' of enthusiasm'. Later, he would call it 'showing off'.

John heard, in 1953, from Dutch agriculturalist friends, of the huge reclamation of land that the Dutch government had put into action. And he had thought the Zuider Zee still existed! He made up his mind to see the phenomenon for himself - and write about it. (The result was two broadcasts and three articles.) He wrote offering some advertisement of the new polder of Wieringermeer to the mayor of the area, and was accepted.

In 1933, having made a lake out of the Zuider Zee by enclosing it with a dam, the Dutch state was to reclaim a total of 540,000 acres from the old sea bottom, planning it into farm holdings and villages. Twenty-one years later, at a point when roughly one-eleventh of the new land had been created, John wanted to see how 'a country of rock-ribbed individualists was to begin an agrarian socialism for the express purpose of stepping up food production in an uncertain world.'

(He found the long straight roads planted with characterless poplar trees depressing, and he missed his blackbirds.) The efficiency of the farm management, the rigorous safeguarding against pests, the profits made, were admirable. 'Surely', he thought, 'from all this new efficiency and tidy flatness rebellion must emerge and poetry burst forth.' He found both: the Catholics and the Calvinists were quarrelling over the running of the primary schools and their farm co-operatives. One morning while driving through the polder, John and his host saw a bulldozer moving earth from one end of a garden to the other. The mayor stopped to enquire about it of a man in clogs and overalls. John asked what was happening as the mayor, smiling, got back into the car, and was told: "He's making himself a miniature lake which he wants to stock with fish. And then he'll buy two swans. He likes swans." 'I am all for that little man,' John wrote.

A talk about being a teacher, an idea he had had brewing since the end of 1953, was on the typewriter. He was pleased with his title, 'Putting It Across'. When the first draft of his script had circulated there were nervous memos between Harvey and three of his bosses in the Talks Division. John was warned not to be indiscreet about the old bears among the staff at St Paul's. 'Dammit, why be dead serious at 9.00 am?' he wrote back to Patrick Harvey. He had to cut his script drastically. The talk was broadcast in May 1954.

(John hated to be tamed. The question 'Isn't one ever allowed to be light-hearted about serious matters?' - also asked of Patrick Harvey at the time - epitomises his iconoclastic attitude. The experience of the intercepted letter from Wales in 1941, to him, rather than a lesson, was simply bad luck.)

'You know, the besetting temptation of schoolmasters and schoolmistresses is towards laziness. And the opposite of laziness I'd say wasn't hard work. No, the opposite is zest or, a word I'm apt to suspect, enthusiasm. In other words, so long as you're teed up by your subject and are fired with the itch to communicate your zest, you'll communicate it all right. Because there's nothing so galling to a keen teacher as the realisation that he's not getting it across and therefore has no ambition so strong as the one to find a way of getting it across and, therefore, while the zest lasts, the ability to teach emerges and flourishes. But zest is an exhausting virtue, and schoolmasters aren't, alas, super-human or even super-ordinary. There comes a weary time when you've spent yourself and oh! still there's so much more to get through. And then you'll have to persuade them to listen to you when, quite candidly, you're not worth listening to.

'... But an experienced teacher knows his rhythm and is ready, so to speak, to take up his slack. When his zest passes, he must bring into action other facets of his personality, other tricks in his repertoire. This is where, for some, the cane comes in - or the threat of it. This is where, if you're clever, it's so easy to be lazy.

Caning - the punishment for the crimes of lying, cheating and bullying - was rarely used at St Paul's (nevertheless it was not abolished until 1980). During his early years of teaching John used it on some junior boys, when he had not yet learnt to read the mood of a class, or how to control his anger. He regretted it deeply, and never spoke of it.

In his composite picture of a bad teacher, he wrote, he would not put much emphasis on an inability to keep order. He knew well that it was his responsibility - at the start of a lesson - to communicate his own enjoyment for the subject he was teaching by relaxing with it. 'Then comes the call for framework and facts. Then comes the discipline.'

'Once a teacher drops the slightest hint that he finds his pupils tedious and irritating, the compliment will be quickly returned and he will be on a very sticky wicket indeed.' Occasionally risks had to be taken: when - for example with boys who had come from an art class - by giving them a punctuation exercise, he had to be 'the ruthless martinet, a role they know I hate, and the period could sometimes be more successful. This is where I sometimes - and very sometimes - admit the failure of all else but the cane. Yes, it is a failure, but so long as they know I will and can use it, it is not a disgrace, and one never really loses control. Yes, I am glad to have the cane available because I am not a good enough teacher to do without it.'

Because of his educational broadcasts, John was classified in the BBC files as a teacher. In January 1954 he was a guest adult with four teenagers on *Under Twenty Review*, a forum for the discussion of films, books and plays, on the Light Programme. John Boorman, now one of our best-known film-makers, was an honorary teenager, aged 21. Another, Bruce Bennett, an actor, was a pupil of John's at the time. ("All right, Bennett," John had said to him when a class was reading *The Merchant of Venice*, "I'll let you read Shylock, if you promise to speak up!" And as Bennett has told me, he has been speaking up ever since.)

At the school John was adding publishing to his teaching. He revived in 1954 a dormant school newspaper called *Folio*. Robin Alden, a young master who joined the English staff two years before John left in 1963, wrote in his obituary of John for the paper:'...it was the fun of putting his experiences into words, and offering them to anyone interested, as something personally observed and re-created, that John hoped to foster in "Folio", and in his own special brand of English teaching. That is why "Folio" mattered so much to him, even in its dimmer moments, and why he continued to contribute personally to its columns from time to time after he left St Paul's.'

The Dutch experience had made John curious to compare another type of agrarian socialism. An idea had been simmering in his mind since he had seen an article in *Farm Quarterly*: the migration from Montenegro, in 1950, of peasant farmers, to start a collective farm in Serbia, 300 miles to the north.

The *Geographical Magazine* and the BBC expressed interest in the idea. To obtain the information he needed, John had persuaded himself that he would have no alternative but to travel to Yugoslavia as a bum: '...the joy of solitude and silence,' he described in a letter to Patrick Harvey, 'of lying down at night unsheltered and exposed to the curiosity of nocturnal creatures, of waking up, of walking on...'

Milena - who had happy memories of a visit to Dubrovnik as a girl - allayed his fears about going to a Communist country, encouraging him to see it as an adventure. At home we tried out dehydrated meals of the type used for arctic expeditions. John's pilot friend Roland Alderson had a Dexion trolley made for him at London Airport. It was to carry all his luggage behind him as he walked. He was delighted with it, and christened it Kolica ('Little Wagon' in Serbo-Croat).

He had read that the region of the farm, a vast fertile landscape called the Vojvodina, had been part of Hungary until the end of the First World War, with almost half its population Magyars and Germans. By 1944, when Hitler's army was driven back, both those colonies were gone for good. Many of the Montenegrin migrants came from their poor land voluntarily, eager to farm where the soil was fertile - and where they could be good Communists for Tito.

John's articles and talks in the offing were seen as potentially good publicity for Yugoslavia, which - in the five years since it had become a republic - remained relatively remote and unexplored by Britons. It was a good year for an adventurer to be visiting: Soviet propaganda against Marshal Tito was stopped and trade negotiations started between the two countries.

John was to leaven his informative text for the *Geographical Magazine* with a good story. A genial 68-year-old Montenegrin, John Kasanegre, took him into his Serbian home for the two days of his stay; he and his wife enjoyed giving him good coffee and slivovitz, and some rest after his long uncomfortable journey from Belgrade; and telling him, in broken American English, their chronicle. They had emigrated to the Western United States just before the outbreak of the Second World War, when Montenegro was a political tinderbox. Homesickness for their country brought them home thirty years later - in spite of the good dollars Kasanegre was earning - to find that this time Montenegro was fighting not the Austrians but the Germans. Their two sons and their daughter joined the communist partisans; the sons were both killed, one by execution, the other in battle. Their daughter survived; she and her tractor-driver husband were there to embellish the story told to John.

With Serbia behind him John was in mountainous country for the rest of his stay: he walked with his trolley in the wilds of Bosnia; he visited the hydro-electricity plant at Jablanica; he walked again, along the Neretva valley to Mostar, and from there by train, bus and on foot to the Dalmatian coast.

In Braici, a mountain village five miles from Budva, he talked to Montenegrin peasants who, when they were offered an easier life in Serbia, had decided to stay. Since clearing up after the break with Russia, they were now workers rather than fighters, turning awkwardly to road construction, building Titograd out of a small town and putting hotels along the coast. On the land, John was told, life was marginally better, assuming a pattern very similar to that of the old pre-communist days. He could see that for the men the task was growing easier, whereas for the women there were still few benefits. They were still carrying faggots for several miles on their backs, carrying baskets of soil from low to high land, which they would laboriously shape into terraces.

Montenegro had had an alliance with Russia since the early eighteenth century, and had fought with Russia and Serbia against Turkey in the Balkan wars of

1912-13. The country's bloody history had always interested the classicist in John. With its beautiful coast – in particular that small area inland from Budva – Montenegro was to become one of his great passions. When I first stood upon Lovćen – the mountain that is its historical centre – and gazed at the Adriatic,' he wrote three years later for *Harper's Bazaar,* 'I had some inkling of what Cortes felt like on that peak in Darien. But whereas he had stood silent among a band of conquistadors, I had sung, danced, prayed, and finally wept in an access of spiritual and physical energy... never have I been so enchanted as by that road leading from the coast over the first spur of Lovćen range to Cetinje, the old royal capital of Montenegro.' He learnt that 'Black Mountain', the meaning of the old Venetian name Montenegro, does not derive from the physical appearance of the mountains (which is the ash grey of white limestone) but from – in the eyes of its people – the blood spilt on them in centuries of battle for independence, against Greeks, Romans, Slavs, Venetians, Turks, Austrians, Germans and Italians. 'Being more romantic than geologic,' John wrote, 'I am delighted to be bewitched.' (What would he have made of the Balkan upheavals of the 1990s?)

He continued south-east to Macedonia for his last few days. (Throughout the trip, each bird he identified was annotated, with the date of its sighting, in the margins of his *Field Guide to the Birds of Great Britain and Europe.*) Over Lake Ohrid in the evenings he watched red-legged falcons, common as starlings in the area, catching flies.

★★★★★★★★

From the moment John returned from his trip he was on the telephone, trying to sell a new idea: to make a film, during the next year's Easter holidays, about that historic and beautiful 21-mile stretch of road in Montenegro. BBC Television wouldn't supply the film; eventually approval came from an ITV television producer and the Yugoslav Embassy. John's aim was to form a team of experts among his friends, for wives to come too, and for everybody to have a holiday.

Windlesham friends of John and Paula, Jack and Mary Clifford-Wolff, two elderly sisters, and two young masters from our local prep-school joined the party, making a total of 25 people. The 'ologists' – as my mother called the members of the film-making team – included two other St Paul's masters: Ted Gawne as historian and Arnold Monk-Jones as ornithologist, with his wife; a geologist, a botanist; John's brother Tommy as photographer and botanist; Mervyn Peake, writer and artist, and Robin Jacques, a well-known illustrator, who had been commissioned to draw by *The Sunday Times.* The party crossed Belgium, Germany and Austria by train to Rijeka, then cruised for 35 hours down the Adriatic to Split.

'We were to pick up our Jugoslav cameraman at 5.30 am (in his handwriting, formed while learning Classical Greek, John always wrote the letter 'J' with relish, never crossing the capital; he would still be spelling Yugoslavia with a 'J' if he were alive today.) in the harbour of Split on Easter Day,' he told readers of *Folio* a few weeks later, 'and start filming the famous beauties, scenic and otherwise, on that coast as soon as the sun got up decently.' The cameraman never found the party. 'Everything was very Balkan,' Ted Gawne told me, 'the cameraman's replace-

116

ment arrived (after John had spent far too many sunny hours ranting down tele-
phones before locating one and ordering him to run all the way to Budva) in
city-slicker clothes and when his brief was to photograph us trudging through
the Montenegrin hills, and when I - the historian of the party - was photographed being shown round a lovely 7th Century chapel by the local priest, he
had forgotten to put a film in his camera!'

Ted Gawne in 1994

Professionally, the team agreed, it was a fiasco. Thank God the party was intent
on having a holiday; it did, laughing a lot and enjoying the sunshine, the scenery
and the cheap wine. Still remembered is the bath several of them took, one after
the other, so scarce was the supply of hot water. Paula, Mary, Robin and Mervyn
made a happy foursome exploring Dubrovnik. The two artists, watching and
sketching, captivated the whole party. Mervyn, when he wasn't portraying with a
brush the hook-nosed Turkish profile or the peasant woman exaggeratedly bent
under her load of kindling, sat and wrote copious illustrated letters home to his
wife Maeve; Robin's pen with his careful dot-technique recorded the tall, handsome town people and the narrow precipitous streets.

Planning the television programme together after their return, John and
Robin visualised a friendly 20-minute discussion between themselves and
Mervyn, Ted, and Tommy. 'When he had film in his camera, the things that
Serbian photographer did take,' Ted Gawne told me, 'were rejected by ITV as
being of inferior quality, and the nett result of all this was a five-minuter when
John talked to a highly nervous Mervyn Peake, who sounded as if he had a heavy
cold but was actually over-fortified with whisky.'

At the end of 1955, the atmosphere at home was not happy, and John felt
responsible for it. In addition he had caused a commotion locally. Early in

October he broadcast a talk about Windlesham, called 'Portrait of a Village'. It was to cause threats of a libel action to the Director General of the BBC from a deputation of Windlesham people; that in turn got into trouble the many producers who knew John. One of them, Dick Keen, said to me: 'Obviously deep down he hated Windlesham, and the talk made me aware of social dissatisfactions in John which I hadn't previously suspected... I think the protesters only wrote, they didn't visit Broadcasting House. But our bosses - who treated us like children - were quite scared for a short time.'

Dick Keen continued: 'Another little memory has come back to me, which amused me even at the time, while I was being hauled over the coals: one of the grievances of the complainants was that a group of residents had been assembled in some hall to listen to the broadcast. And this was what they heard:'

(The hall belonged to the Village Institute, about a quarter of a mile from our house, where, for the village, there were billiards, bowls, country dancing and a weekly film.) 'I'm sorry about Surrey. I live in her, I hate her, but by hating her for as many years as I can remember, and by living in one of her most typical villages for fifteen years, I know how to love her very dearly.

'...Bagshot Beds make poor farming land, but excellent golf courses. Just right for expensive preparatory schools, Rhododendrons - and Privet Hedges. In the very old days of yore its inconvenient distance made it a paradise for rogues. Kings hunted through it, highwaymen hid in it and gypsies scarred it with their squalor.'

'But John was always getting into trouble!' said my uncle Dick, on being reminded of this episode. (It was brave, he said. Neither Tommy, Henry nor Dick ever took their youngest brother aside. It wasn't their style. They would have thought, as usual: 'John's bad luck again!)

Windlesham was a straggly village; and rather unfriendly - not only because my father had antagonised a fishmonger, a market-gardener and a few others. My friend Ann D'Arcy-Smith, two years older than me, remembers now, about fifty years later, an odd mixture of characters. For their different reasons, they appeared true blue - but they weren't quite; the undercurrents of the self-made were felt. Julie and I used to tip-toe past gaps in some people's hedges, not wanting to be seen. There were eighteen big houses in the village; most of them were behind trees, at the end of long drives. In her dotage, the widowed Countess Alice of Athlone, a grand-daughter of Queen Victoria, lived in one of them. Timothy Tufnell, the property magnate, owned a huge white mansion near the church. Big Ann, Julie and I found it creepy as we passed it on our walks to the Windle Brook, never seeing any sign of movement there. On two or three of our most familiar roads, there were stranded rows of workmen's cottages. We knew the children living in them only by sight, we being middle-class and they being 'village children'. And - a Home Counties feature at that time and for many more years - there were dank reminders of the war, evil-smelling derelict Nissen huts half hidden by undergrowth.

Before the broadcast John had shown his script to our rector, a friend of his, and a fair man. He had approved the facts. After it, in his letter of apology to Patrick Harvey, John wrote: 'I feel the BBC may have a somewhat exaggerated idea of what the village really felt. One pointer to it may be the fact that the cricket team which I was accused of insulting elected me at the height of the affair, Vice-President - and pretty much against my will. I'd very much like to make my peace with your department.'

Harman Grisewood, the BBC's Director of the Spoken Word, wrote a memo about John to Mary Somerville, the Controller of Talks, saying: 'He has shewn himself to be the sort of man we had better avoid at any rate for the present and I am in favour of sending him the kind of letter you spoke of yesterday'.

Although nervous for his three last talks on Yugoslavia, John still simmered in a letter to Patrick Harvey, laying down the law to the BBC: 'Here's my first instalment. I've sweated blood to tell the truth without offending anyone it is adviseable [sic] not to offend and without causing anxiety to your department. And I feel pretty confident that this script at any rate is both adequate and innocuous.'

★ ★ ★ ★ ★ ★ ★

At Sandy Lane Cottage money was very tight; fees paid for both John's writing and broadcasting were low. Like his colleagues he often felt demoralised and insulted by the paltry salary that schools on the Burnham Scale paid their masters. Robert Perceval, a Balliol contemporary, who was one of the Clerks of the House of Lords at the time, had lunch with John at St Paul's. He was 'very shocked', he told me, when he heard that he was earning £744 per annum, only 15 per cent more than the pay - even more shocking - of a state schoolteacher.

'It really is about time the public were shaken into appreciating the rapidly growing responsibilities of us teachers and the disgraceful neglect of us by a public that is not encouraged to think,' John, typically, wrote to a BBC producer in November. As an English teacher, he felt that a large part of his work went unrecognised; and that as a subject English was still unappreciated. ('There were the sportsmen, the classicists, and the great mass of us in the middle' Nicholas Bromley, one of John's mid-1950s boys told me.) Chris Arnold, one of his wartime pupils, then a young architect with two or three years of experience working on the west coast of the United States, was back in London. He dropped into St Paul's and, probably in the masters' Common Room, had a short conversation with John about life in California. Sometime after this he received a letter from him 'asking, in general terms, about working in the United States.'

Although America was to seduce him again, John's enthusiasm for Yugoslavia will spring to the minds of many of his friends when they remember him. His five nephews were all schoolboys in the mid-1950s; they remember, at Henry and Pam's annual fruit-picking camp at Evesham for us eleven cousins and our friends, their youngest uncle recounting his adventures. Tommy's youngest son Julian's anecdote is of John telling his favourite story: of waking one morning in the wilds of Bosnia to find a steaming pile of bear dung a few feet from his head. When Geoffrey Dearmer was adapting John's talk 'They Call It Cnra Gora' for 'Children's Hour' he told Patrick Harvey in a memo that he thought it 'awfully good'. Harvey agreed: 'Yes, excellent if a bit nasty in parts: corpses, blood, vultures, exhumed grandmothers. We ought to watch this tendency of his, and I think it's worth putting to him.'

At St Paul's he got away with it. With his fifth-formers the opportunity to indulge their bloodthirstiness always amused John, remembering himself as a boy. Andrew Montagu, in his first year in 1960, told me that John asked his English class to imagine a poor family at the time of the Great Plague, and to write about the impact this terrible scourge had upon each member of it. 'I think that my recall is probably enhanced by the fact that I gained a good mark for my efforts despite his criticism that my descriptive passages were "not lurid enough". Wonderful stuff for a thirteen-year-old and the start of a disgusting classroom discussion from which he seemed to get as much pleasure as the boys.' John also shared a favourite comedian, Frankie Howerd - with a pupil, Geoffrey Kendell. Kendell can still, to this day, remember the gleam in John's eye when he enthused about Howerd.

His boys were aware after a few lessons with John that his travel broadcasts, and his writing - even the columns in *Folio* which he wrote for their readership, were as important to him as his teaching. They knew his teaching had something extra. Peter Moakes (whose father Jack Moakes - a good friend of John's - was a St Paul's colleague), told me: 'I put Mr Usborne on a different plane from many of the other teachers.' 'He had a Bohemian touch,' said Nicholas Bromley. 'Beside the other grey-suited masters, I remember him wearing sneakers.'

Robin Excell, a clergyman, wrote: 'I bet John has locked no end of little pockets of information into people's minds through his unique style.' Excell remembered a Latin lesson. 'He had set us a vocabulary test; and whenever he did that he would always say: Don't leave any blanks. If you don't know the answer, guess. Well, one of the words in the test was "cruelly", and I had no idea what the answer was; but I followed his advice and tried "crueliter". Twenty minutes later he was coming round and he saw it and said "No, that's wrong. The correct answer is "crudeliter"; in fact it's such a good guess I'll let you have that.' Paul Leppard remembers a Current Affairs lesson when John asked the boys to bend down and look backwards through their legs to get a different view of life. None of them did; they were too embarrassed.

John didn't like Antony Gilkes, the High Master from 1954-1962. John was one of a group of masters, who, as a form of protest over his cruelty, would absent themselves from his morning prayers. At the end of *Folio's* first year, and its editors' struggle to produce two issues per term, Gilkes had forbidden John to publish *Folio* more than four times in the year, to prevent the boys on the editorial committee spending time away from their school work. John's motive in publishing *Folio* was as a newspaper, to maintain for the boys an interest in current affairs, and to encourage good factual writing. He was furious that it was forced to become a magazine.

John was better tuned in to boys than to girls. Once - when I was fourteen and very self-conscious - he treated me rather insensitively; my mother, when I complained, ticked him off for it. Although in this instance both schools broke up for the holidays on the same day, I had to leave mine at the end of the morning. He arranged to meet me at the top of the steps at the main door of the Boys' School. I remember feeling acutely exposed as I walked behind him, in my hated school tunic, the length of the Dining Hall to the Masters' Table, past three hundred Paulines as they ate.

At home, for fun, he gave Julie and me little projects - for him they were just extending his own amusement. He suggested we made an alphabetical list of the then 48 states of America, because he adored their names. He earmarked limericks for us to learn, and Ogden Nash animal verses such as 'The Firefly' and 'The Jellyfish'. Naturally Julie and I were used as guinea-pigs when he had books to review for 'Children's Hour' - and our remarks were mentioned, very gravely, to our pride.

An important part of John's teaching job were his duties as tutor, to about 20 boys annually - a system unique to St Paul's, founded by Tom Bell, the High Master who preceded Walter Oakeshott. He fought for his wards when problems arose with other teachers. David Morris, now living in Canada, suffered bullying from his classmates, having transferred from a state school. 'Your father was faced with making this pubertal misfit feel at least partly at home. At any hint of a problem my mother would be on the line to him, or standing outside his door. He responded to the challenge with charm and dignity. He gave me hope that I was not doomed to spend my life friendless and isolated, and by feeding my imagination, gave me back some intellectual pride.'

Dick Keen sees John 'as a person who was early in his concern about what used to be called "an explosion of leisure", which is very much with us now and has proved to be much more intractable than was then foreseen.' In the autumn of 1955 John submitted a talk called 'Boy Into Man' to Lorna Pegram, who was then deputy editor of 'Woman's Hour'. It was pure hustling, I think, because, characteristically, he could never accept the 'mumsiness' of the programme; in his letter to her acknowledging the rejection of his script, he argued back: 'In my job children who find things meaningless are urged to go on thinking about them till they mean something. And if your women are never to be made to think by being offended, then once again why go on spending public money on them? And what on earth is Gilbert Harding for but to offend into thinking? But seriously, if this 'Automation' is to be taken seriously, then everyone, even the sensitive females who mustn't be shocked by 'Woman's Hour', must get wise to the fact that everyone is going to spend longer and longer being educated; otherwise there's going to be serious unemployment and even more serious neurotic boredom.'

★ ★ ★ ★ ★ ★ ★

My father's visits to Milena after school continued to be crucial to his life. He needed her affection and support; he needed her to tease him and to hold his demons down - and as a sounding-board for his ideas. He was now 41, 'feeling his age'. When he smiled, he was a handsome man, but some photographs taken then show him looking tired and more than usually thin; his face was acquiring a lop-sided look, his eyes beginning to drag down at the outer corners. His strong dark eyebrows were starting to beetle, his small amount of hair going grey. 'Poor John!' said my mother's old beau Vivian Spong, looking at those snaps, 'He didn't look well.'

One of these photographs was published in our local 'rag', the *Camberley News*, and captioned 'Windlesham's well-known writer and broadcaster Mr John Usborne spends a lot of time at his typewriter'. It's comic. He's caught off guard, or, more likely defiantly not posing for the photographer - on a December Saturday. He appears exhausted, teeth clenched, eyes bleary, his old sweater unravelled at the neck; the little Olivetti is before him on his desk, galleys laid out beside it.

His blood-pressure was regularly too high. Winters were always grim: mouth ulcers were frequent and he had difficulty throwing off colds. Relaxation at home was snatched, in the only form he had known for a long time: playing the piano 'very badly' and listening to records of Bach, Brahms and Britten.

Vivian Spong visited us with his wife one weekend, John's and his first meeting. While the women were chatting, I imagine John listening to Vivian talk, as I did recently, of General Sir William Slim, his C in C during the Burma Campaign. He questioned him about his job, and discovered that since Vivian had retired from the Army in 1947 he had been working for Calmic Ltd. (then a company under the Rentokil umbrella). He was in the Hygienic Services Division. 'On each and every flush' of a lavatory, he explained, 'Calmic's little copper container - attached inside the cistern - let out a powerful disinfectant into the water.' John's wicked public-schoolboy sense of humour was instantly kindled; he was already planning his sales ploy to the school bursar. He managed to get Vivian some good business at St Paul's. (Apparently the school had the longest row of stalls in London, for the boys... but only two for the masters.) 'The Lavatory Man' became John's nickname for Vivian when he felt like teasing Paula.

I've never wished he was a different sort of father; but I feel I have suffered by not having been taught even the bare bones of a business sense by him. Another father, perhaps, would have sat us down and explained shares and old age. He had no business sense himself, so - out of pique as well as his principles - he hated it, and money too, and was a snob about the business world. He tried not to let his snobbery get the better of him. He teased Michael Barton about dealing in, among other products, senna-pods, in his import-export business. A group of bowler-hatted commuters (as we know from his BBC talk of 1951 'More Eccentrics Needed') always made him want to run in the opposite direction. Not so, however, a few individuals; I know that over the years he made good travelling companions of a few businessmen on the Aldershot and District bus home. Their conversations, Julie told me, gave him something to talk about at the rather subdued suppers I missed.

Chapter Nine

'How much fonder I shall be of my family when I get back, and they of me, perhaps.'

These lines ended a letter John wrote to Patrick Harvey on 3 April 1956,
expressing pleasure that Harvey was to handle his 'forthcoming trans-Atlantic
business'.

Poor Daddy. We were all growing away from him. His attachment to Milena and
her children meant that at Sandy Lane Cottage a cold wind was blowing. My mother, of course, knew the reason. Julie was closest to her, and, fragile as the unit of both
parents was, she accepted and needed it. I was being shown great affection by the
family of a schoolfriend in London, and I spent many weekends with them.

Thinking about that time now, I'm wishing my father had had a son; led by
my mother, I suppose we three females, having our gender in common, shut him
out. For both Julie and me our mother's company was easier; she was the more
demonstrative, and, though I was unable to respond, it was good to know that she
cared. Our father, as a teacher, was uncannily intuitive at recognising talent in the
boys he taught, but rather ham-fisted with his daughters.

Having wanted to go to art school herself, my mother recognised my artistic
'symptoms'. Somehow my work at school never fully recovered its originality
after I had some bad reports at the age of fourteen. I started crying in my room
then - probably because I knew I wasn't measuring up for my father. (He took
me to see the pioneer psychiatrist William Sargent at St Thomas's Hospital, who
smiled at me as he told me that he didn't think I needed pills.) His disappointment over my lack of enthusiasm for English Literature wasn't obtruded on me.
I'd become dreamy, which made me incapable of being analytical.

If Milena and her children had not been so necessary to my father's life for
those six years, would we - his daughters - have had more of his attention?
Probably not. Milena certainly listened to him - and my mother didn't. So my
mother's attitude permeated through to Julie and me: he was an odd husband and
an odd father.

As a result, maybe, of having lost a loving mother at a tender age, he was
uneasy physically with both Julie and me. His tension made us uneasy. Having that
lively mind of his, so much enjoyed by his St Paul's colleagues, meant that his ideas
were whirring away, and we were often overlooked. His power of concentration,
in the many subjects which caught his interest, was astonishing; but now he felt
intellectually lonely with his family. One of his daughters, he had hoped, would
follow in his footsteps and show some promise as a writer; he'd waited and
watched, and I suppose, having lived with disappointment for a while, he was giving up. With me he was too solemn - puzzled, I think, to find that he could not
really share my interests.

Julie remembers our father's roars of laughter during telephone calls with friends; but she feels that he spent very little time communicating with us. When she was tiny - roly-poly, with masses of golden ringlets - she used to ride on his shoulders. She remembers one time being up there, close to the laden boughs of our Blenheim apple tree. While he and my mother and some friends were talking, she spat on his bald head and rubbed the spit over it to cool it for him. There was laughter all round as she was abruptly put down.

While I was away in London, and Julie, aged nine or so, was at Hurst Lodge School in Sunningdale, she had a good outdoors rapport with her father. It had much to do with play after school. After supper in summer the three of them were often outside; Mummy would weed her borders, while in the field Julie would look with Daddy for new shoots emerging, and they would chat as he dug up couch-grass. Micky, with mud round his nose, would be digging near them, snorting and snuffling as he pounced on imaginary animals emerging from his holes. Daddy rigged up a rope for Julie on a beloved old oak tree; she remembers watching unnoticed from a branch hanging over Sandy Lane, as a crocodile of chattering prep-school boys walked below her, from nearby Woodcote House.

Bill, her tame jackdaw, had been brought down from the nest as a fledgling by our father and Mark Paterson. (In those days no one frowned on such an act.) He became an affectionate pet; and, jackdaw-fashion - with his head often on one side as if he was listening - a comedian: Daddy would let him out of the old hamster cage when he let Micky out in the morning - and he would fly up and tap on Julie's window to wake her up for school - even on Sundays. He knew the time she would be nearing home on her bicycle, and would fly to perch on her handlebars. Even Micky's head became one of his perches.

One day Daddy suggested that he and Julie should test Bill's intelligence. He took the jackdaw to the open barn in the far corner of the field, and released him when he heard Julie - a hundred yards away under the oak tree - call his name. To their astonishment Bill flew straight to her shoulder and stroked her cheek affectionately with his beak. It became a regular game; he liked Julie's cries of 'Good bird!' and her rewards of extra corn.

Every year we had good fruit, both hard and soft, from the garden. I remember on summer days hearing a faint popping noise as Micky pulled the blackcurrants off the bushes with his teeth. Agricultural experiments went on continuously in the field, my father usually growing American versions of fruit and vegetables. We had blackberries as big as loganberries; furtively, we had tobacco; once the whole area was covered in buckwheat, another time with rye. Since our corn roast parties in the Augusts of 1948 and 1949, when friends came to our field to eat our corn roasted in a bonfire and drink cider and orange-squash, growing sweetcorn was a Sandy Lane Cottage institution. We ate cobs and cobs of it over the years; it was a great help to the family budget.

My father enjoyed shaking us women out of our conventionality. He wasn't a smoker - but he tried smoking the 'silk' (which grows like a green web round the corn cob, under its leaves) in a pipe just like Popeye's. And Julie remembers a day when my mother sighed 'Look what I have to put up with!' as she showed our charwoman the clothes-line; my father had borrowed the clothes-pegs to hang his tobacco leaves up to dry. He bought a cider-press to make cider from our windfalls; again he commandeered kitchen equipment, this time all the bowls and saucepans he could find. The juice didn't ferment, so it was poured on the compost heap. 'After dinner,' wrote his friend Rupert Kinross, 'instead of conventionally explaining the "geography" of the house to his guests, your father would steer the menfolk into the garden to pee on his compost heap, of which he was very proud.'

We used to tease him about a tiny toy of his, sent to him by another keen ornithologist, Howard Johns - whom he had met in 1946 in Hamburg, New York. Called the Audubon Bird Charm - marketed by the Audubon Society - it consisted of an inch-long, unvarnished wooden cylinder with a tight metal stopper, which, when twisted, would squeak to simulate bird sounds. The object was to attract a bird to show itself. The Charm only really works on American warblers, most of whom make a 'pishing' sound; in Britain the odd squeak from it may attract one of our native warblers. My father loved experimenting with the thing, and his listening expression as he stood in the garden was ridiculous, especially to my mother: '*Really*, John!'

My parents found their modus vivendi. Old friends knew the truth about their marriage, but it was typical of the 1950s, I'm told, that to most of our neighbours our ménage appeared contented. My mother invested much of her energy in her home and worked hard at keeping up appearances. She was extremely presentable - indeed, glamorous, as were all her chums; she contrived always to dress beautifully. (My father and - to his annoyance - her mother, kept her supplied with the scent, good gloves and Jaeger sweaters she felt were her due.) At weekends they were good hosts to friends who dropped in for tea and drinks.

Milena, a very different sort of woman from my mother, in a different sort of marriage, lived in the comparative anonymity of a city. In July 1955 my father offered a talk to Patrick Harvey, called 'Night Walk through Kensington', written white-hot - probably on the coach home - after leaving her. No other reason would have kept him in London to notice the scents of its gardens on a summer evening. Patrick Harvey - who knew of my father's relationship - rejected the script with the comment 'too private for broadcasting'.

On occasional Saturdays, Milena brought her children, Charlie and Jane, down from London to Virginia Water. My father would borrow a van; he, Julie and I, with Micky on his lead, would meet them off the bus, and we would all troop round the lake having a nature lesson from my father. I associate Virginia Water with rainy weather, perhaps because I, the grumpy adolescent, was dragged away from reading or sewing in my room. My father would point out the crested grebes. Grebes and rhododendrons - not Milena and her children - are etched on my memories of Virginia Water.

★ ★ ★ ★ ★ ★ ★

Milena knew of John's excitement while he waited, at the end of 1955, for a decision concerning him, from Bowaters, the paper-making company. In the summer of 1956 it was to send him on his most important journalistic trip so far. His connection with Bowaters began during the war, in his work as educational adviser to the Iron and Steel Federation. Since he was at Oxford John had been moved by the Depression in the United States and Franklin Roosevelt's plans to improve the lot of the Southerners. His curiosity about Geography and Current Affairs shows a characteristic combination of the romantic and the realist. Philip McGuinness said: 'There was a certain detachment about him – it was this, I think, which gave him the sweeping look-around interests which must feature in the make-up of all real journalists.'

He was awestruck by the magnitude of such as he had seen of the North American landscape – but equally romantic to him was the massive machinery employed on it, sometimes to physically change it. In the United States for the first time immediately after the war, teaching Geography, the experience of living a short distance from Niagara Falls and the Welland Canal stoked his inspiration – for the region's interesting geology and ecology, and its role in the American economy. He had been quick to set up visits to steel mills on the shores of Lake Erie. The scale of Roosevelt's New Deal in motion thrilled him.

Over many years he had observed a remarkable success story unfold: he knew that from the end of the 1920s Eric Bowater, an Englishman, had been determined to establish his London firm of paper merchants as a manufacturer in North America. In 1938 Bowater's (the apostrophe explained the charisma of one man) had bought a small mill in Newfoundland for $6,000,000 from a Canadian paper company. The island was a British Dominion, but mostly as a result of neglect by Britain since the Depression, its economy had recently been declared bankrupt. In return for the obvious benefits the islanders would derive from the capital invested, the rights for cutting the pineforests of the island's interior were granted to Bowater's by the Newfoundland government. The revival of the industry by Bowater's was easy; and it rescued the island's economy.

Bowaters – the apostrophe had now been dropped – was a name we heard at home often as my father planned his trip. Eric Bowater had announced to his shareholders in May 1955 a Master Plan to expand not only the British mills, but those in Newfoundland, Tennessee and Nova Scotia. John was to visit the North American mills and report on the progress of the ambitious building programme. In Nova Scotia he would have a part of his expenses paid by the Geographical Society's Trust Fund for the Advancement of Exploration and Research, while he did research for two articles for the magazine; and the *Yorkshire Post* had agreed to an article on the descendants of the province's first emigrants from Yorkshire.

'What I'm after on my next escape,' John bubbled over to Patrick Harvey, 'are caribou, loons, porcupine, fireflies, bears, hill-billies, Acadian French-speaking negroes, English-speaking Frenchmen, Gaelic-speaking Yorkshiremen, blackfly and Poison-Ivy.' Geoffrey Dearmer, like a fond uncle, pacified him in his nervous excitement, well aware that he was piling up too many responsibilities for the trip. John felt suffocated at the prospect of hours confined with millworkers and noisy machines; he wanted some interest from the BBC in his plan to go off the beaten track to do some birdwatching and exploring of his own. He asked Dearmer for guidance on what he should research for some forthcoming talks, and was gently told: 'I don't think it is any good anticipating experiences.'

Though he needed to get away, he told Patrick Harvey, he never wanted to escape for good. One of the best parts of his English working day at St Paul's was the gathering of a fluid group of masters at a table in the basement tuck shop after school.

Philip McGuinness was one of the last stragglers at the table one afternoon while the tea-ladies were preparing to close; the others, he remembered, were John and Tony Richards, whose conversation went something like this:

Tony: 'I must go. Procrastination is the thief of time.' (He rises.)
John (still seated, sipping his tea): 'Don't you mean that punctuality is the thief of time?'
Tony (sitting again): 'Should it not be "Punctuality - dash - the thief of time?"'
John: 'I don't like dashes. Isn't a colon better?'
Tony: 'Do you mean "Punctuality - colon - the thief of time?"'
John: 'Yes, something like that. I prefer a colon to a semi-colon.'
(Now ensued a ten-minute conversation on PUNCTUATION.)
Tony (rising again with a handful of books): 'I must go.'
John: 'Yes, procrastination is the thief of time.'
Tony: 'No, punctuation is the thief of time.'

Philip McGuinness in 1994

An American connection with the school kept John busy for more than two years, and out of it he made a good friend. Paul Longland, John's colleague, said to me: 'In the Common Room we did get tired of hearing John's talk about Eric Wiseman!' Wiseman was an Englishman, who - with his wife - taught at St Mark's School in Massachusetts, one of the top Ivy League 'prep' (private) schools in the United States. In June 1954 the couple brought a party of eight boys from different Eastern Seaboard Prep schools to join a debate held by St Paul's debating society. Wiseman and his parties repeated the engagement twice. The last, in June 1956, not a debate but an Anglo-American Discussion, included six Paulinas. 'A nervous and possibly hostile gathering fought out the issues of education in the respective countries,' *Folio* reported.

In the early 1950s the excitement of Franklin Roosevelt's New Deal passed. To British people who had rejoiced in his reforms, the old stereotypes of America - as the last fortress of capitalism, a repressive and conservative nation - returned. But Hugh Gaitskell, who became the Leader of the Labour Party when Attlee resigned in December 1955, was sure that the progressive impulse there still survived after Roosevelt's death.

John flew to Newfoundland on 31 July 1956, three days after Nasser seized the Suez Canal. A war could have erupted during his stay away - but that was the least of his worries. He was happy to be distancing himself from the British Press, and curious to experience the frosty American political attitude towards Britain voiced by John Foster Dulles. Nasser's mischief delighted him; he found Eden's reaction to him difficult to stomach.

Not once mentioning the crisis, John wrote 21 letters to Milena during his 45-day absence, the last from St Matthews, Kentucky on 13 September. 'I shall be burdening you with my random thoughts in lieu of a diary. Don't read it if you feel bored.' He would have been deeply hurt if the diary had bored her. Apart from the obvious need of a lonely journalist on a very difficult assignment to write to the woman he loved, the letters formed an interesting document. Unlike the ones he wrote to his radio producers, these are not meant to humour or impress. 'It should show you how much I love you and need you with me that, as soon as I get in from being out or am left alone, I sit down to talk to you this way.'

★ ★ ★ ★ ★ ★ ★

John's plane arrived in Gander at 6.45am. While waiting for a small plane to take him across the island to Stephenville, he wrote a euphoric letter-card to Milena telling her that the flight had been wonderful and that he was enjoying reading her parting present of Colin Wilson's new book *The Outsider*, and that he was about to accompany an eleven-year-old English boy for a walk round the airport 'to look for salmon and birds'. The small plane was delayed, so they walked into the forest and down to a lake. There they watched another co-passenger, a Newfoundlander from Clapham, in a city suit and waders, catching trout as he waited for his plane to take him to St John's, his family's home town. The boy turned out to be thrilled by my bird-love and we both shrieked with delight when we saw a Sandpiper and a White-bellied Nuthatch and a Brown Thrasher and so forth. But he was listening all the time for six-foot Black Bears to come out of the dense forest!

> 'Well, the plane finally came and we flew across this fantastic island. Corner Brook smells of sawn wood; the rest of Newfoundland of evergreen forest. Corner Brook's a typical N. American boom city sprung up in the last 20 years out of almost nothing. Big American stores, car shops, super-cinemas - but only rutty, dusty roads. And all round, mountains and forest'

> 'Something's beginning to take shape in my mind,' he wrote two days later, 'I feel something very strange and new and exciting about Bowaters in Newfoundland. I know I have a feel of what's happening here of which those

who work here have no capacity. You can see them as through a microscope. You fly over the country; you look at it from a mountainside; you see endless rolls and swathes of forest and lakes and rivers. You see ants. What queen directs them? They have American cars. They're rich - what from? I''s Newfoundland, the oldest found land in the Commonwealth, and the Newfoundlanders, for over 300 years, have been subsisting, inbreeding God-fearers, clinging polyp-like to the rocks below the primeval forests - semi-cretinous over-Anglo-Saxons, fish-eaters, wife-beaters, God-fearers, polyps. Suddenly almost, they take to the forests and climb up from the cod-laden sea.'

He was to be flown by seaplane to Hare Bay, on the north-eastern tip of the island, to inspect with 'bug-experts' some diseased forest. 'Needless to say I'm bubbling with excitement,' he wrote, 'and needless to say I'm grateful I'm able to be so excited that the time simply gallops along and I can't brood on your absence till the evenings, when I'm too tired to let it keep me awake.

'I wish I didn't get distracted by little things so easily. I can't help star-ing wide-eyed at an American Robin and miss something important an ant is telling me about Mill Statistics. I visited a logging camp yesterday to take photographs but was distracted by a forestry expert who showed me wild flowers, orchids and honeydews - and I miss an important photo showing the difference between a Balsam Fir and a White Spruce tree. A Canada Jay flies out of the woods carrying a red object in its claws - I can think of nothing else for a while. Life is so exciting, so pulsating in so many direc-tions that nothing has a setting, nothing fits into an integrated picture - there's no meaning and no direction and suddenly I get frightened and depressed and want you, my darling Milena, as the only thing in the world that has meaning and importance quite remote from Canada Jays and Wild Orchids and Newfoundland Ants.'

The plane was prevented from taking off by three days of storms. 'Blast the rain, blast it!' he wrote, 'I long to see the sun and smell the woods.' As he waited, John fought off loneliness by going out to meet people and listen to their accents. When the sun came out:

'I can't tell you how exciting it is standing still in a forest in a strange, distant country and listening. I was half expecting a large Moose to appear (they are very common here). I stood in a secluded spot and played my lit-tle bird-charm. Soon four different kinds of birds appeared and looked at this squeaking intruder. I was able to study them at my leisure through the field glasses. One little thing, a VIREO, which makes a noise like its name, was so puzzled by the charm that it followed me down the track for about 50 yards. I saw two Rose-breasted Gros-beaks. What glorious colours! The forest is full of flowers; A purple veitch they call Creeping Charlie is every-where. Sorry, my darling, I know you enjoy my enthusiasm when we're together in the country. But at this distance it can be downright boring!'

He didn't write again for nearly a week for there was no spare time, no privacy and no post office. 'I won't go into details about this Monday-Saturday trip to the North. Enough that it was highly adventurous, infuriating and exhausting. I was miserable all the time I wasn't being frightened. Everything went wrong, connections missed, boats broke down, roads were morasses or canyons & radio messages never arrived. I slept in roadmakers' camps, woodmen's camps and depôts. I ate hugely but what quality! – yesterday a filthy ship's cook reeking of tobacco and old socks cooked us stewed cods' tongues! Whenever I wasn't being shown something & felt myself sinking back into misery I slipped away into the forest with my bird-charm and got dozens of adorable birds to fuss round me as I stared at them through binoculars.'

John confided to Milena his feelings about Paula's affair: 'Naturally I'm worrying. I feel something catastrophic will come of it. I've written to her to suggest that if she wants to marry him & not be embarrassed by the class problem, she must take him to Canada or the States where such things count for so little and he, with his engineering skill, could get a job easily.

'But I don't see how our children and Jim's fit into this. Paula would hate to be so far from them & I can't see them being very happy with Jim...My bet is that when I get back she will have decided on a complete break from him and be utterly miserable and probably blaming me for much of her misery.

'At Hare Bay I was fretting all the time about you and Paula, but most of course because I'm terrified the family's going to be left high and dry by Paula and I'd had no news since leaving England. Of you, my darling Milena, I fret only because I love you so passionately and can't stand being away from you & hope you're happy but looking forward to my return and will continue to. You save me from unimaginable terrors.

'I fly to Halifax, Nova Scotia on Monday. Please write often. Can't tell you how wretched I am. Never again, please God. Darling Milena, keep me from this abject misery. Over 4 more weeks of it! J.'

The next day, Sunday, he was a journalist again, planning a broadcast for CBC, to go out within a few days in the maritime provinces of Canada; for the last hours free of Bowaters' harness, he enjoyed himself. 'I've got over a dozen people to come to the CBC studio at 8 o'clock this evening to be interviewed by me about their background. What would surprise listeners to the BBC are the English rustic accents out here; settlements such as the one I was in yesterday in which almost everyone is either a Bennett or a Hutchings & speaks pure 18th century West Dorset. Now that Bowaters attracts them all from the coast and their codfishing, these Old Country relics are vanishing by integration into some thing which will soon be merely Newfoundlander and more Canadian than English. It seems I'm catching the old types just in time.'

Gathering his information on the Nova Scotia mill was easier. It had been already mature and self-sufficient when the Organisation had bought it earlier that year. Built in the early 1930's, it faced Liverpool Bay, on the Atlantic coast, about 80 miles south of Halifax, the capital. Nova Scotia's principal industry was newsprint; since the beginning of the mill's career, its two machines had supplied some of the world's most important newspapers, the *New York Times*, *New York Herald-Tribune* and *Washington Post*.

John realised that the forest and bad weather of Newfoundland had oppressed him. His spirits always lifted when he was within sight of human efforts in agriculture. After a week in Nova Scotia, having seen much of its landscape, and revelling in its history, he was to write that he was already in love with it. He was comfortable and content in his Liverpool hotel when he wrote to Milena - after a Sunday of some good hospitality, spent in the open air at the lakeside cottage of the mill's manager and his family.

'I'm quite absorbed in this genealogical business of these Nova Scotians. It is a unique province in this way because the phase of immigration lasted for seventy years and ended almost totally in the 1850's. Since then very few have emigrated here and few have moved away. Communities which come - say - from Wales in 1832 are still recognisably Welsh. But this will last not much longer. Big things are happening to the West of Nova Scotia and the Nova Scotians will soon move gradually to the flesh-pots leaving just as many behind as it takes to man a few industries, and these industries in enlarging will take on Europeans. It is History in just the way I love it; - really human and warm, like you, my darling!

'I can't bother overmuch with the Conventions. But I am put out to learn how very tolerant Canadians are over Nixon. *Time Magazine* has recently devoted most of one issue to him and it is read so avidly here that Canadians must be quite happy at the not-too-unlikely prospect of his being President.' (Two days later, on 22 August, Eisenhower and Nixon were renominated by the Republicans to run for the Presidency.)

Next day, having heard from Paula, he wrote a confident letter - a confidence born of relief, perhaps. 'Paula's last letter was a little reassuring. She says she has no intention of breaking up the family yet, if ever. She has not contemplated marrying Jim, though he'd like it. She seems grateful of my offer of freedom and understanding, but wants us to go on living together, so long as it doesn't get too unbearable. Poor girl: not much of a life for her.'

He juggled work for Bowaters, the BBC, the *Geographical Magazine*, the *Yorkshire Post* and CBC all at once. (With glee he told Milena how he spent some of the pocket-money earned from the CBC broadcasts: a pair of galoshes for the Newfoundland forest, nylon underpants, and two drip-dry shirts for when he needed to be smart. And how his teaching would profit: 'My American history has improved about two grades!')

Henry Harrison, aged 84, lived with his sister on their farm 150 miles north west of Halifax. John had heard they were the only two of the Yorkshire stock that settled the land in 1774 who were still on the original holding, granted to their great-grandfather. 'Henry was charming in a beautifully rustic way and tickled pink I wanted to write him up,' John wrote. 'He took me round the farm and then I walked into the forest by myself and gorged myself on huge blueberries. Supper at 5.30 and a good one too, with Henry talking…he calls his animals "critters". The "danged" raccoons eat his ripening corn-cobs. Chews plugs of tobacco and spits black quids. At first he did't know a thing about his early forebears. But bit by bit I extracted good stuff, particularly when his sister brought me a letter written home to Yorkshire in the 1780s by a Harrison, complaining that the muskeetoes were bigger than the English ones and seemed to go for the English more than for other people - a pure jewel for my Yorkshire Post article.'

The Harrisons put John up comfortably and he set off early the next morning to reach Antigonish, about 130 miles east. It was a day of what he called Peak-in-Darienism; apart from boosting his spirits it would enable him to inject his articles and broadcasts with the right flavour. Looking at the panorama, he visualised the north of the province as it might have looked to the first French settlers in the seventeenth century. In warm sunny weather he walked a total of about 20 miles. As in Montenegro he walked on a mountain road, looking down on a coast; this time it was the beautiful Bay of Fundy; he saw fertile farming country, and infinite square miles of forest stretching west.

Late in the evening, after a series of lifts and a busride, he arrived at St Francis Xavier University, the power-house of the Antigonish Movement. 'Settled in by Professor Laidlaw after a cup of tea with dozens of priests (Jesuit) all called Campbell, Cameron, Fraser, McCallum or McTavish. Tomorrow I tour farms and talk about modern methods of co-operative agriculture.

'Antigonish was settled in 1802 by 370 Jesuits from the Hebridean island of Barra, all farmers. It was a revelation,' he wrote to Milena after the visit. 'The Jesuit priests turned out to be radical socialists to a man. Their cooperative movement, started among the poor fishermen and farmers of Eastern Nova Scotia and Cape Breton has extended to most corners of the world. It's most impressive what they've done - or rather what they've made others do for themselves & no Catholic proselytising. I met several of them and talk about fires in the belly: they all burned. Wonderful people.'

Two days later, in Halifax, John had made two broadcasts. On his last day before flying south, he had a worrying task - set by Michael Huxley - to find, and photograph, a descendant of a black slave for one of his articles, about the pattern of communities formed in Nova Scotia since the early seventeenth century.

'I tried to get the 10-12 miles out to the negro quarters, but found the buses weren't running that far. But luck came my way. On the walk over the new suspension bridge across the harbour, with the sun behind me and the bridge looking beautiful over the very blue sea, suddenly five enchanting little negro girls came towards me laughing and singing, dressed rather colourfully. They posed perfectly for me and went on!'

From New York, John wrote crossly: 'A pretty bloody day, all told.' Fog in

Newfoundland had made him miss all his connecting flights to Tennessee. 'You can imagine my mood!

'Last week I inadvertently bit my tongue very hard. Two days later an ulcer formed in my mouth. The two wounds are now so bad I can hardly talk audibly.

'Buttons are falling off my only suit and I've sat on a nail! Darling Milena, fly out and be my wife or I shall have to buy myself a terylene suit before I leave for Tennessee. I look a scarecrow. When shall I have your next letter? Mad social whirl again? Don't forget me, please. I love you always. J.'

★ ★ ★ ★ ★ ★ ★

As early as 1944 Sir Eric Bowater had considered establishing a mill in the United States. By then the newsprint industry, profiting from the cheap electricity provided by the Tennessee Valley Authority's new dams, had revitalised the South. Bowaters' new mill, at Calhoun in East Tennessee, opened in October 1954.

The economy of the Tennessee enterprise was based on the southern pine, which matures for pulping in twenty-five years, three times as fast as the northern spruce or fir. The area had excellent communications. Upstream were three giant TVA dams to provide almost half of the requisite electricity.

'God!' John wrote, 'The heat simply slapped one in the face!' Tennessee, in the Deep South, was a state whose character he had been aching to experience since before he first taught American History; for its Civil War battlegrounds, its Great Smoky Mountains, its colourful birds... and other qualities extolled, I'm sure, by *Farm Quarterly*. He was agog to look at his surroundings, to imagine the devastating soil erosion before the changes made to the landscape by the TVA. From the Buick station-wagon taking him from Knoxville to the mill, he was thrilled to see 'the red eroded gashes healed up, or rather healing up.' He asked the black driver about the TVA; 'Yes sah! De TVA shure has done Tennessee a power o' good, yes sah!' And then a view he was to hear often from the blacks he spoke to: 'De Republicans are aimin' to git deir hands on it and dey won't do de TVA no good, no sah!'

He was given a good lunch at the mill, and a quick tour round, 'which as usual means very little to me except colossal noise, smell and heat'; taken to his hotel to change his shirt; to a drugstore where 'a sort of glorified horse-doctor proceeded to cauterize my tongue and the ulcer on my inner lip. I've seldom experienced such exquisite physical pain.' He was driven a hundred miles to a village in Georgia called Burning Bush, for a barbecue supper (a new word for John, so written in capitals for Milena) with a group of prosperous farmers and their wives. 'Artificial lakes, willows, crickets, dusky servants and yelling farmers, drinking rye and Scotch on the rocks (ice). "Wehll, Jahn, y'ole surn 'v a gurn, ah dew d'clare, doggone it, good to see y'". I listened to some South Tennessean and Georgian accents which are pure music to me.' He ate with delight some "Hursh Purpies"; and procured the recipe for Milena from the cook.

In spite of his 'blasted tongu' on his second day he recorded the voices of farmers, bankers, shopkeepers, railwaymen, doctors. He wanted to include the voices of black people in his recordings, but was refused and lectured at length by the general manager of the mill. (At the time the town of Clinton, Tennessee was under a state of emergency, with attacks on black children on their way to school.) Characteristically, John often had difficulty in restraining himself from speaking his mind to the businessmen he met. 'Si Henry, a mill-man, says: "God must have meant them to keep separate or he wouldn't have made them two colours." But when Si had his tank filled with petrol by a coloured man he patted him on the back and said: "Thanks a lot, old timer." Was he talking to a horse or a man? Sounds awful to me, but I can see their viewpoint.'

'But I love these drawling people; I love this sizzling weather &, darling, you should see these mountains and the rich forests and the red earth. Tomorrow I'm being taken about 130 miles to Atlanta, Georgia and round some forests and will give the broad economic picture of Bowaters' impact on the Tennessee region. I have a terrific program, which includes a carnival on Labor Day, to get money for a baseball pitch when I shall be expected to be very hearty.'

'I bought two pairs of "Wash and Wear" Terylene trousers today at a sale for $5 the pair! That's less than £2. I also bought two gay shirts for £1 each! Fantastically cheap'. (My father loved those trousers. They were made of a horrible floppy greyish-mauve fabric. My mother hated them for the two years one pair lasted; she immediately put the surviving pair in the dustbin. She found my father fishing them out again. 'Really, John!')

John spent another week pleasing Bowaters and accepting Southern hospitality; he made more recordings of local voices, met an old hill-billy in the Great Smokies, saw a six-foot bear rummaging in a garbage bin; he was hurtled to Atlanta for a nude floor-show - and 'got stewed' on mint juleps. He bought a tropical suit in Chattanooga. And 'What a relief' his mouth started to heal.

He was persuaded to go to an Episcopalian service by Jim Henry (no relation to Si), a friendly tree-farmer. While kneeling in the church, he noticed an advertisement for chicken manure on the back of a fan. The devout Jim, when John pointed it out to him, thought about it for a whole day. 'Finally he decided Jesus would not have approved and he's now "awful vexed" about it.'

'I do get to like Americans more and more. AND to admire their extraordinary technological genius. They are materially minded to an astonishing degree and by compensating through tremendous addiction to organised religion, they do it with such sweet simplicity and perfect faith, one can't help loving them for it. They do love their neighbours (except at elections) and they do act in neighbourly ways which I'd find oppressive.

'Did I say Americans love their neighbours? Only white ones. Race riots subsiding at last, though more to come in other parts of the South. At this rate I believe Wm. Faulkner was right when he predicted Civil War.'

For his last few days John was to stay with Howard Johns, his old friend from upstate New York, who with his wife had moved down to the Blue Grass Country of Kentucky. For the ten years since they had first met they had exchanged letters about birds, and John was longing for sightings of the many species which Howard promised him. 'He gets the cardinal all through winter and much of the summer,' Milena heard. 'It's bright scarlet except for a black ring round its bill and eyes. Goldfinches go for his sunflower heads. I saw the red-eyed vireo pecking at the suet and the proud-strutting glistening grackles on the lawn. I saw the gorgeous purple finch and the astonishingly greedy chickadee.'

A couple in their late seventies called Tom and Lucy Usborne (Tom was a distant American cousin whom nobody in the family can now connect - John was the one who had discovered him in 1947) had come down from their small town on the banks of Lake Erie to see John. They had introduced him to the Johnses. Milena heard about a party their hosts gave for them: 'Beautiful evening - as the sun went down the noise of crickets and tree frogs came up. We drank highballs and ate caviare on our cheese biscuits till our host had cooked our steaks and sweetcorn, when we sat down and tucked in. The rector was there and his over-succulent wife who overdoes her Southern drawl and the ice-cream manufacturer who's proud of his English name, Entwhistle and his even honey-childer wife. Sooner than later I was announced as a Socialist, and the target for bombardment. I spent most of my time defending their TVA and kept my temper till Entwhistle said: "I like you Englishmen OK, you're fine. But that Attlee, he put your country back 50 years." And then I became a 100% Socialist and no holds barred.

> 'Today I hope to drive into a wild Kentucky forest and stay there for hours, so that I don't have to listen to Lucy reminiscing about her family or gassing about the Democrats. Elsie Johns is almost stone deaf. Howard goes to his canning factory. Tom is likely to fight Lucy every ten minutes. Yesterday at the wrong moment he announced: "I'm so hungry I could eat the ASS out of a rag doll."'

This was my father's last letter to Milena. There followed instructions on how they would meet four days later at the Victoria Terminal IF my mother, Julie and I didn't meet him at the airport. We didn't...so he and Milena had lunch somewhere and talked, and he stared at her and loved her to distraction.

Chapter Ten

John's letters to Milena were the nearest thing to a diary that he committed to paper. At the same time, – and of course my perception is coloured by pique - his topics seem to be carefully 'edited' to entertain her. Being allowed to read these letters to Milena forty years after they were written, in the course of writing this book, I was to learn from them that she was the main object of his affection. Naturally I was hurt – but of course I was never meant to read them. They had their language for each other.

Julie and I – aged 14 and 16 – were in Laren, Holland, staying with friends of friends. We weren't writing to him, he complained to Milena. 'What a family!' he spluttered on to his airletter. His guilt about leaving us dispersed when our letters eventually reached him – describing our first experience of flying, having to eat margarine like we did at home instead of the good Dutch butter we'd heard about, and a thick tablecloth that seemed to us like a carpet.

John wrote also to California, to his first cousin Jenny, second daughter of Aunt Dorothy and Uncle Hubert. She and my father were a month apart in age. The two of them had had an animated correspondence since writing to each other from their respective boarding schools in 1928. (A letter he wrote at the age of fourteen caused a flurry in the family when it was intercepted by a Benenden mistress; he told Jenny he had discovered the meaning of the verb to fuck.)

Now divorced from her American husband Kenneth Ross, an administrator in the Los Angeles Art Department, Jenny lived on the edge of a canyon above Pasadena, in the foothills of the San Gabriel Mountains. When Ken left her for another woman in 1955, she and her four children stayed on in the bootlegger's cabin that she and Ken had converted early in their marriage. In spite of her domestic and economic struggles, she never regretted leaving England. Her American way of life suited her. She loved mothering, but far away from Englishwomen's frowns; and as a woman, she revelled in her cultural freedom.

Jenny, with ripe-corn-coloured hair and fine-boned looks, had arrived in the United States as a shy young bride in 1938. 'Remember, the great Depression was still on,' Ken Ross told me in 1998, 'we stood in line once a week to buy a loaf of bread for a nickel. Yes! Jenny was a courageous pioneer who had emigrated from security and the English aristocracy to a comparative wild west, where one had to be resourceful to survive.' Since her divorce this shy Englishwoman had made the most of Ken's contacts; she worked at three part-time jobs: Art Critic for the *Pasadena Star News*, Curator of Exhibitions at the California Institute of Technology, and market researcher for the Lou Harris Poll.

Jenny had brought her family's socialist principles to California. She would always be ready – with humour – to encourage a maker of the fast buck to help the less fortunate. When she wrote to John in Newfoundland in August 1956 she was continuing their exchange on the man they both revered, Adlai Stevenson. An Englishman's American? Thrilled that Stevenson had been nominated

Jenny Ross in 1995

Democratic candidate, they were anxious that his health should not let him down as he fought against Eisenhower for the Presidency. Jenny teased John in her next letter, adding a message for Milena: 'Would she mind if John married *her* and brought his daughters to Hollywood to make them all rich?'

★ ★ ★ ★ ★ ★ ★

October 1956 was a horrifying month: the military build-up of British and French troops in the Mediterranean culminated in the British bombing of air-fields near Cairo. On the 23rd, the Soviet leader Nikita Khrushchev, taking advantage of the bated breath of the United States, Britain and France as they looked towards Suez, sent his tanks into Budapest to crush an uprising. In three days of fighting 7,000 Hungarians and 3,000 Russians died because Hungary had dared to ask for an end to Soviet occupation. No other nation came to her rescue.

That month, home again and a few weeks into teaching his new sixth-form sets 'general work', John, as usual, was using - for reliable reportage - *The Times*, *Observer* and *Economist*. 'Wasn't it better,' he asked in the teachers' weekly maga-zine *School and College*, 'that they should mis-spell, mis-punctuate and suffer from word-starvation than go up to the universities with no interests outside, say, chemistry, rowing and sex?' He had started experimenting with a counter-balance by stirring in the opinions of the *Spectator* and *New Statesman*. 'Frequently boys were unsettled and angry at the Socialist view', he continued, 'but on the whole were surprised it could be expressed so genteelly and reasonably.'

'When the Anglo-French forces intervened in the Israeli-Egyptian war,' John wrote, 'I was deeply shocked and, perhaps rashly, said so. What would the Spectator and New Statesman say? The boys waited with excitement. When both were forthright in their disapproval of Eden's decision, about seven-eighths of them were horrified and irate. All the serious papers I'd taught them to respect were against them. In the middle of the following week a form of senior biologists demonstrated their feelings by letting off a small laboratory-made bomb near my desk.'

The bomb went off just as John was coming into the room - but caused no damage. The school authorities did nothing.

Soon after the event, the boy who was the editor of *Folio* brought him some manuscripts for inspection before going to press. John continued: 'There was a pastiche account of "The Bomb Attempt" in which the intended "victim" was referred to as "Comrade X". I pointed out that this was dangerous because some of the parents would think I was really a Communist. This merely amused him. So I committed a whacking indiscretion. I told him that in the 1955 General Election I had voted Tory and it might interest the anarchists to know that.'

'The news [untrue] evidently spread quickly. They were a very respectful and studious lot from then on.' John was genuinely surprised that the view he had expressed often - that a schoolmaster in his position should have no politics - had not been taken seriously by the boys. (Couldn't he see that they enjoyed him as the school's political renegade?)

Many at St Paul's remembered John's disappointment when Gaitskell lost the election. He couldn't resist sailing too close to the wind, because - while he whipped up the drama in a situation - he had the knack of detaching himself from it. He manipulated with ease: 'I made them write essays about art and poetry for a while.'

By gaining a strong reaction to the Suez Crisis from his pupils, John felt that at last his methods were vindicated; but for the moment, the episode and its repercussion provided him with a good article. The pace of his article 'Opening Sixth-Form Minds' was so good, his convictions so plausible, he made such a dashing figure of himself, that the reader could forget he was reading a magazine for teachers.

That autumn I was in my first term at Farnham Art School, and was thinking of not much more than clothes and art materials and skiffle. Lonnie Donegan's number 'Rock Island Line' was of the utmost importance to me. I remember my father muttering about Anthony Eden with icy contempt, but the seriousness of the Suez Crisis went over my head. The horror of the Hungarian Revolution, however, was very real, particularly as three art students from Budapest were taken into my art school.

★ ★ ★ ★ ★ ★ ★

Out of John's trip to Canada a series of four 'Children's Hour' talks called 'Exploring Forests in North America' would be broadcast weekly in May 1957; he would produce four articles for the *Geographical Magazine*. The article - well-written but sober – for Issue Four of *The Bowater Papers*, Bowaters' stylish biennial house magazine, was published a year later.

In December 1956, after a school day, John spoke at the Horniman Museum about birds and frogs. Much of his knowledge of the behaviour of small mammals, birds and insects came from watching them in our garden. In the kitchen one day he had heard a persistent piercing squeal coming from the garden. On the path a frog was being swallowed by a grass-snake. When the snake saw John it disgorged its victim and disappeared. The frog was so paralysed with fear that John was able to turn it over and in three minutes it recovered and jumped away. This event was the subject of FROG'S TERROR, a letter published in *The Countryman* magazine.

He had turned out in 1955 a BBC talk for Schools, 'Growing Corn in the Middle West', which included dialogue between himself and an American, composed from nine-year-old notes. In September 1946 he had been flying over Tennessee on his way to visit steel mills in Chicago. Pointing out the Cumberland Gap below them, the man who sat next to him started to talk. He proudly described the route his great-great-great-grandfather had taken in the 1770s with thousands of other pioneers, over the Allegheny mountains from the east to find new land to farm on the other side. In the prairies, he said, where his ancestors finally settled – corn now grew in place of the grass, and hogs now took the place of buffalo. These flat lands of the north west, beyond Chicago, were now the Corn Belt, the richest farming country of the United States.

The story of Bob Mullard's ancestors pushing west again from their dairy farm in the Ohio Valley fifty years later, after trouble with Indians, touched and excited John. It prompted him, on one of his four hot days in Chicago, to drive out to the eastern fringe of the Corn Belt, where he got a glimpse of huge expanses of 12-foot maize...and no doubt tried to hear (he knew it was possible) the ears creaking as they grew.

His interest in maize had never dimmed since he had first eaten it at the age of twenty-two. Ten years later, in an Illinois farm kitchen on that day out from Chicago, a month after leaving famished post-war England, he had eaten a lunch of corn-fritters and corn-fed ham. Maize was the subject of his first book, published by Rupert Hart-Davis in 1956 as number nine in the *Countryman's Library* series, just before John's departure for Canada.

Within the parameters of its readership *Corn on the Cob* sold well. (Folded between the pages of John's own copy of the book I found a six-monthly royalty statement for June 1961 – six years after publication – for £48.10.6.) It was a very readable handbook for the farmer, the market gardener and the amateur gardener. Like his later book *Unscramble*, it was considered a gem by his friends. 'A book about maize!' his nephews – especially one who is a publisher – still laugh, but admiringly. Monica, John's American sister-in-law, had helped him to compile three and a half pages of corn-recipes, mouth-watering to both of them. Ralph Gabriel, John's old friend and corn-growing colleague, says he knew no more about the subject than John, but remembers 'being consulted' over the 'phone. He still appreciates the humour in the book.

Patrick Harvey was looking for ideas for the BBC's South East Region in November 1956. 'What about the Ghosts of Battle Abbey?' John suggested. They had – he swore – waylaid him when as a small boy he walked along the Monks' Walk (his sister Margaret, who was at school there, says it was called the Ghost Walk) to his organ lesson there. 'Or would you rather wait till 2066?' Another idea, one of six in what must be his wackiest letter to Harvey, was headed 'Way With Pigs': 'This swineherd boasts that his farrowing is achieved with fewer casualties than any other pig man's. He beds out with the expectant sow and gets to know her in a sort of affectionate porcine way. As the piglets are being born he removes them from the vast and unwieldy mass of sow flesh and manages to comfort the old girl simultaneously. He doesn't believe in runts.' "I think not" was written in the margin.

★ ★ ★ ★ ★ ★ ★

For John the winter of 1956-7 was more than usually gloomy. 'Recently I became so overwhelmed with other work that now I cultivate only a small corner,' he told a local reporter, who had asked him about his field. He was tied to his typewriter. Denied fresh air, often feeling 'liverish', he felt his wife and daughters were unsympathetic towards him. 'Oddly enough,' commented the reporter, 'no other member of the family – and this includes Mick the 10-year-old spaniel – shares Mr Usborne's love of the countryside and yen for far away places.' John must have been feeling particularly hard-done-by to have said that. He knew well that Micky took his walks on his own, exploring – and being 'The Lover of Windlesham'.

In the back of John's mind – with the prospect of months of unremitting slog to meet his deadlines – was a plan to spend Easter of 1957 in Dorset with his Aunt Dorothy. 'The Aunt' had been living in Ryall for ten years, with her spinster niece Agnes; she was now sixty-nine – tiny, brown-faced, tweedy, ankle-socks-worn-over-lisle-stockings, sensibly shod. Church and visiting 'problem families' kept her busy. It was time he got on that Royal Blue coach again. She was able to offer him the peace he needed for some difficult writing.

He looked forward to hearing the views of his *Guardian*-reading, radical old aunt. She wouldn't disturb him as he worked in the 'chicken-house' at the top of the garden, with the paraffin-stove keeping it cosy. He would allow the birds around him in the hedges to tempt him out sometimes. With gulls muttering on the thermals above him, he would walk in a sea breeze to the foot village of Stanton St Gabriel and the cliff-edge of the Golden Cap. His bird-charm, his field-glasses and his tape-recorder would be his walking equipment. And at that distance from the bloody Green Belt he could give up shaving...

He would listen to 'old Ag', his cousin, talking of her four Jerseys and milk prices and the Axminster cattle market. A great attraction was the chance to do some of his favourite research: matching the old Dorset speech he had recorded in Newfoundland with that of the old men in 'The Five Bells', the pub in Whitchurch Canonicorum, half a mile down the hill into Marshwood Vale. He had recorded old Charlie Wills, who had been discovered by the Dorset broadcaster Ralph Wightman, singing Dorset folksongs there as he drank the local cider with his friends.

The Easter break helped. He enjoyed writing the 'Children's Hour' talks, espe-

cially because Geoffrey Dearmer was producing them. Animals featured prominently. He ended the second one:

'The Modern Bear
Doesn't Care.
Why should he?'

In August John bobbed up from his writing for a fortnight at 'Camp', the annual
get-together of the Usbornes at Totterdown, Henry and Pam's house in the Vale of
Evesham. Henry had made him foreman to the team of about sixteen fruit-pickers,
made up of Usborne teenagers and their friends; we were picking plums, damsons,
apples and pears - as we had done for the last four Augusts - in Henry's beautiful
eighteen-acre orchard sloping down to the river Avon. The adults lived in the house,
while we, their children, slept under canvas in the small garden orchard.

'Most fruit picking camps are pretty serious and humdrum affairs,' he
said in a broadcast for schools six months later. 'This was different. And the
difference lay in the pickers being my daughters, nephews, nieces and their
friends; in the fruit belonging to my brother, and in the atmosphere being
charged with lunacy.

'It was my job to see that the fruit was picked without pulling the trees
down, sorted without sending the best fruit to the pigs and sheep and the
worst to the markets, and despatched to a variety of wholesalers. At the end
of each day I tried to estimate the earnings of each so-called worker and
pay out. Each picker had a ball of wool, different in colour from every
other picker's wool colour, and was supposed to tie a bit of it to each box
of fruit picked, so that we could identify it at the end of the day, and work
out the wages accordingly.

'But most of them lost their wool or left it in another pair of jeans. One
benighted picker would stick a buttercup on the top of his basket instead,
or a teazel or a clover head...'

The grown-ups were there to celebrate Aunt Dorothy's seventieth birthday. On
the lawn a masque was performed for our ancient granny or great-aunt by us children. Paula didn't come. Her excuse for declining the family reunion was that she
must mind the dog - the fees our local kennel charged were exorbitant. Without
her, John fell easily into the role of the youngest brother, and was teased and fussed
over by his three sisters-in-law. Like a schoolboy, he laughed as he pelted his smallest niece Joanna with little apples as she was in a doorway on the way to find her
mother. He caught up with the family gossip, told his dirty jokes, and played tennis
doubles with his brothers for the first time for years.

★ ★ ★ ★ ★ ★ ★

Apart from his teaching, the pressure of my father's work at home at the end of

1957 must have seemed a wry blessing for him as a means of keeping Milena from his thoughts. She had started a job - as a psychiatric social worker in a South London hospital - and wanted to end their relationship. I remember a winter evening in 1958, when I arrived home from Farnham later than usual and ravenously hungry, to find the house empty and unwelcoming, my supper burnt in the oven; tramping crossly to our sitting-room, opening the door to find my father - grey with cold and completely still - sitting in his armchair, without any heating. The sight of him so still, looking so unhappy, staring into space, stopped me at the door and froze the words on my lips. He only mumbled something, and I think I left him, embarrassed, to go up to my room. Nothing about their relationship was ever explained to me by my parents. The atmosphere at home wasn't fun, it wasn't affectionate; it was quiet and passively angry.

Paula was cruel to John in little ways. She didn't give him enough to eat for supper; he used to get up with a grunt after it and cut himself a hunk of bread. He took to staying in London sometimes for a rest from her nagging and the cold waits for his buses. Alec Harbord, an older St Paul's colleague, and his wife Joan would put him up at their house in Barnes. They enjoyed his visits. Joan told me the little she knew of Paula from John's confidences. "She made him take his shoes off before he came into the house!" He'd known Joan since the war years in Crowthorne; she, I think, was one of the very few at St Paul's who knew of his despair.

Stephen Boyd, a pupil who became a deputy editor of the *Sunday Times*, was a fifth-former in the academic year of 1956/7 - when John was at his lowest ebb. The boys, especially if he won their attention in their first year, brightened his days. The affection was mutual. Boyd said:

> 'He really was like a good deed in the grey, grey world of Fifties London. Most of the masters at St Paul's were frightening either through the ritual and arbitrary misuse of their power or the choleric and violent nature of their personalities. John Usborne had neither of these. His weapons were an urbane civility and wit and an infectious enthusiasm that could charm and hold the most recalcitrant thirteen-year-old.

> 'I'm happy to say that he is the man responsible, some years later, for my becoming a journalist and I still thank him for that most days. This came about when he was teaching me English. One day he set the class the project of writing a scene from a film script. When he came to mark our scripts he announced that anyone receiving a certain mark or over should think about a career in writing. I found that he had awarded me such a mark and the seed was sown.

> 'He was that sort of teacher, actually destined to change the people he came into contact with. I'm enormously grateful to have met him and to have been taught by him. He was also a beacon of elegance in the drab, frowsty Fifties. His lanky figure would float round the school and make even inky little teenagers realise that style and elegance were attainable in a Britain still haunted by the war.

'I can see him now in his classroom, towering over those around him, bald head and glasses flashing in the light, always surrounded by toppling piles of *New Statesman*, a magazine which had a special discount system for students and whose distribution he organised. And he is laughing, something of a rarity for a St Paul's teacher in those days. And there's a buzz in that room that you get when someone is passing on to others something that's important to them.'

Bryan Lask, a consultant child psychologist, told me that he was a real plodder at St Paul's. 'Your father was one of the few teachers, Tony Retallack another, who made me feel good about myself and my abilities.' Richard Rathbone, now Dean of Postgraduate Studies at London University's School of Oriental and African Studies, came to St Paul's as an unhappy child and had a wretched first year there. John and Tony Retallack became immensely important figures to him also.

Tony Retallack in 1995

'Your father introduced me to Coleridge, by playing a magical record of John Gielgud reading 'The Ancient Mariner'; he followed it up by showing us the Gustave Doré illustrations, and only then sent us off to read it. He taught me about the links between Impressionism and Debussy and Ravel, which the hairs on the back of my neck had suggested but which seemed "soppy" to talk about. He introduced me to *Dubliners*, and Tony Retallack followed that up by lending me his, then contraband, copy of *Ulysses*. It was an enormous relief to learn that others, and especially others in gowns, thought that my interests were somehow respectable.'

Playing the piano had been a great comfort to John. Paula had persuaded him that to help pay the bills, our piano should be sold – an awful thing for her to do to him, because she knew that playing it for a few minutes relaxed him when his writing was difficult. She sold it – the old upright Bechstein from the billiard-room at Windrush – to a local school. Since it had gone he heard his music on records, played in the evenings while he marked his papers. He loved Bach, Brahms, Britten. Michelangeli playing Ravel's 'Concerto for the Left Hand' was a marvel to him.

Henry – in his third term as Labour MP for Yardley, and a successful business-man – kept a big-brotherly eye on John. John's other two brothers, enjoying a better standard of living now that their children's school fees were almost all over with, were also concerned about him; in spite of his increasing stature as a broadcaster, after ten years there was no let-up to keeping his writing going alongside his teaching, to make ends meet. The overdraft was no smaller; life was no more com-fortable than before. I was living at home, had a grant, Julie was earning her keep, but Paula still went shopping on her bicycle, and we had never yet had holidays without imposing on family or friends.

'Dear Henry,' John wrote in May 1958, 'We both decided, as soon as I saw the cheque, to send it back immediately. I had had words with my bank about three weeks ago. They've been putting the pressure on to reduce the overdraft and actually taking off £5 per month without my consent. I protested and said Paula was on the edge of another breakdown with worry, which was about true. So they relented and agreed to extend the limit on condition it was back to the original before the end of the year. So I felt it was possible to return your very kind gift. Then in the course of the week – I've been back at school and thus too tied up to write straight away – the nail-biting in the kitchen began again: how are the bills to be paid etc.? So most reluctantly we've decided to accept.

'My earnings from writing are negligible now as the last American trip's almost exhausted and I am spending almost all my spare time organising the next in August and writing educational articles for 5 guineas a time. I am now searching madly for a job. Two came within reach. Both worth a lot of money. I must go back to regular journalism or public relations; preferably foreign correspondent or, second string, educational correspon-dent. My present dualism of teaching and hacking is far too hard work and too little rewarding.'

My parents bought a Mini van, the cheapest four-wheeled car on the market at the time, later that year. John Turner, a pupil from Windlesham to whom John gave a lift up to St Paul's in the early 1960s, was to call it 'the pea-green van'. Paula loved driving and had longed for a car. John only drove on sufferance. (He once backed the pea-green van into his friend Guy Burn's smart car in the forecourt of St Paul's.)

Paula and her mother pined for a better life for us. By now, almost all my par-ents' friends had more ease and security in their lives. A family who had come in

1957 to live in the Dawkins family's old house, became delightful neighbours. Ralph Walker, about seven years older than John, was an engineer, from a wealthy family with property in Argyllshire. (John never discovered where his money came from. Whisky? he wondered.) His wife Katherine had had a tomboy childhood in backwoods Canada; she didn't quite fit in with Paula's glamorous friends. She was girlish and slightly awkward, sandy-haired with a shy gap-toothed smile. Julie and I found her motherly.(Our own mother, I always felt, never wanted to be in her daughters' company for long.) We all loved their Jack Russell bitch Jolly.

The Walkers were wonderfully welcoming to us, having us all to supper often, making each of us feel for a few hours that the Usborne family was doing all right. John and Ralph - who was just retired and was starved of congenial male company - got on well. On cold evenings the two of them would closet themselves in Ralph's study to listen to music and talk at length. They would go out birdwatching together (sometimes as a foursome of two pairs of brothers, with John's brother Tommy, and Ralph's brother Dick). As Guy Burn had been, Ralph was amused by John.

For fun, both men used to keep a look-out for examples of odd and comic writing from the most diverse sources. (In 1959 an idea was forming in John's mind, for an English textbook; he would use his pupils as guinea-pigs.) Ralph revelled in this game and came to be relied upon. Predictably, many of the passages they looked at were American.

One of John's pupils of the late 1950s, Nicholas Bromley, suffered 'relentless American literature in English lessons - too much...but your father was a splendid English master who made it interesting despite the awfulness of having to read *Lord Jim* for a year. In my day at St Paul's there were the sportsmen, the classicists and the great mass of us in the middle. Your father - if I recollect correctly - managed to encompass all these.'

America gave John pleasure that he couldn't restrain himself from passing on. John Turner had to read out loud Alastair Cooke's 'Letters From America' as John drove them up to school. Norman Evans told me: 'He taught me how to pronounce Connecticut!' 'He had a relaxed and adult attitude to teaching,' said Michael Cottrill... in an American way.' (Cottrill remembers him reading the American story *Shane*, by Jack Schaefer, unusual for British students of the English language at the time.) Geoffrey Kendell wrote: 'I even had the excitement of your dad sending my essay on "The History of the Cowboy" to the Cultural Attaché at the American Embassy! Such teachers can make silk purses out of sows' ears!'

Andrew Montagu wrote: 'I particularly remember that if the class had been uncharacteristically good or, more likely, if John was feeling benign towards humanity in general and pre-pubescent hooligans in particular, he would finish the lesson with a reading of modern, humorous literature. These would include P.G. Wodehouse, Ogden Nash, James Thurber and Jerome K. Jerome amongst others. These readings were an excellent gauge of his good humour, the better his disposition, the longer and more uproarious the extracts.'

'He had been one of the first people to impress on me,' wrote Peter Ceresole,' - and on the class as a whole, as there are few more narrow-minded and chauvinistic than the young - that the United States was a place that it might be nice to know, even to live in... He was especially careful to explain to us that the inhabitants of this huge place, of which we'd heard so much, were quite unaware of Europe, and he told us how once, in a petrol station in Kentucky, he had been asked where he came from. "I said England, and he said 'What, New England?' and I explained that it was the other England, in Europe". The gas station man had then said that he had heard of England in Europe, so it must be pretty large. John told us that he had explained that it was smaller than the USA, smaller than Texas, smaller than (I think) New Jersey, at which he had been physically seized to stop him leaving while the man shouted into the back "Hey Joe! There's a guy here says that England is smaller than America!"

'I may have got some details wrong here but I vividly remember John standing like a balding beanpole in his slightly distressed jacket and the first yank-style slacks I ever saw, shouting "Hey Joe!"'

I found the following doggerel in the St Paul's archives in 1994. Entitled 'More random thoughts on marking 5n English', it was for the Summer 1958 issue of *Folio*:

'I still deplore some 5n rabbits
For their unliterary habits.
With microscope it's hard to read
C.Richardson's space-saving screed.
And what could more erratic be
Than Swain's unique orthography?
When Rubens-Rathbone's feeling low,
He dams his rare creative flow.
How disappointing for a chap
Who has so many gifts on tap.
Massara tends to find exhaustin'
All work irrelevant to Austin,
While Trimby's literary taste
Finds all but poetry a waste.
But there are others I could name
Who stoke a thickly clinkered flame
With teaspoonfuls of slag-heap dust;
I'll indicate them if I must.
The Editor, I'm glad to say,
Asked for twelve couplets. I obey.
I'll use my last remaining space
To mitigate the form's disgrace.
I can't help liking you, 5n.
I'm sure you'll all be worthy men.'

'He was, I remember, a teacher who used real things in his lessons,' wrote Robert Friend - who became a diplomat - 'He once brought in a bundle of letters written in violet ink on foreign-looking airmail paper. They were from a school in Krasnoyarsk in Siberia. (Because a friend of his had been going to Moscow, John set his Geography Eighth a project letter-writing to English-speakers in the USSR; these were some replies.) It was then that I realised there were considerable cities and enormous mountains and rivers in the Soviet Union. Before that it had just been a large green area in my school atlas.'

'He treated his 14-year-olds like adults and never imposed his authority by any means other than by the strength and charm of his character,' said Robert Silman, a consultant in Reproductive Physiology, 'I have vivid memories of some of his lessons, e.g. play-acting, where I played an actor manager in Elizabethan times berating Shakespeare for not appreciating the needs of his audience...'

Nicholas de Jongh is now a well-known Entertainments journalist. He told me: 'I have an abiding suspicion your father didn't like me. But I do have affectionate memories of the drama competition which he organised for all the Fifth Form English sets. It was judged by James McKechnie (the now long dead radio actor).

'I played Brutus in the quarrel scene in Julius Caesar. Your father presided over the finals of the competition, judged on a tape recorder. I think that I was judged best performer. It struck me as a terrifically imaginative scheme.'

In February 1958 the Campaign for Nuclear Disarmament was founded. At St Paul's John wrote the leader for *Folio's* Easter issue of 1958 on the H-Bomb, out of frustration at the school's apathy over the issue. The policy of the paper's editors previously had been to keep clear of ordinary politics and international affairs, but his strong feelings inspired him to change, with his article, the look of the front page.

John was very angry with his 18-year-old daughter, too, for treating the Aldermaston March as a two-day party.

(Four and a half years later, in October 1962, Christopher Atkinson, now a teacher himself, was to be impressed by John's anger towards his class when the Cuban Missile Crisis was at its height. 'Of course, as politically naive 13-year-olds, we sauntered into his lesson musing loudly on which of us might be picked to play in some minor school rugby match scheduled for the lunch break. On hearing this he told us angrily that what we really ought to be thinking about that autumn morning was whether we would all be still alive to see the day out.')

As for John's discipline, in the letters I received there are differing views on it... or the lack of it. Keith Howell-Jones, a solicitor, remarked:

'You can mess some masters around; only once did we do it to John. We hid Elliot Berry in the cupboard before John came in. He taught for a quarter of an hour, whilst we were clearly in high spirits, thinking it a huge joke. Suddenly he said, without emotion, "You can come out now, Berry", smiled and then carried on where he had left off. He had worked it out from the beginning. No one felt better or worse for it, he or us. It was a small joke shared, not one of the best, and that was the way to deal with it.'

John Simpson, our distinguished TV war correspondent, wrote to me:

'In 1957, at the age of 13, I was decanted into your father's formroom and observed his tall, rather elegant figure. Later, I realised that he was a profoundly liberal person, though at first I assumed that because he wasn't a tyrant he must simply be lenient: a pushover. I was something of a savage; and when a friend brought in some magnesium wire one day I lit it while sitting at my desk. There was smoke and a blinding light, followed by a dreadful silence. No one even laughed. Your father looked across at me, calm and unruffled. "You're being extremely tedious," he said languidly; "don't do it again." I was shamed by his civilised reaction, and never again misbehaved in his periods.'

★ ★ ★ ★ ★ ★ ★

On 2 August 1958 John 'was Montreal-bound BOAC-wise'. For this six-week round trip of 18,000 miles, spanning Canada, he was to invest his own money in a part of his travelling costs; his stay would start in Baie Comeau, Eastern Quebec, and end in Montreal; stopping just across the border in Westfield, New York; Cornwall, Ontario; Detroit, Michigan; Winnipeg, Manitoba; Vancouver, British Columbia; and the Yukon in Alaska.

The editor of the *Geographical Magazine*, Michael Huxley, had asked John to write three articles: two on the St Lawrence Seaway, which would be opened in June 1959 by the Queen and President Eisenhower; and one on the Peace River power development project in British Columbia. Five new broadcasts for a 'Children's Hour' series, to be called 'Our Canadian Cousins', had been agreed on by Geoffrey Dearmer. *The FBI Review* and *The Economist* were interested. John was to be a guest of the Hudson's Bay Company (after 400 years still British, with its headquarters in Bishopsgate, London) for a week in Winnipeg, while he researched for them for an article on the history of the company.

'A thing that interests me enormously about Canada and the United States is the British way of putting down roots', were the first words of John's 'Children's Hour' series. He continued: 'I enjoy meeting my own countrymen out there and watching their various ways of becoming North Americans, whether Canadian or American. I feel happier about people becoming Canadian than American, because I think a Canadian is usually a delightfully happy mean between us and the American. I feel completely confident about the Canadians. They are too British to be full-blooded Americans and too American to be full-blooded Britons, and that's just how I like it.' Geoffrey Dearmer was obliged to cut the paragraph for political tactlessness.

John's first week in Canada - for his own amusement, and an investment on behalf of his Geography pupils and his 'Children's Hour' listeners - was spent 500 miles from Montreal, at the easternmost extremity of his itinerary. A colony of Scottish Highlanders settling in a French-speaking part of Canada - where the St Lawrence river is so wide you can't see across it - had intrigued the ethnologist in him. Baie Comeau in 1958 was a small town on the North Shore, founded in the 1920s by those Scotsmen who had come to join the aluminium industry. (Canada's aluminium was first manufactured because there was water power to spare from its huge rivers after its use in making paper.) John visited the plant to meet the Scottish employees, study their backgrounds and watch the way they coped with the French language.

Knowing that within a week he would be in urban areas, furiously gathering facts on economics and engineering for his most exacting articles, he escaped Baie Comeau one morning for an early morning walk. 'Turning my back on the new town,' he told his 'Children's Hour' listeners later, 'I saw in front of me mountains and forest exactly as it must have been for hundreds of millions of years. For this is the edge of the Laurentian Shield, the oldest exposed rock in the world. I stood and listened. Not a sound except the throb-throb-throb of the great aluminium smelter.' On his way back to his guest-house for breakfast, he heard 'the Canada bird' (the white-throated sparrow), saw many downy wood-peckers, a slate-coloured junco and an American robin. (The American robin is like an English blackbird, twice the size of a robin redbreast, slate black, with a chestnut breast and white round its eyes.)

A day or so after his early-morning walk, he stood on a tug, midstream, look-ing through his field-glasses: '...the river seemed to me tremendously old and venerable and terrifying. The small whales and large porpoises that cruised past us seemed ancestral rather than new, young, living things. The shrieks of the gulls and the thin whistles of the sandpipers made me too feel thousands of years old. Old Man Mississippi's a kid in comparison. A most uncanny river.'

Back in Montreal he went to work. He followed the river by train to Cornwall, Ontario, to look at the new Seaway and the huge system of dams being built to make electrical power. John's first article on the 114-mile Seaway dis-cussed the geographical and economic background to its opening, from the mid-1940s when it was mooted, to the years between 1947 and 1951, when the American lobby against its building was promoted by all those profiting from the overland transport of American exports. The St Lawrence Seaway Authority was established by the Canadian Parliament in 1951 without securing a treaty with the United States. 'The British Press reaction was one of delight and admiration. "CANADA GOES IT ALONE" said many headlines.

'The second article deals with the engineering problem of the building of the Seaway, and the enterprise as an international achievement. John described the giant machine which lifted and wheeled houses and their contents to new sites, to make way for 30,000 acres needed for a headpond for the powerhouses.

He loved Winnipeg. Its people seemed so friendly and easy going. Hudson's Bay Company, his hosts, added to its charm. Here he became interested in Inuits. Among the people who helped him in his research in Winnipeg, he met a Frenchman of his own age, Charles Gimpel. Charles was the eldest son of a native of Alsace, René Gimpel, a Paris art dealer and friend of Monet, Renoir and Proust. Charles and his brother Pierre - when they founded their gallery, Gimpel Fils, in London - were the third generation of the family to be art dealers.

Charles's wife, Kay, was a Winnipeg girl. He had met her during the last war, in Paris. The Gestapo had caught him there. His health was not good, the result of a year and a half in concentration camps. In Winnipeg in 1958, Charles was preparing for his first trip to the Canadian East Arctic. He had always been interested in the Great North; in his gallery five years earlier he and his brother had mounted an important exhibition of Inuit Art - the first of its kind in Europe. Since then there had been a great demand for Inuit carvings, drawings and prints from collectors not only in England, but Switzerland and France as well. Charles, a good photographer with a passion for sculpture, was off to search for himself. John was intrigued by this eccentric and comic character, a mixture of an urbane art dealer and a lover of the wild.

In 1957 John had bought himself as a Christmas present *Wild America*, a new book by the two eminent ornithologists Roger Tory Peterson and James Fisher. He was fired with the desire to see for himself some of the American waders they described. He hired a Pontiac for a day and drove out of Winnipeg into the Prairies, on a straight, flat road, as far as Lake Manitoba. Here he watched red-winged blackbirds, Bonaparte gulls (like our little gulls in summer), yellow-legs sandpipers and dowitchers (the last species is also a sandpiper, migrating between South America and the Canadian tundra; bright yellow legs, rusty summer plumage.

'As for British Columbia: why did I ever leave it? Or did I? Some part of me is there and one day I must go and collect it.' John was intoxicated, as he'd been in turn by Tuscany, Montenegro, Virginia. This, though, was real wilderness - seen on the eve of mind-blowing changes to be made by man in the Peace River Project.

While he organised his short stay, a London-based economist named Bernard Gore had given him the background material for his *Geographical Magazine* article. (Gore was to be regarded as one of the brains behind the Peace River Project.) From Vancouver, since the early 1950s, industrial development had been expanding massively (in a north-easterly direction because the rivers flowing south from the Northwest Territory provided power), due first to Dutch and, in 1953, British capital. Bernard Gore was the chief adviser to Dr Axel Wenner-Gren, the multi-millionaire Swedish entrepreneur. In 1956 Gore had advised his client to invest five million dollars in preliminary surveys of the Rocky Mountain Trench and the Peace River up to the Alberta border.

John told the listeners to his 'Children's Hour' talk:

'Briefly, there's a long straight trench, running north and south all the way up British Columbia from way down into the States. Flying over it one can hardly fail to gasp in amazement. In the middle of B.C., in the Trench, are two rivers, one the Finlay, the other the Parsnip, which run in opposite directions towards each other and meet at a place called Finlay Forks. Where they join, the river becomes the Peace River. Well, a number of enterprising people are planning to build a great dam across the Peace near Finlay Forks and start a flood in the Trench which by 1975 will have become the biggest man-made lake in the world: 260 miles long and about 15 miles wide. It'll take seven years to fill the new lake and by then they hope to be able to generate 5,000,000 horsepower of electricity and transmit it about 600 miles over the mountains and forests to Vancouver and all the industries that will grow up in the area. It's quite the most fabulous enterprise I've ever had anything to do with.'

Jenny Ross flew up to Vancouver from Los Angeles on 1 September to join her cousin on his five-day inspection of the Rocky Mountain Trench. (Alcan, the Canadian aluminium company, persuaded by Bernard Gore, would foot the bill.) Paula never knew that they met. Apparently, at the early stage of his planning John had expressed to her the hope that Jenny could meet him in Vancouver; and her comment was - according to the letter he wrote to Jenny, inviting her - that she, Jenny, wouldn't be able to afford the flight up there. He had kept quiet; and in that letter told Jenny not to let her know they would be meeting. 'Let's just say, Ann, that they were very good friends!' my aunt Pam, Jenny's sister, said to me on one of our blustery walks together.

A small P.W.A. Barklay aircraft and pilot were put at their disposal, to inspect the dam-sites - and to fly low 'exploring' for uranium. They visited the Peace River at Hudson Hope; and on the third day flew more than 400 miles NW just over the border into the Yukon. They did a little of what bush-pilots are strictly not allowed to do, diving on moose and grizzly bear. One grizzly, he told them, instead of running away, had stood to its full eight feet or so and tried to box the plane out of the air!

On one of their inspections of the Trench, in an area of almost solid anthracite, they measured - 21 inches across - one of six perfect dinosaur footmarks. 'They were so vivid,' John told Geoffrey Dearmer, 'that it made me imagine a sort of Charles Addams cartoon and I hardly dared look over my shoulder just in case...!'

They heard a pop tune while at Watson Lake, called 'Squaws Along The Yukon'. John couldn't resist including three lines of its lyrics in his article for *Folio's* autumn issue:

'Her skin I love to touch
But I just can't touch it much
Because her fur-lined parka's in the way.'

Back home again in September, John found that a satisfactory job in a more lucrative profession was not going to materialise. After 18 years as a schoolmaster, he was realising that his strength lay in his teaching. '...and the less time and inclination I seem to have for earning that extra fiver or two by writing. I find myself wanting to teach more, not less, but unable to teach better also wanting to earn more.'

'He was a honey pie!' Kay, Charles Gimpel's widow, remembered meeting John in January 1959 in London. He went to the Gimpel Fils gallery in Davies Street to hear about Charles's August visit to the Canadian Inuits, and to see his photographs. John recorded part of their conversation, about the history of Inuit carving - of animals, kayaks, sledges - first sold to Scottish whalers in the early nineteenth century as souvenirs of the Eastern Arctic. (It was a happy reunion on that cold winter day; John came away with a small sandstone walrus in his brief-case, which Charles had persuaded him to buy.)

John's idea - to help promote this 'Art made for strangers' - was never used by the BBC, because his recording was of poor quality. He continued to record badly interviews and birdsong. The producers warned each other of this built-in prob-lem of John's - they in turn had been ticked off by 'the quality boys' - but he never could quite accept it. His enthusiasm got in the way. Here's an example:

'Dear Miss Rowley,
    An idea for a light-hearted TODAY triviality. I have a wren in my gar-den which, when it is angry, sings without taking breath for 15 seconds. I have recorded it twice and timed it; I have halved the speed of the record-ing and listened carefully for any breath taken - incidentally the slowed up version of the wren's song is quite exquisite - and I am staggered by the pure physical effort. My idea for a three-to-four minute piece is that I should introduce my recording - or, if it's not up to quality, a better one - and ask listeners to time it; then slow it by half. Finally ask a teacher of singing to explain how he thinks the breathing and voice production is managed. I, an untrained and bad singer, have tried singing loud without taking breath for 15 seconds and find it very difficult. The wren's breath capacity must be about five hundred times less than mine.'

By contrast, without recordings but stuffed with lively material to interest chil-dren, parents and teachers, John's five talks on Canada for 'Children's Hour' were very professional.

His 'dualism' [teaching and writing], after almost 20 years, was a habit; it contin-ued long after the letter he had written to Henry. In July 1959 John offered for a BBC magazine programme a batch of short plays on Abraham Lincoln by some pupils, and - as late as April 1960 - six comic anecdotes about animals. For 'Children's Hour' he set a competition for a ballad about a Canadian bush-pilot; he sang the winner's verse on the air to the tune of 'Marching Through Georgia'. He wrote on Canada for *The Economist*... and regularly on education for *School and College*.

In 1959 John made his final decision to plan for a livelihood that would not depend on a city employer. He knew that he was locked into a harmful way of life that was to a certain extent self-inflicted. He used to mutter about his infer-nal blood pressure. He knew that he was too thin, and suffered from bad headaches, insomnia and mouth ulcers.

In a passage from a talk broadcast in the Home Service's after-breakfast slot in March 1963, he looked back on his career:

    'I chose to be a schoolmaster because I wanted to teach for a living rather than write, as I'd tried to do before. I chose day-school teaching because I couldn't see ourselves enjoying the company of boys and schoolmasters and schoolmasters' wives, however pleasant, enough to stand being with them for more than nine hours in 24, and five days a week. And I settled for a

London school because the money we needed beyond the poverty I'd earn from teaching could best be eked by maintaining my journalistic contacts in Fleet Street and Langham Place. I chose to live in what then passed for country, partly to be as far from my colleagues and pupils as possible, but largely because if I had my way I'd never go near a town.

'I could, I suppose, have given up my London day-school teaching and found a quiet country day-school not too far from my London contacts. But my school is not easy to leave, however one might detest Hammersmith and Baron's Court and the revolting pile one has chosen to work in. It's a good school, make no mistake.'

Keith Howell-Jones, a pupil, listened to the broadcast. 'I felt so pleased to hear him say that,' - he remembered his relief at hearing John's praise for St Paul's. 'It would have seemed to me, then, disloyal and treacherous otherwise. And I think, even now, that he did love his work there.'

Howell-Jones' description of John at the beginning of 1960, to me, illustrates a more contented demeanour. His tension about his politics was gone. I sense that he'd made his decision to leave St Paul's, and was counting his blessings:

'The man was tall, and always dressed with a completely unaffected raff-ishness. He wore crumpled cream linen suits and looked as if he had just come from Havana. He had a slightly languid delivery when speaking. You never knew what he would say next. He was no mere eccentric, or effete dilettante, but a refreshingly different person, with clear, and, to me, novel views on life and the subjects he taught. He taught us what the word icon-oclast meant, and now I know he was just that. He held political views, socialist, which he happily talked about, without proselytising, when Supermac's "You never had it so good" philosophy prevailed.'

John and Paula spent the summer of 1959 together in the British Isles. A happy week was spent with their friends Tim and Haidee Coghill and their ten-year-old son Anthony on a barge, floating from Wargrave to Lechlade and back again. Afterwards he told his radio listeners of his earlier returns to teaching in the autumn after strenuous assignments abroad:

'I have returned to the classroom more bushed than beaten, sustained only by the satisfaction of having first-hand boast-material for A-level geo-graphers and low-level dining out, and wondering when, just when, I would grow up and stop, as Henry Thoreau put it, counting the cats in Zanzibar in favour of water rats and purple loosestrife along the Thames.'

My parents' uneasy truce was holding. Paula had badgered John into admit-ting he needed a rest. His talk about that week, 'Slow Enough for The Times', went out on a Sunday afternoon about 16 months later.

'I brought 10 books with me and for two days fretted because I hadn't brought two others. Perhaps the most lucid symptom of my paranoiac state was that I took the current issue of The Economist.

'It took me about 48 hours to learn that water-rats and purple looses-trife made better reading, better relaxing, better wisdom than all my books. No, not quite all. 'The Scholar Gypsy' improved itself, the country and me with reading. And not only did I not identify the distant Wychwood bow-ers, the Fyfield Elm and Thessaly, but it seemed delightful enough to know they were there.'

My parents went on to stay with the Walker family in Argyllshire for three weeks. Neither of them had seen the Highlands before. That experience also made a talk, for 'Children's Hour'. Geoffrey Dearmer had asked John to look for wildcats, and to write about them. The result was a grown-up talk for teenagers, featuring wildcats, eagles and deer, based on the exciting stories of three game-keepers.

Julie, at the age of 17, went to Paris for a year and worked au pair for three successive families. Her letters home were entertaining. From Neuilly she described being watched from the balcony by the monsieur as she dressed in the morning. Her grasp of French was quick - she had an actress's ear, developed at a school where drama was important.

At the end of 1959 I was in my fourth and last year at Farnham Art School, and was now living in the town. (Did I tease poor tired old Daddy about having my own top-of-the-milk at last? For years he had pinched it for his breakfast cof-fee.) To protect me from the uneasy atmosphere at home, my father wanted to send me to the United States. He and Peter O'Connell, a young colleague who had taught in Massachusetts, pulled some strings for me: St Paul's, Concord, New Hampshire (no relation) - one of those prosperous Ivy League prep schools - cre-ated a job for me in its new Art Department.

Chapter Eleven

Signing himself 'Idealist' in 1961, one of John's pupils wrote for *Folio*:

'Macmillan has not cares nor woe
From politics he shirks;
He leads an easy life to show
That "Tory Freedom Works".'

Like John, his brother Dick was at both Macmillan's prep school and his Oxford college, Balliol. Before Macmillan's Government - I asked him - had he ever had it so good? 'Yes, my three years at Balliol in the early nineteen-thirties.' he said, 'I had no idea that there was a war coming. I worked hard and played soccer and tennis for the College in season; I had no guilt - but I much appreciated my privileges.'

(Three of John's nephews were at Balliol in 1960.) John also, his colleague Philip McGuinness told me, 'was pleased with Balliol'. His contentiousness, bred in him early by holding his own in argument against three older brothers, was perpetuated by the College's disputatious tradition. He was sentimental about contentious and combative men in the past and his own day; men who agitated, who were philosophers and journalists of protest - such as Edmund Burke, William Cobbett, Richard Jefferies, Henry David Thoreau, Fred Hoyle. He thought them better still if they were countrymen. (Cobbett, 1792-1835, had all the right attributes: he farmed in both England and the United States, he was a naturalist and a bird-lover; he hated London; he knew well the downland part of Berkshire which John loved; and he brought maize home to England.) From 1942 and his gauche efforts by reading to his first pupils about the Irish revolutionary Eamon de Valera, John encouraged his Paulines to rebel.

In July 1960, when 'the dog-days of the summer trail heavily to their end', he was, as usual, getting rid of some frustration on to his typewriter. He had narrowly avoided a Common Room argument with classicist colleagues about the state of arts teaching: 'We are a thoroughly third-rate lot,' he wrote. 'To have kept this stuff about the Delian Confederacy and the private speeches of Demosthenes going for about four and a half centuries is the mark of third-rateness. If man's mind is clever enough to produce rockets to go round the sun and land on the moon, it is clever enough to learn how to deploy man's inexhaustible vitality in the arts of world peace.'

He enjoyed introducing his 14-year-old Londoners to the beauty of nature: 'They MUST keep their eyes and ears open. After a whole period on Wordsworth's 'My Heart Leaps Up When I Behold', I accuse all the readers of never having seen a rainbow in the sky. "But, Sir!" they protest. "No, no!" I say, "you couldn't have or you wouldn't have read that poem like that." One day, while I was on that act, a mistlethrush began to sing from the plane tree outside my form room. I could see at once that not one of my pupils had noticed it. I paused and remained silent for a few seconds. "Something tremendous has happened," I said solemnly. And I held my finger up. Gradually the whole form cottoned on. "A miracle," I whispered, "specially for the Lower Fifth." And then, while they were still bemused, I re-read 'My Heart Leaps Up'.'

'I have a dog.
I have a dog, which bites. (My dog bites.)
I have a dog, which, though it looks harmless, bites.
(My harmless-looking dog bites.) (Some dogs that look harmless bite. Mine does.)
Although some dogs look harmless, some, including mine, bite.'

Called 'The Sentence', this was John's introduction to his book *Unscramble*, which was to be published by Hutchinson Educational in October 1961. The idea inspiring it had come to him a year or so earlier, from the suspicion that most of the boys in his English classes had never properly learned to read. When he set them chunks of prose "for comprehension" he realised that the long words - instead of acting as a stimulus - had the effect of a narcotic.

While writing one day he hit on an experiment to help himself reproduce the gist of a passage. 'From an article in the *Spectator* I took one paragraph which contained very interesting information, some history and some wit conveyed in middle to high-brow English. I left the first line at the top and the last at the bottom, but jumbled all but two or three of the rest in such a way that only an alert, trained reader would see at once that it was meaningless. I shall try it on a Sixth Form. First I shall note who is the first to find it meaningless, and then I shall set them all to unscramble it. They will enjoy it as a parlour game, of that I'm sure. But they may, if I continue with the game, find themselves not only learning interesting information, history and wit, but the habit of being permanently unfogged and demisted.'

The Sixth Form guinea-pigs unscrambled a few texts from John's eclectic choice of writers: Cicero, Bunyan, Milton, Jane Austen, Rex Warner, Harold Nicolson, Max Beerbohm, Julian Huxley, S.J.Perelman, journalists of the *Observer*, and writers of small-ads in American newspapers.

I remember, as a teenager, urging my father to read a book I'd liked, and being told almost proudly: 'I don't read right through a book these days. Maybe I will when I'm retired...' At the time, he was telling his radio listeners: 'I realised that I was growing illiterate, but now, far from feeling guilty about it, I am growing querulously uneasy about the very foundations of conventional literacy.

'Every summer for years I've read Julius Caesar, because it's one of the best Shakespeare plays for my 14-year-olds, and it's often set for 'O' level. I must say I'm very fond of it, though I think it a bad play, and hardly a page but I find myself excited and enchanted by the luxury of talent that the man devotes to the old story.

'But enchantment is the word that counts here, the dangerous trap that the great magician sets for all who value literacy. The other day, I was listening excitedly to a broadcast of a production of the play, when I was summoned to meet a daughter off a London coach. I drove fast, and when we returned I was still keen to go back to Shakespeare.

'But, as I was walking up the path, I heard a nightjar churring. Somehow that sound in the dark wood was more important to me than what had kept me in suspense a few minutes before. And I stood by the wood in another, deeper enchantment, knowing that no poet, try as he may, could put into communicable words the urgent truth that was coming to me over the night air.

'Of course, the poets have always been nearest to it. Wordsworth waxed lyrical about a lesser celandine, a violet by a mossy stone, and so on. But they enchanted him to cultivate the vacant and pensive mood on a couch indoors, and to think he'd hit an artistic jackpot.

'It so happens that along a hedgerow in my garden there is a patch of lesser celandines. About two Septembers ago, after planning some of my teaching for the Michaelmas term, I was on my knees with a pair of sheepshears shearing down the long grass at the foot of that hedgerow. About every square foot, as I rolled the grass back, I found a nest of about 40 slugs' eggs among the celandines, off-white soft things like medium-sized pearls. Now what about old Wordsworth? I thought. Did he ever see this?'

David Richardson, a pupil of John's, told me that by organising a talk about *The Times* by a member of its staff, John, by dint of a couple of telephone calls, brought a breath of fresh air into a timetable that was at times stiflingly traditional. Bradfield had done it for him and his classmates and he remembered the thrill of it.

Showing the boys the workings of journalism was - apart from his English lessons - a spur to encouraging them to write. *Folio* - which John nurtured for eight years - was their vehicle. Once a boy had published an article or a poem in Folio, John knew that the spark had ignited.

It was difficult recruiting contributors and helpers for *Folio*; Once a boy joined the staff, he was expected to show John his determination - and that he could be relied upon. John gave a little advice on layout, but otherwise left the boys to run the paper themselves. Robin Pumphrey, David Aukin, David Brown, Nigel Maslin, Elliot Berry, Michael Cottrill, Robert Friend - each speaking independently - told me how much they enjoyed the freedom John gave them.

As St Paul's 'unofficial' Newspaper, *Folio* became - according to one of its editorial team - 'rather scurrilous and even anarchistic.' Usually this was a stance taken in reaction to a High Master who had many strong critics among the boys. He was a man too shy and self-conscious ever to be popular with teenagers. In those days,' David Aukin, now a director of a film company, told me: 'we had an awful High Master called Mr Gilkes; the name has a Dickensian ring and he was indeed born out of his time. He tried to instil an atmosphere of muscular

Christianity which of course was accompanied by regular beatings of little boys.'

(Gilkes had allowed four boys to interview Field Marshal Montgomery in John's classroom in the summer of 1959. At the time Monty was probably the school's best-known Old Boy; he had come to inspect the school's Combined Cadet Force. 'I never wanted to go to University,' he told David Aukin, 'I would only have learnt to be idle.')

Equipped with John's Stuzzi Magnette tape recorder, 'a little band of "Folio" pilgrims' paid a visit in 1962 to the offices of the new satirical magazine *Private Eye*. One of them was John Simpson, aged 18, the paper's editor. Nicholas Luard, drinking Scotch, gave them a rather pompous interview. 'Private Eye', Willie Rushton boasted, 'is taken by the British Museum, Mr Butler, Randolph Churchill, John Betjeman, the Bishop of Rhodesia and sixteen or seventeen thousand others.'

As President of St Paul's Tennis – his role from 1947 to 1963 – John used *Folio* as a means of fighting for recognition of the game as a school sport. (At the time, Millfield was the only school known outside educational circles for its tennis.) While reviewing the progress of his teams, whetting the curiosity of non-players, John enjoyed some sports-writing. In an article in December 1957, he cherished the loyalty of his tennis-players and urged them to resist being poached away to play cricket; he mentioned his own 'rabbiting' – playing tennis for his school between cricket matches. St Paul's First VI had won the Youll Cup (the Blue Riband of public school tennis) twice during his Presidency, he boasted – that summer and in 1955.

Roger Ambrose – now the Club Secretary of the All England Lawn Tennis Club, Wimbledon – was John's Tennis Captain in 1958. There being no tennis courts at the West Kensington school, the boys played on four courts made available to them at Queens Club, a few minutes' walk away. They played during lunch breaks, and on sports half-days. (John loved playing at Queens himself, and did, as often as he could.) His teams briefed and consulted him at his classroom tennis meetings; otherwise they were left to organise their teams themselves.

David Martin was appointed Captain in 1960, the year John was to pronounce the best for tennis the school had known. David's parents were keen tennis-players, living in London, and in 1956 they chose St Paul's for him with its good tennis reputation as a criterion. Looking back, he feels that, at the time, St Paul's offered him a unique opportunity.

★ ★ ★ ★ ★ ★ ★

It was extraordinary for me, impressed already by my father's journalistic energy, to discover at a late stage of my research a treasure trove of 64 more articles by him, written between January 1957 and April 1964. The name of the magazine, *School and College*, didn't register itself on my mind at the time he was writing for it. My father was usually at his typewriter, writing; what about, I didn't ask.

While I was searching – in a London University library – I looked for his name in the contents lists of about six issues of 1960. (The magazine was published monthly.) It didn't appear. I knew he was in there somewhere. Another name,

Peter Gascoigne, occurred very frequently, I noticed. I turned to one of his articles, entitled 'Moods and Dreams of Masterly Rebellion', and read a few lines. Immediately two little references, unmistakably my father's, jumped off the page at me: 'At this time of year I need my Thoreau' and 'I have little hair to tear out'. I laughed out loud.

By comparison, his radio talks often seem mild, almost 'easy listening'. In these articles, hiding behind another name, he was able to be controversial or playful and chatty. Using a pseudonym was a common thing in those days and for his purposes - literary and emotional - it was essential. Even with the pseudonym, his tact is skilful. St Paul's was described and its methods were cited often, but in the Peter Gascoigne articles, never by name. A few days later I discovered that for all those years the articles were a secret John kept from his colleagues. Tony Retallack told me that *School and College* was never read in the Masters' Common Room at St Paul's - indeed he hadn't known of it. Mr Gilkes, however, would probably have had ex officio copies of the magazine in his study, if only for him to read its profiles of other headmasters of British Independent and Higher state schools.

The themes of eight Usborne-signed articles were safe enough for Mr Gilkes's eyes. One described the Old Boys' Day cricket match played at Summer Fields, in 1959 (Gilkes was a keen cricketer). Another, 'New Broom for Punctuation', a well-known hobby horse of John's, may have made him snort. Two advertised books, one gently promoting *Unscramble*; another described the meeting at St Paul's of Paulines and American schoolboys. 'Royal Visit Backstage' was short and light-hearted, about the school's preparations for the Queen's visit in 1959, and John's amusement that he had hardly noticed them. 'Never since Bluff King Hal had there been a better-looking or more popular partner in top royalty than Prince Philip; never has there been, to the youth of England, such an attractive Queen as the one who, on Friday, May 22, spent two and a half hours watching a privileged fraction of that youth trying to pretend they were behaving as they would any other day of a school week.'

Sometimes, of the Gascoigne-signed ones, an article's link with teaching is tenuous: the theme of 'Seasonal Philosophy' is birds, slugs and earwigs; but it has John describing how on July nights 'edgy and depressed from long bouts of exam-marking, my buttocks itching from inhibited circulation, I torch my way through the holly hedge to look at my maize.' One concentrates on his weary summer dog-days: 'Is it only me that sees the classrooms and passages full of sheep?'; in another he's crabby: 'If schools were as good as they ought to be, I wouldn't have got my job.'; some are anxious for his pupils - and searching on the parameters of a subject: 'Must I teach History?'. Howlers and pre-exam worries are remembered: 'Please, Sir, you wrote on the top of my last essay: "You won't pass anything till you improve your vocabulary." What can I do about it now, Sir?'

In a 1960 article entitled 'Wrastling with Unpleasantnesse' - (title by John Aubrey, 1626-97) on the writing of end-of-term reports - John described quite accurately, several years before such a thing existed, a word processor database. 'For 1,100 years, three times a year, regiments of tired, undernourished, myopic polymaths have gnawed the ends of their quills and squeezed out scintillating epigrams... "The Infernal Machine" would contain thin rolls of paper bearing a termful of the master's comments, in his own code, on each of his pupils. 'At a button-touch each name will light up prominently...a graph of every pupil's progress - or otherwise - is drawn electronically as the term moves on and at the end of term it has a spool completed which is sent in a special container to the parents.'

He was delighted, in this article, to publish a salty report, filed away for just such an opportunity. 'Once in a moment of rebellion I wrote of a boy whom I not only knew by sight but remembered to have shown no talent or industry throughout the term:"He is egg-bound, and if he doesn't lay the blasted egg early next term, I will ask the Head Beak to cull him." It got no further than his house-master, who framed it and asked me to be more sensible.'

He airs his feelings on the personality a teacher should project: 'First, make it quite plain you are on their side and haven't yourself completely grown up. Then try to appreciate the strains and exhaustions and excite-ments of growing up in a school environment, and having done that, try to get no more out of them than you calculate they can give at the time. Rhythm works here as in all else, and a child's is more complex than an adult's.

'My pupils are more attentive on Monday mornings, not because of my teaching but because they are chastened by the thought of a full week before them, physically tired by the weekend and relaxed by the fug that has been building up in a heated, window-shut classroom for the past two days. I must open windows figuratively and physically all round...It is important to know what lesson they have just had and with whom and it is no less important to take the temperature with regard to the day's sport-ing events.'

★ ★ ★ ★ ★ ★ ★

While I was away my tiny bedroom became my father's study; from his desk he had a good view - with his field-glasses handy - of his Allington Pippin apple tree and the birds in its branches. Julie told me recently that the atmosphere changed radically at Sandy Lane Cottage after the death of Micky in the autumn of 1960. It was a terrible blow, particularly to my father. When he was away from his work, field or garden, Windlesham was made bearable for John by the proximity of Ralph and Katherine Walker. According to Katherine - with their daughters away and Micky dead - there was tension between my parents whenever she went to our house.

The Walkers found Paula flighty. (Why should Katherine and she have any-thing in common? A girl from the Canadian wild and a Sydney socialite?) But they gave John some peace. On his way home, even on days when he drove the van up to school, he would call in on them - only three minutes short of our house. There he would sink into one of the armchairs in Ralph's study, allow Jolly to jump into his lap, and fall asleep.

In 1958, probably at the Glanvill Cup Final at Queen's Tennis Club, John met Jack Meyer, maverick, sportsman, schoolmaster, gambler, philanthropist and eccentric. He met him often again. 'Boss', as he was known, had founded Millfield, his school in Somerset, in 1935, one of the pioneers of the English co-educational system. It had an extraordinary success. Meyer's magnetic personality, his brilliance at individual teaching, and his accent on the glamorous sports charmed the international élite to send their children to him.

Meyer offered John a job on his staff, very likely at their first meeting. John's morale was given a very necessary boost by the compliment. The job would have brought him a better salary, more appreciation of his talents, smaller classes, country air. But he declined, after much thought, because he had already decided to move to the United States.

In September 1961 the Berlin Wall was rising. During a huge Ban The Bomb demonstration in Trafalgar Square 850 people were arrested. Under *Folio's* headline 'Stop The World...We Want To Get On!' Nicholas de Jongh, aged 17, reported: 'The hoardings scream their message: Signpost to a sane world. The black and white posters no longer surprise us. Vanessa Redgrave sits down again. Canon Collins leads new delegations. Fifty megaton bomb alarms committee of 100. Earl Russell warns Government.'

At school, John encountered the new bottom class of the school, 'the notorious and evil 4b'. Robin Dodd was a member of it:

'We had a particularly nasty way of ragging masters. Three boys would start a diversion in the back, then I would start up from the front row. I would put my hand up, smile and ask an innocent question, but frame it in such a way that it would send the class into hysterics. The art was to do it in such a way that the master couldn't accuse you of anything, rather like the House of Commons!

'One day, we really gave it to John Usborne, and I remember, he sat at his dusty desk, put his head in his hands, and said words with such feeling that Laurence Olivier would have been proud: "Oh My God, 4b!" The class whooped with delight, the bell rang, we made our usual exit, trampling and tipping over everything, and playing a few notes on the old upright piano by the door - that would always wind him up!'

'What ARE you doing?' John had shouted at a class of Fifth-Formers five years earlier, Christopher Musk remembers. John gave them an English lesson on Monday afternoons. The boys were dressed in their uniforms in readiness for 'Corps', immediately afterwards. Their berets were put carefully on their desks. One day, at a signal, they started polishing their brass beret badges, with increasing momentum, between their serge-covered thighs.

Unscramble, a small mushroom-coloured paperback costing four shillings and sixpence, was published in October with hardly a murmur. It fell between two categories: a textbook and a puzzle-book for literary adults. At the time of publication, apart from the publisher's advertisement in *The Times Educational Supplement*, there were no reviews, until six months later, in *School and College*, a favourable one from a teacher. John received an advance of £40 against royalties of 7.5% on the first 10,000 copies sold. It was in print for ten years.

About his job in the autumn term of 1961 I found the most glowing lines in all John's writing about teaching: '...those glorious days in October and the first half of November when you're sticking to the plan you drew up, on average, on September 7th, and you're actually looking forward to next week, and the boys are making highly satisfactory progress, and you tell them so, and they believe it, and you apparently have no morons this year at all, and the thrushes have started singing again.'

His approach to Geography, though, was getting him into trouble. Michael Orlik, in his last year at St Paul's at that time, remembers that John was obliged to stop teaching the subject after a complaint to the High Master by the father of a fifth former. He was given a History class to teach instead.

In an article earlier in the year about Geography as a study, John had written:

'It is precisely because the teachers are honestly dissatisfied with the methods by which they have studied and are trying to teach what they know to be at the apex of all education that they are steadily drawing off pupils from the older, smugger, effete courses, which have known their definitions so long that, like honi soit qui mal y pense, they have forgotten the translation or ceased to find it relevant.

'Geography holds the key in education to peaceful co-existence. The more, as a geographer, one studies man in his environment, the less dogmatic, the less hubristically scientific, the more humble one becomes in one's search for peace.'

★ ★ ★ ★ ★ ★ ★

For years, Eric Wiseman – the man who brought parties of New England schoolboys over to meet their counterparts in England –had been bullying John to find himself a teaching post in the United States. In January 1962, with the help of a letter from Eric explaining to him how much of his salary, to the last dollar, he would save each month, he made his decision: to accept a post teaching English at Woodberry Forest School, Virginia.

Lilian Moore of the English Speaking Union clinched the post for John. Baker Duncan – the 34-year-old Texan stockbroker who had recently become headmaster of Woodberry Forest School – favoured Englishmen for his English department; he was at the time looking for a teacher of John's stature. He had good connections in England with schoolmasters; he told me recently that John was suggested by several of them. He came to England frequently, and probably met John at St Paul's. He may even have watched him teaching.

'I regret to say it's the money that talks loudest. I look forward to the mocking-birds and that gorgeous drawl and the weather. But without the money, they wouldn't have got me.' 'I've been putting it off, shaking it out of my system for at least ten years. But now I'm forty-eight; if I don't go in 1963, it will be too late. If I'm sensible with money, the prospect is thirty-six terms on a private estate in over a thousand of the loveliest acres I've ever seen, thirty-six terms of teaching only what I most enjoy teaching, for eighteen periods a week instead of twenty-three.'

Those lines were published a year later, when John had still only seen Woodberry Forest in photographs. He and Paula planned that he should spend the first year there on his own. Paula would put the house up for sale as soon as John was sure the job suited him; he would return in July and together they would go back with all their worldly goods in August 1964.

★ ★ ★ ★ ★ ★ ★

John had more writing on Henry David Thoreau than on any other man. He was determined to have one last attempt at a broadcast on him. In 1949 his offer to 'Children's Hour' of a Thoreau package - a talk and a homemade medley of Massachusetts woodland sounds - was rejected. A year later he recycled that talk, plus the noises off, into a lecture at St Paul's. In August 1951, straight from the dock in Boston after his tramp-steamer crossing of the Atlantic, he had made a pilgrimage to Walden Pond. Turning a blind eye to the hoardings and hot-dog stands, he had stripped off his clothes, jumped in and exulted. He had put a stone from the bottom of the pond into his haversack as a souvenir.

'I think that did it,' he said. In his talk in May 1962, to mark the centenary of Thoreau's death, he described how his view of Nature had changed during those 11 years. (From his 1950 vantage point John had asked: 'What is nature? It has a capital N. Bee-loud glades and lake water lapping and Thoreau, as someone had said, getting more out of ten minutes with a chickadee than most men could get out of a night with Cleopatra...one falls for a lesser celandine; one's heart leaps up at a rainbow and a wee, tim'rous mousie, and one knows what one wants to escape to.')

'Thoreau's 'private business' was the tricky one of watching himself, a man with a capital M, in the setting of Nature with a capital N, he thought. Thoreau wasn't escaping at all. He was facing. Facing the fact of his own and all men's dislocation.'

Another Thoreau-worshipper was the great American satirist and humorist E.B.White. This was one of the many components of John's admiration for White. (All the four Usborne brothers and their sister admired him. "Those literary coves!" said Henry, the businessman and campaigner for World Government, of his siblings; his admiration for White was tuned differently.) White contributed ballads, sketches, reviews and picture captions to the *New Yorker* in his early twenties; for about a decade, anonymously, he wrote its opening page of editorial. During the Second World War, with his characteristic good humour, he stated his case for Federal Government; the four editions of collections of these comments from the *New Yorker*, called *The White Flag*, became famous books.

E.B.White had been taught at Cornell University in 1919 by a certain William Strunk Jr; a professor who made required reading for his students a little book on English usage called 'The Elements of Style', written by himself and privately printed. 'T.E.O.S. was Will Strunk's parvum opus,' White wrote, 'his attempt to cut the vast tangle of English rhetoric down to size and write its rules and principles on the head of a pin.' When he was 58, E.B. White wrote a piece about the book for the *New Yorker*. 'The editors of Macmillan', he told us, 'got hold of [a copy] and arranged to re-issue it, using my article as an introduction. They asked me to make revisions in the text, and write a chapter on style, and I have done both these things.'

'If you use a colloquialism,' Strunk advised in his chapter 'The Elements of Composition', 'simply use it; do not draw attention to it by enclosing it in quotation marks. To do so is to put on airs, as though you were inviting the reader to join you in a select society of those who know better.' 'A wise little book,' says Dick Usborne of what he calls "Strunk and White". (John's copy - with annotations illustrating his enjoyment of it - was given to him by Paula after John's death.) It's clear - and the timing of its publication is right - that the spirit of *The Elements of Style* had something to do with the flavour of John's book *Unscramble*. John didn't care whether his book was a success or not. He'd done it, that was all.

John sent his Thoreau script to E.B. White, asking his permission to quote him on their hero. 'I think you did very well by HDT in so short a space,' White replied, 'and I am happy to be in there.' In 1963 one or two philological worries and the news that he was using some E.B. White prose in English examination papers gave John the excuse to write two more fan letters. White rose to the bait and produced two charming letters in return. Asked whether he remembered his old professor's rules about the pronoun "one", he didn't - but added: 'As for me, I try to avoid the impersonal "one" but I have discovered that it is like a face you encounter in the streets and can"t always avoid bowing to.'

★ ★ ★ ★ ★ ★ ★

In the summer of 1962, a few days after John had given in his year's notice to Gilkes, he and Paula set off in the pea-green van to the French Riviera. They were to have a short stay with Eric Wiseman and his French wife Marinette in their rented villa at St Aygulf. In spite of the hours of shared driving in an uncomfortable car in boiling August heat, they had a good holiday. John had been edgy, panicky, overworked as usual, Paula preoccupied with her ailing mother, now - to John's irritation - living in Windlesham. Away from their cares for a couple of weeks, they got on well; with the Wisemans they made a good foursome, eating out, celebrating America and John's decision. Paula, apprehensive about leaving England, was cosseted and reassured.

Both adored the hot sunshine. They drove on, along the coast to the Costa Brava - hardly developed then - taking a few days en route. They would stop to swim if a beach looked inviting. Paula was a good French-speaker, a strong swimmer and a strong car-driver, all things she did better than John. Her self-confidence revived. For the first time for years she could bask on a beach in the sun, being reminded of the beautiful beaches of her Australian childhood. John took with him a few books to dip into, a scholar's choice, to suit the places he planned to visit. Paula photographed him holding a fat edition of *Imperial Caesar* by Rex Warner ('*Really*, John!' I can hear her saying, watching him load it into the van) against his chest, sitting on the balustrade of their hotel balcony, looking out to sea.

I had arrived home from California in May. We were all four based in Windlesham that summer. Julie, aged 20, had recently - because of her aching legs - resigned from a job at Sandersons in London, giving advice to customers on décor. I had discovered that, to find the work I thought I wanted - neither in teaching nor in Fine Art - I would have to take a fifth, post-graduate year in printing and graphic design. I was an expensive daughter.

Julie had been badly ill while I was away. From a small child she would often complain of leg-ache; sometimes she would be put to bed to rest, missing school. I had never seen her during her bad psoriatic arthropathy flare-ups. At the end of August, after weeks of drought and no end of it in sight, she and I decided to take our bikes over the Channel, and work our way west from Dieppe to Fécamp and back. In spite of fears that the trip might be too much for her, she wanted to go. We both had romantic visions of the Normandy countryside: easy biking along sun-dappled roads, living on bread and camembert and cider, helping ourselves to apples from the orchards. Planning to sleep under the stars, we took no tent, just our sleeping bags. We spent only two and a half days away; on the second night we were caught in a deluge as we were dropping off to sleep under a tree. Soaked to the skin and our teeth chattering with cold, we caught a bus the forty kilometres back to Dieppe, and took a room in a pension while our clothes were dried for us in its kitchen. We caught the next ferry home. Soon afterwards Julie spent several weeks in the Middlesex Hospital.

★ ★ ★ ★ ★ ★ ★

'What have I gone and done?' (John never expressed his worry about Julie in the letters he left, but I know it weighed very heavily.) He made enough of his other emotions, panic and sentiment, for an article - entitled 'Hold Me Tight, England' - at the end of the autumn term. He had suffered several black days, hating the thought of going to America. Of his colleagues and pupils, only the 14-year-old John Turner knew of his decision. 'I don't know why I don't want anyone to know. It could be that they won't approve of my going for the Big Yank Fleshpots, of taking even the first steps to becoming an American citizen.

> 'This Christmas will be my last in England for at least twelve years, pos-
> sibly for ever. Last night I saw my last Maigret, and this coming weekend I
> shall use my cider-press for the last time. Tomorrow I give my finger-prints
> to the American Consul in Grosvenor Square.'

At Woodberry Forest he was to teach, in his own words: 'the top two thirds of the top (sixth) form, 52 boys divided into four classes, English lang. and lit. only, and all aiming at the best universities.'

During John's last year in England, 1962-3, his brother Dick was assembling contributions from Old Summer Fieldians for his book on their old prep school, *A Century of Summer Fields*. Dick told me that John sent him a long piece, well written - but in a teasing vein: 'If you were in a tight corner on a battlefield you could rely on the Summer Fieldian...' Dick said no to it- and never afterwards quite convinced himself he had done the right thing. The governors of Summer Fields, who had commissioned the book, would not have been pleased, he thought. It was the only piece that wasn't right,' he said. 'It was trenchantly true...more of a Guardian piece.' John was hurt. Tommy got it wrong too, Dick said; 'sounding off about roses... page after page on roses with Latin names. But Tommy wasn't a writer; John was.'

'I confess I am an escapist,' John told listeners to a talk he gave a few months before he left St Paul's. 'I feel sure I shall be able to teach better where I'm going. Teaching Vergil and Milton there...will, for me, harmonise far more closely with growing Virginian peaches, big black figs and Country Gentleman Sweetcorn. Almost never to worry about money, about not keeping pace with the work, about the tax man.'

One of *Folio's* reporters interviewed him. What were his reasons for leaving? There were three, he said: that he felt he was growing into a rut in his teaching, and Virginia would give him great scope for experiment; that he wanted a warm climate, and to get away from cities. The last was money. 'What do you want to do when you retire?' he was asked. 'I want to potter, to study ecology, to live in Dorset in a large garden, and write a book or two.' His 21 years at St Paul's were celebrated in *The Pauline* in the autumn. 'He will be sorely missed in the Common Room, which will not be the same without his wonderful laugh, audible however crowded the room, his unassailable good-humour, or the supply of apples or Indian corn or sticks of celery, with which he would unexpectedly fill one's pigeon-hole. He is the right man for America. His countless Pauline friends wish him well and will miss him badly.'

★ ★ ★ ★ ★ ★ ★

Woodberry Forest School lies 85 miles south-west of Washington, in the piedmont country near the Blue Ridge Mountains. Orange is its nearest town; Charlottesville, the site of the University of Virginia, is about 40 miles to the south. The school's setting has always charmed its visitors. Its original buildings have a breathtaking view of the mountains to the west. There's a sloping sweep of beautiful green grass in the foreground and the Rapidan river flows through the grounds. 'The country I'm describing', John's recorded voice told English radio listeners a year after he arrived, 'lies mostly in the counties of Orange and Madison, an area not much larger than, say, Huntingdonshire; various shades of red soil, rolling to hilly farm and forest, cattle to horses, small-holding to big farm to stately homes. And the whole caboodle fringed, dominated, inspired by what for me is now an essential part of every landscape: mountains.'

The school was founded in 1889 by the parent of a pupil. Small home schools for young children were prevalent in the post-Civil War South because farms were too remote from any town. Captain Robert Stringfellow Walker had fought bravely for the Confederates. When he was 34, nine years after the surrender of Appomattox, he and his wife took over Woodberry Forest, formerly one of the best dairy farms in Madison County. The buildings and land were neglected after the war, but the soil being rich, Captain Walker soon made it prosper again.

Captain Walker's three older boys were the first pupils; three more local children were enrolled soon after. Their teacher was 19, a graduate of the University of Virginia. Everybody lived and studied under the roof of the 1794 Residence, the nucleus of the farm. By the end of the century the school flourished, and Captain Walker's eldest son was its headmaster.

The little bedsitter, above the school's main entrance in the Walker Building, was John's living space for the first year. The next spring, he sent Paula a biro drawing he'd done for her on a scrap of paper - of a barn, a silo and a row of trees, captioned 'Farm scene where our cottage will be.'

John was at a loss to know how to 'place' all he was noticing, the extraordinary panorama, the voices, the air of affluence and 'landedness' of this school compared to the cosmopolitan, grimy, jostling, confined atmosphere of St Paul's. In September 1963, a fortnight after his arrival at Woodberry Forest, John's BBC producer Dick Keen received a letter from him. Apologetically - he hadn't planned to bother Dick with his impressions for at least two months - he broached the thought that, since he had:

> 'at this juncture very strong feelings and reactions to this radical change in my life, listeners in England might be interested to catch me while my iron is hot, even if the bellows are in the wrong place or may shift their angle later.'

> 'For me the most enjoyable thing so far is the estate or campus of 1000 acres, with its farm, its golf course and all a super-country club could want for a high subscription for membership. The boys are Old South to a Gone With The Wind in manners both to each other and to us...' Dick Keen told him that he should try again when he could give 'a profounder impression and one less likely to contribute, however unintentionally, to superficial anti-Americanism.'

John tried again, and the result, much edited, was broadcast on the Home Service as 'A Private School in the South' in March 1964. This paragraph was excluded: 'Highly expensive, the school has two locally powerful reasons for existing: one, that the Southern public high schools are very poor and give almost no chance to an ambitious family of getting the boy into a reputable college; two, that since there are almost no prep. schools in the British sense, no Southern public 'grade' school can prepare a boy for passing easily into the top-class New England 'prep' (public in U.K.) school like Andover and St Paul's. Unquestionably for Southerners north east of the Deep South and those who prefer something genuinely southern, this is THE school that is most likely to get good places into college and even to move up into the Ivy League class. The money comes mainly from tobacco both in Va. and N.C., but there's plenty of livestock and plain business money from small townships in and around the mountains. Washington provides a few who don't want to lose their southernness.'

(Dick Keen told me that he felt John's writing lost its vitality a year or two before he departed for the United States.) The following excerpt was included; and of all at St Paul's who heard the broadcast, it was remembered especially by the younger English Department colleagues:

'My new pupils are charming. Their manners are almost impeccable; they work very hard and they still stagger me for their religious devotion... But what in my opinion bedevils the whole system is the grisly word grades - or what British students call marks. An American parent will ask his children if they're 'keeping up their grades' and will be happy to know a child is, as he puts it, 'averaging', say, '86'. If a student isn't graded for some work at least once a week, he'll get a bit edgy; and if, at the monthly returns of grades, he gets less than 70 in any subject, he's flunked, he's in trouble and he's determined to make up for the lapse next time.

'I complained about this one evening to one of my most intelligent pupils. If he'd think less about grades, I told him, and more about being original and imaginative, his work would please me more and he'd have a good chance of being a scholar. He looked at me for a while before he spoke. He wanted to get into Princeton, he said, one of the best universities in all America and there was little hope of doing that if one got less than an average of 85 in all subjects...it was a lot easier to get a high-salaried job if one had graduated from Princeton than if one graduated from, say, the University of Delaware.'

Just 37 days after he had arrived John was writing an article for the school newspaper, *The Woodberry Oracle*. He was still, he said, 'in the heart-leap state that Wordsworth got into when he saw a rainbow in the sky. Who would dare to insinuate that Woodberry's campus can be rivalled anywhere in the world?' With his light touch and some flattery he encouraged the boys to found a Virginia Society. He was excited himself: he could imagine a beautiful book on the ecology of Madison County and Woodberry. He would edit it. The headmaster, he told them, had given his backing; time was already set aside for field work - by budding biologists, geologists, sociologists, ornithologists, and artists. The best writers among his Sixth-Formers would get into print.

★ ★ ★ ★ ★ ★ ★

Julie and Jenny Ross's eldest daughter stayed with John as guests of the school in the autumn. Susannah left after ten days; she was on her way home to California after a stay in England. Julie had come 'to check on Daddy'. The people she met at Woodberry were kind and welcoming, but he was so much in demand for consultations by pupils that she saw very little of him. 'We swung a golf club together at lunch time once or twice.' She left after six weeks for the West Coast to stay with Jenny and her younger children. Her doctors had suggested that her psoriatic skin and arthritic joints would benefit from the California climate. She hoped to find a job in Los Angeles, as Jenny had enabled me to do earlier.

Julie and Susannah remember hearing the singing of the black cleaners, arriving in the early morning from their shanty town on the school estate in huge old Cadillacs and Pontiacs. John had anticipated that the segregation in Virginia would make him uneasy. Of the white Virginians, he wrote to Dick Keen:

'They're Anglo-Saxon to the last negro - who claims descent from the Washington who held General George's horse. I'm sure America's race distinction is nearer to resolving itself more decently than our class-distinction.

'Yes, I'm learning a new language and have to watch my step. Just as it comes, here's a sample: Bells ring here; they never go...but to revert to breakfast and other meals; the glossary is rich. Grits, succotash, banana-bread, oatmeal, limas and pah. Know any of them? Pah is a bit unfair. No Southerner can pronounce the open I-sound. Ah lahke ahce-cream on mah pah.'

John knew he would need a place he could escape to, a place where he could dig, and between digs lean on his spade and look at the view.

'For my precious spare time I have been given a piece of rough land, about 10 miles from my bed and board, to turn into a garden. The site looks gently down at an arena of field and forest, bronze, gold, dark green - and gunmetal-coloured as the seasons change. With the land goes a beautiful replica of a Cotswold country house belonging to a colleague of mine with the old English name of Latham. Usually I go to Elly - that's the village where the house and garden is - in Mr Latham's lovable old jalopy. But I often start the trip on foot and am picked up later. The walk is almost as lovely as what's at the end of it.'

Arthur Latham was a true Virginian - England was his spiritual home. Born and brought up near the capital, Richmond - in his early fifties when John met him - Arthur was a tubby, jovial and dishevelled bachelor. (I remember him in a flapping, badly-fitting brown suit and a little black hat on the back of his head.) He was devoted to his black dachshund, Miss Hop. Arthur made Elly welcoming to many of the teachers and their families, and pupils; guests were served toast and honey, with tea out of a English silver teapot, by a black maid wearing a white apron. After a visit to the Cotswold town of Chipping Campden as a young man, he had started a thirty-year task, building himself a house, with one black helper.

In December John worked with a pickaxe at the red and rocky ground of his plot, stripped to the waist. A pileated woodpecker - as big as a crow - 'drums louder than any English woodpecker I remember' he wrote to his friend John McNair in Gloucestershire. In February 1964, as he dug, he watched turkey vultures circling; mocking-birds sang all day. Four bluebirds watched him from a telephone wire.

At Elly, John had many surprises. The strong sun, the absence of the right bugs and the presence of the wrong ones meant the gentle emerging of flowers that his English spirit looked forward to would not happen. Pawpaws, persimmons and strawberries would flourish; mimosas were like weeds. Grape-hyacinth bulbs, ordered from England, flowered well in the spring; but he noticed at the same time a carpet of wild Virginian grape-hyacinths growing at the edge of a nearby barley field. He planted - too late - zinnias, petunias and pansies, from seed packets he'd bought locally. 'I've learnt my lesson, which is: in Virginia, if you want to avoid endless watering and hoeing, plan only for a Spring show of flowers before the weather gets blistering.'

169

Swarms of people, it seems, were anxious to meet John; he made a strong impression from the start. There were 300 boys and forty masters at the school. Among the Faculty, John liked especially Joe Rowe, who taught Mathematics. He shared John's interest in trees. Once, near Elly, they walked together to the top of a hill attempting to identify all the trees they passed.

Ed Crow, a young blond North Carolinian, about 27 when John arrived, taught English. "John was my hero," he told me. Ed reminisced to me that John had noticed that the yellow line along the middle of the country road he walked to Elly stopped dead at a certain point, adjacent to a house. Because the garden gate, front door and window-frames were painted with the same paint, John had decided that a woman in the house had watched the man working, got talking, and invited him in.

Ed Crow in 1994

Tom Bethell, another Englishman, teaching Mathematics and Philosophy, had come to the USA a year earlier after coming down from Oxford. On most evenings he would drop in on John. His love for Traditional Jazz - he had made a record from his recordings of jazz musicians in New Orleans - impressed John, who had enjoyed recording singers himself. John Stillwell taught English and was deputy headmaster - a kind and reliable source of support. Wilfred Grenfell, a Canadian teaching History, was the son of Wilf Grenfell, the great doctor and explorer of Newfoundland.

Did I ever hear any comments from my father on John Kennedy's assassination? He wrote only occasional fatherly letters to Julie in California, and me in London, cheering us on in our jobs. He was to be back in England in July. He was happy to be in Virginia, and he was obviously a success. I was happy for him. My parents would be settling in America - something for me to show off about - and I had an idea that I might follow them.

Chapter Twelve

John was convinced that descendants of English settlers living in isolated pockets in the Appalachian Mountains spoke a language closer to the dialect of Shakespeare's actors than present-day Englishmen. Robin Pumphrey, one of John's pupils of the late 1950s, remembers him telling him of the archaic English he had heard when walking there.

Five years later he was excited to find that some of his Woodberry pupils had that very accent. He wrote to Dick Keen:

'I've discovered - or think I have - that much of my pupils' diffidence, or, even, backwardness over English poetry is due to their accent-shyness. Because whenever they hear or see Shakespeare they hear an accent they think more English than American - and it is, usually - they may give up developing their own voices as instruments for playing their own language at its best. I am determined to break down this diffidence and shame in this school. I genuinely believe that when a well-enunciated Virginian or North Carolinian voice tackles, say, a Hamlet soliloquy, it makes sounds that Shakespeare would have found more musical than mine or yours doing the same.

'I feel, as an Englishman, that I have a special mission out here. These boys, I told myself, must be persuaded that they have as lovely voices as most Englishmen know they have, if only they can be made to articulate clearly. I got one form to read, verse by verse and boy by boy, some of Shelley's ADONAIS and to vote afterwards on who had been the most effective reader. I thought they did it beautifully; I really did. In fact I nearly burst into tears it was so musical. And I told them so. I said it had been one of the most moving experiences of my whole life.'

'I would like, if you agreed, to record my favourite Falstaff from this school, who has a rich mountain accent from North Carolina, and the same boy doing the gravedigger in Hamlet with a fellow mountain boy. As for Hamlet, I have a lovely South Carolinian for that.'

'I, for instance, would be fascinated to see Shakespeare's reaction to my way of speaking a bit of Hamlet to Polonius and then to what you'll hear in contrast:

'Give me that man
That is not passion's slave, and I will wear him
In My Heart's core, ay, in my heart of heart,
As I do thee.' '

'A Private School in the South' ended with two North Carolinians, John Yates and Jim Tatum, each reading - immediately after John's versions - three lines of *Hamlet*. Then the gravediggers' conversation, lasting two minutes, was read by two Virginians, Harrison Armstrong and David Lyne.

John's original idea for this broadcast was born of his plan to stage a festival in April to celebrate Shakespeare's 400th birthday. The most cherished memory of him is probably this particular orchestration of the school's talents. 'No one but John', Baker Duncan told me, 'could have gotten the boys up to it nor helped us to enjoy it more than he.' In a grassy amphitheatre, under a starry sky and in a cold wind, staff members, a wife, and boys (and some girlfriends, who were there for the Festival) played parts in nine scenes from both the tragedies and comedies. Tributes to Shakespeare from Jonson, Arnold and Eliot were read, songs sung, guitars played. A staff dog howled eerily during the "Out damned spot" soliloquy.

Arch Harrison ran WJMA-Radio Orange, the local radio station where John had recorded his script and the boys their contributions for the BBC broadcast. He and his wife Marion became good friends to John. At Arch's suggestion, John started - a month before the Festival - seven weeks of twice-weekly readings of his own anthologies of poetry and prose. (He earned $2.50 for each fifteen minute session). Arthur Latham and another colleague and his wife, Corky and Mary Shackelford, used to listen to him together on Thursday mornings. He read De Maupassant's story 'The Vendetta', Christopher Marlowe's 'The Passionate Shepherd', and Walter Raleigh's 'Nymph's Reply'; Herrick, 'The Song of Solomon', Browne, Belloc, Shakespeare's sonnets; D.H. Lawrence's poem 'The Snake', and Gerard Manley Hopkins' 'Pied Beauty'.

'Boys of Woodberry, I love you;
But Elly of hill and valley
I love better. There is no war
For me moving through Woodberry,
Only peace breathing from the best
Of campuses; crickets from outer
Sycamores breathing to crickets their
Peace to inner tulips and maidenhairs,
Mimosas, walnuts and beeches. Peace for
War, southern courtesy for continent-
Al competition, grades for the grim
Polish of Princeton. I love your enchant-
Ing manners, your English faces and your
Marmalade drawls...'

'Most of all he impressed me as being truly happy,' Harrison Armstrong has said. In truth - as this verse from a poem John wrote for Arthur Latham shows - he wasn't, except when he was at Elly. The teaching day started at 8.00 am. Classes finished at 12.55 pm. After lunch 'Consultation' - private tuition - went on until 3pm; and it continued after supper from 7.20pm. 'They keep me very busy here and I'm the sort that worries that I'm not doing some job I ought to be doing,' John wrote to his friend John McNair six weeks into the term, 'Trouble is I've been given a pretty blank cheque: no specified syllabus but merely a number of 'recommended' books in a number of given categories of literature, mainly English but not starved of American. It's a good course if I can manage it, and a lot depends on it for the boys.' And then fatigue speaks: '...Point, however, is that merely organising this course over-occupies me and I'm sinking more and more under water as far as teaching and so on goes...' In December he wrote again: 'Term drawing to its close and so is my endurance. Longest term I've had: Sept 7th to Dec 19 and no half-term break...And I've caught my 4th cold since I arrived - it's all this over-heating and the obsession with 'shots' or inoculations against 'flu, which merely circulates germs in hot dry rooms on swollen mucus membranes.'

From a letter to John McNair, 13 December 1963

However...he was doing very well, delighting in re-discovering literature, and wanting only, as the boys listened to him reading, that his enthusiasm would infect them enough to go away and read themselves. Harrison Armstrong - in spite of an important exam looming - read 50 books that year.

* * * * * * *

My father had decided on arrival that Woodberry was the school for him. But even after three months there - in his letters to my mother - he was still trying to persuade her to join him. She was committed to making her mother comfortable during the cold weather, and could not contemplate uprooting.

I'm glad that he had that year at Woodberry on his own. It allowed him time away from domestic chores, from city pressures, from being labelled an eccentric. Although he felt obliged to overwork, as a bachelor he could escape most afternoons to walk, to dig his plot, to watch birds and dream. In 1963 he wrote to Dick Keen of his feelings for Virginia, still unchanged since he recorded them in 1951: 'I fell in love with it at once because it seemed to give reality to a romantic nostalgic dream of an England of my earliest boyhood; a sunny, meadowed and wooded England, a very

173

lightly inhabited England, a quiet England that didn't smell of petrol or rumble with motor bikes, a huge playground with just a few nice big houses and, apparently, no factories. A sort of Camelot with modern plumbing. And something I've always reckoned as an essential for paradise: mountains that go blue in the evenings.'

In May Paula found a buyer for the house, and wrote impatiently to John of her need for him to help her with the packing, especially with his books and papers. That spring of 1964, after a fall in her tiny rented cottage, my grandmother died. Paula dealt with the funeral briskly. She knew that she must now have faith in John; and that to look forward to living in America was all she could do. Julie - still fragile - was working for the Feigen Palmer Gallery in Los Angeles. I was living in Notting Hill Gate, working as a junior graphic designer at Penguin Books in Harmondsworth.

'My Year in Virginia', the talk that Dick Keen had wanted all along, was still not written. While walking in long grass in June, John was bitten on his left ankle by an insect. By mid-July, during temperatures seldom below 90 degrees, he had suffered two weeks of a bad chill, caught - he thought - by falling asleep under a fan after a game of tennis. 'With a full teaching programme and come-and-go-fevers I've been in no state to turn in a lively radio script, though I've had the odd bash.' Four days later, on the 19th, he wrote from the Martha Jefferson Hospital in Charlottesville. 'My trouble has today been diagnosed as an infected arthritic ankle and I've just been admitted here for intensive treatment.' The 'infected arthritic ankle' was a mis-diagnosis by Woodberry's local doctor. John was home in England at the end of July, still suffering from fever.

I went down to Windlesham to welcome him back. I was shocked to see how slowly he moved. There was a fatigue in his expression that was new to me, and no sign of the old spark. His grey eyes, when last seen so humorous, were drawn down at the outer corners; the set of his mouth was tense and uncertain. My father knew then that he was seriously ill. On the days he went to London for tests at St Thomas's Hospital he met his London friends and told them his news. James MacGibbon and Milena Thomas each had lunch with him; each was struck by his slow walk and sad expression. He dropped in on his old colleagues in the Common Room at St Paul's; they too were sobered by his appearance. Guy Burn later passed on my father's news to the others: he had Sub-acute Bacterial Endocarditis.

There is a heart weakness in the Usborne family. John had discovered at his medical for the RAMC in 1939, when he was 24, that he was born with a heart defect, called Coarctation (narrowing) of the Aorta. Because he had not had rheumatic fever (one of the causes of heart disease), the doctors deduced that his breathlessness almost certainly signified that he had two cusps on his aortic valve instead of the normal three. Two cusps cannot close as securely, with the result that the blood - while it is being pumped - leaks back into the ventricles from which it has come. This means a risk of infection to the heart lining and the valves, called Endocarditis. With his habit of driving himself too hard - so becoming easily run down - John had a history of mouth infections. Bacteria from the gums can enter the bloodstream and damage the heart. John's heart was extremely susceptible. The insect bite introduced yet more bacteria.

The Cardiology Department at St Thomas's Hospital in Lambeth had had John's case on file since his first collapse in 1940, while he was working as a journalist. Before he departed for Virginia in 1963, he kept an appointment with Evan Jones, a consultant in Cardiology at the hospital. Working in that department also was one of John's end-of-the-1940s St Paul's pupils, Peter Reed. John had watched Peter's career with interest and several times during his regular check-ups at the hospital they had chatted about St Paul's and talked over the implications of John's condition.

In late August 1964, to his surprise, John was told at St Thomas's that he would be admitted for a six-week course of penicillin injections to kill the bacteria, Streptococcus Viridens: 'breeding merrily on the kink of the aorta (a kink that shouldn't have been there but has been from birth),' John McNair was told. He would be spending most of this time at the convalescent home, Hydestile, the hospital's old wartime evacuation site near Godalming, Surrey.

It was hot and dry that summer and my father persuaded the nurses to wheel his bed out to a spot on the parched lawn under an old oak tree. A striped parasol was rigged up over his head. Friends and neighbours from Windlesham, Usbornes, St Paul's colleagues, parents of Paulines, old friends he hadn't seen for years, went to greet him there.

My mother didn't visit my father very frequently. When she spoke of him I noticed an irritated tone in her voice. For me Hydestile was a difficult place to get to by public transport from London and I went there only once. I made excuses; I found it acutely painful to see my father an invalid.

In early October – after six weeks during which there was 'an episode of left ventricular failure' – he came home to Sandy Lane Cottage to convalesce, feeling very feeble. Not too feeble, though, to bully his doctors for permission to resume his teaching in Virginia. He was to fatten – as he put it – for an operation to repair the valve at the end of the month. Already his return to Woodberry was delayed considerably; he was restless and worried, and longing to be teaching again. He had been reading and his mind was whirring with new ideas.

Dick Keen was told not to give up hope of receiving the finished 'My Year in Virginia'. 'I may be strong enough to write most of the script before then but I confidently look forward to finishing it after the op. and before I fly off to Virginia about December 15th.'

My parents had had the furniture and most of their luggage shipped; they had left Sandy Lane Cottage after 25 years and were renting rooms from a neighbour. The stress of the move further weakened my father and he caught a bad cold. 'I escaped the operation – postponed indefinitely – and am convalescing here till we can uproot' he reported cheerfully to Dick Keen. He would write the script pretty soon, and Dick could fix a recording time. That time the task was accomplished; the talk was broadcast on the Home Service on 3 March 1965.

On his own John spent a day and a night with Pam and Henry at Totterdown, a short stay which has left Pam with a happy memory. My parents and I went to the wedding of their eldest son Barnaby in December. John, wearing a tail coat, looked thin but distinguished; he loved family gatherings and was determined to enjoy the occasion. He is remembered talking happily about Woodberry.

★ ★ ★ ★ ★ ★ ★

'Usborne To Resume Teaching Duties; Honors Candidates Wait Expectantly' was the headline of an article by Jeff Cothran, one of John's pupils, in the

December issue of *The Woodberry Oracle*. In mid-December (on a working day when I told myself I couldn' take time off to say goodbye) my parents - my father on a stretcher - left for Washington.

Three days after their arrival at Woodberry Forest, after some Christmas shopping in Orange: 'I had what they call a heart attack,' he told John McNair, 'breathing became a struggle and I was morphined etc, and rushed to the university hospital in Charlottesville, where I was 10 days being 'digitalised' and introduced to a salt-free diet and waiting to see if they had to operate to repair my perforated heart-valve. No operation yet; return to school weak as a jelly with poor Paula plunged into despair - as who wouldn't be? - and a long wait till I was allowed to try teaching even half-time.

Soon he had another, milder attack. In 1964 the operation to repair the heart-valve was not yet entirely safe or effective. John was considered strong enough to vegetate. Nobody could prevent him from getting back to work. He needed the stimulus the boys gave him, and the boys were relieved and proud to see him again. 'I've now been teaching two periods a day for exactly a fortnight and am none the worse for it,' he told John McNair, 'so long as I go to bed early and keep a low-sodium diet. Really far worse for Paula than for me. It means seeing very few people, doing no entertaining worth the name and my leaving her to brood while I laboriously mount the stairs - pause after every two steps - and go to bed.'

John was 'sidling into teaching again' from mid-February. In his classes he launched some new ideas with characteristic enthusiasm. At his suggestion - for the first time for about 20 years - he taught some Classical Greek. He had spoken about the Greeks on BBC 'Children's Hour' nine years earlier - and had promised himself that one day he would set aside some time for some re-reading of books he had read as a schoolboy. Evidently he did that in Virginia. Infecting young Americans with his love of the Greeks was equally intense as to young Britons: 'My goodness, those Greeks! What didn't they begin?' 'Children's Hour' listeners had heard. 'The older I get the more fascinated I grow with them. They didn't, as a matter of fact, begin very much. But their minds were so amazingly fresh and energetic that, ideas and arts that came to them from elsewhere grew and flourished and reached a near perfection that is purely Greek and that seem as fresh today as they were over 2,000 years ago... I've got a bee in my bonnet about the ancient Greeks. They were fantastic people to whom we owe a lot of the best things in our lives, and yet our interest in them is flagging... I want to take up the Classics all over again and soak up all I can about my dear old Greeks.'

And, closer to home - finding that the plans for The Virginia Society had been neglected in his absence - John exhorted the boys again: 'We need to work on the book'; he had already gathered a folderful of pictures and notes for it. He gave them a promise that his operation 'in a few weeks' time' would only cause them a short interruption.

He was in fact in depression, intensely anxious about the high fees his private treatment was costing. He'd been advised by his doctor, a man he trusted, to resign temporarily and return to England - as John imagined it - 'for the dole and sick benefits and crabbed penury in a bedsitter near the private tuition market.' Paula's welfare concerned him.

Just before his first attack John had bought a small Ford car to allow them both the opportunity to explore. The sunny days of early spring gave my father a little more energy; on 21 February, a Sunday, he and my mother threw a salt-free picnic into the car and drove up to the mountains. They looked down into the Shenandoah Valley from Swift Run Gap. Paula was as struck as John by the beauty and the sense of history in that view, and enjoyed seeing for herself landscapes he had told her about in his first letters from Virginia. In a letter to her friend Mary Clifford-Wolff she wrote: 'John and I have never been closer.'

It was a perilous time for her. She missed Windlesham and her friends, and John was desperately dependent on her. 'Only Paula ever sees me as low as I often feel. Stiff upper lip otherwise' he wrote on a scrap of paper in early March. On the bad days - becoming more frequent - he was feverish, very tired and in the grip of fear. Paula was angry with the Windlesham GP and the London doctors for having allowed him to leave England. Peter Reed from London reassured John that with Dr Mueller at the University of Virginia Hospital he was in very good hands.

'It's just possible I may be able to have the operation in London,' he wrote bravely to Julie, 'We live for the day. I've heard that Baker Duncan values me highly enough as a teacher to bring us back from England rather than let me get a job over there. It'll have to be a big bribe, though. Mummy really could never enjoy America at her age and you mustn't lecture her about it. I made the wrong decision bringing her out and taking this job in the first place. I should have stayed at St Paul's.'

John hadn't seen his old friend Paul Longland for a few years because he had left St Paul's to teach at Noble and Greenough in Massachusetts. Paul and his wife Helen came to stay on 21 March, from Philadelphia, where they had been visiting one of their sons. John was looking forward to hearing about Paul's reactions to teaching in the United States, and to showing Woodberry off to him and Helen. He had been excited for months at the prospect of showing Paul a haunt of bluebirds which he had discovered. On the morning of the 22nd, a warm sunny day, the four of them set off in the Longlands' car with a picnic. They hadn't reached the school gates before John was suddenly overcome by severely rapid heartbeats; he was rushed to Charlottesville.

By the time he arrived at the hospital he was calm, but he was admitted. The next day he had another sudden attack. The doctors tried to convert the rhythm of his heart with drugs; that treatment failed and he was taken to the operating theatre where electric shock treatment brought his heartbeat back to normal. He was 'again comfortable'. On the 24th, next day, he had another attack, and was again successfully defibrillated. The doctors decided to operate immediately, but before they started he had yet another attack. This time the defibrillator failed to relieve him. 'Very desperate day,' my mother wrote in her diary, 'John very courageous.' That evening he lay exhausted but conscious in the Intensive Care Unit, with my mother sitting beside him. 'I love you' were his last words to her. Next morning at about ten o'clock, during another attack, he died.

Epilogue

My cousin Andrew wrote to me in 1997: 'John had a way with people that hinted at past relationships. He had a long stride and good-looking trousers, and although energetic he seemed delicate, a father of girls, poor, maybe bordering on the feckless – but everybody's favourite; typical of a youngest son.'

My father died in his fiftieth year.

After his death, my mother found it difficult to persuade the local undertakers in Orange, Virginia, to dress my father in his gardening clothes, those trousers a little short for him and an old sweater.

About six weeks after the cremation, with her departure imminent, she realised she must scatter his ashes; Richard MacKenzie, an Englishman on the Woodberry staff, had been keeping them safe in the back of his sports car for too long. So she, Arthur Latham and Joe Rowe met at Elly to scatter them on my father's beloved hillside plot. Joe Rowe wrote: 'The urn was on the mantel. Paula and I had a whisky, Arthur had a Coca Cola. Each of us told happy stories in which John was the principal character. After two drinks, and Arthur becoming impatient, Paula said she couldn't go through with it. The next day was an exact duplicate of the day before. On the third day Arthur called his gardener, a black man named Nelson Morton, who under Arthur's supervision, dug six holes; in one of them he placed the urn. He then covered all the holes. That afternoon Paula and I joined Arthur at Elly again, but the interment was over.'

'Revered Woodberry English Master, John Usborne, Dies of Heart Attack', said the headline of the report of his death in *The Woodberry Oracle*, and there was also a poem, 'In Memoriam', by one of his students. My mother received many letters, from boys, colleagues of my father, and people in the Woodberry community who had liked him and been impressed by his Shakespeare Festival. (In his memory, a nature trail has since been laid around the school's large campus by the Virginia Society, which he founded.) At St Paul's, the news of his death so soon after he had left it for a more comfortable life, was a great shock. Robert Alden, a young English master who had joined the staff two years before my father left, wrote a whole-page epitaph for *Folio*. 'Those in the Common Room who remember John,' his last lines read, 'will remember a friendly, sophisticated, humorous and very human colleague, always ready to entertain, and be entertained by, anyone and anything.'

Ten days after my father's death, I went out to Woodberry to spend a fortnight with my mother. My father's colleagues and their wives were looking after her well. (My sister was then working in California, and she and my mother met there a few weeks later.) The shock was delayed, and I believe the effect of it changed her personality. After only six months in the United States, aged 49, she came home, and finally settled in Sunningdale, about two miles from our old house. She found part-time work in a local dress shop. After a disastrous second marriage, and suspecting that her memory was failing her prematurely, she deliberately lost touch with many of my father's old friends, to their sadness. She died in 1996 at a residential home in Hatfield.

Index of Names